THE NEW ROUTE TO THE EAST.

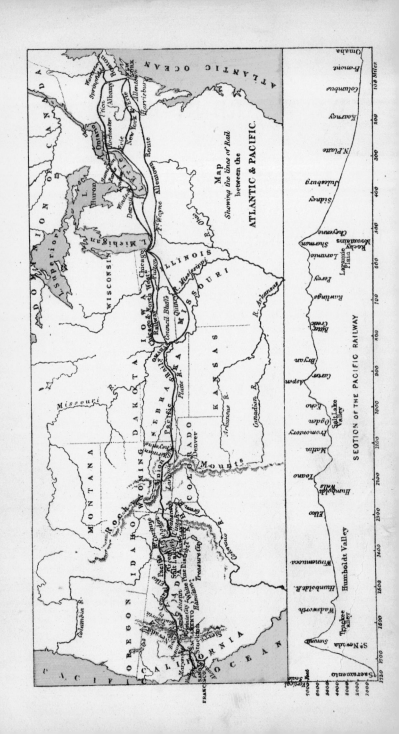

Map
Showing the lines of Rail
between the
ATLANTIC & PACIFIC.

SECTION OF THE PACIFIC RAILWAY

WESTWARD BY RAIL:

THE NEW ROUTE TO THE EAST.

BY

W. F. RAE.

NEW YORK:
D. APPLETON & COMPANY,
549 & 551 BROADWAY.
1871.

TO

MY AMERICAN FRIENDS

I Dedicate this Volume

WITH

SINCERE THANKS FOR THEIR KINDNESS

AND

HEARTY GOOD WISHES FOR THEIR COUNTRY.

PREFACE.

———◦◦◦———

ALTHOUGH two series of letters, the one entitled
'New York to San Francisco,' the other 'A Visit
to the Mormons,' which recently appeared in *The
Daily News,* form the basis of this volume, yet
those who have perused these letters will find that
the revision they have undergone is so thorough,
and the additions made to them are so considerable,
as to constitute the volume itself an entirely new
work in substance, if not in name. Like the famous
stockings of Sir John Cutler, these productions now
resemble, in general outline only, that which they
were originally.

Seldom, indeed, should contributions to newspapers be reprinted precisely as they were when
first published. A journalist must adapt himself
to his readers if he would gain their confidence
and produce a vivid and lasting impression. Every

newspaper has its own circle of readers. The better fitted a piece of writing may be to rivet the attention and gratify the taste of that circle, the greater is the probability of its proving unsuited for the varied and unascertained tastes of the vast critical circle to which a writer appeals, and by which he is judged, when he gives a book to the public.

Articles of a purely literary character may sometimes be advantageously reprinted from newspapers without the excision of a sentence or the modification of an opinion. The brilliant and incisive critiques of the late Samuel Phillips are as sparkling, pungent, and valuable now that they appear in a volume exactly as they were when they informed and gratified the readers of *The Times*. Artistic and thoughtful biographical sketches, like those which Miss Martineau has reprinted from *The Daily News*, would not have been improved if the original form and phraseology had been sensibly altered. No change would be for the better in some of the finished studies in political science and social ethics which distinguished contributors to *The Pall Mall Gazette* and *The Saturday Review* now and then collect and reproduce in volumes. But letters such as mine are in a different category. The space at my disposal being necessarily restricted, I was de barred from making full use of the details I had collected. Moreover, my contributions had to pass through the alembic of editorial supervision. The process may have greatly improved, while slightly altering them. Nevertheless, when acknowledging their paternity, I exercise a natural right in dress- ing them according to my own fancy, and pre- senting them in the garb which I believe to be at once the most suitable and the most becoming. As a necessary consequence of the veil of anonymity being formally drawn aside, all the responsibility for views adopted and opinions expressed is now transferred, from the journal in which many of these letters were printed, to the writer whose name is on the title-page of this Work.

That portion of it which relates to the Pacific Railway supplies information which the public can hardly call stale and may possibly consider to be interesting. Those who have not made the journey will gather from this volume what I hope will be regarded as an accurate notion of the vicissitudes to be encountered, and the pleasures to be enjoyed, while future travellers will probably find the particulars I have given both instructive and serviceable. The accompanying map, which has been specially prepared in order to exhibit the course of the railway, along with a section showing the gradients, will enable both the general and the professional reader to understand very clearly the nature and magnitude of the enterprise.

It is possible that my account of the Mormons will occasion some surprise. In the main it differs materially from the accounts written by several preceding visitors to the Valley of the Great Salt Lake. I could not confirm all their statements without making an unpardonable sacrifice of truth. Doubtless they were honest in their eulogy; but, then, they must either have deliberately shut their eyes, or else have been incompetent and superficial observers. It may be, that, going forth laden with foregone conclusions, they returned home rejoicing that they were in the right. Captain Burton's description of what he witnessed in Utah is permeated with his avowed approval of polygamy. His wife having publicly explained that his practice is diametrically opposed to his teaching, the book in which he has presented a favourable picture of Mormon society must now be regarded as an awkward joke or an elaborated paradox. Mr. Hepworth Dixon, without unreservedly expressing personal admiration for the worst Mormon doctrines and customs, has undoubtedly produced the impression that polygamy is not such a bad thing after all. His volumes about America are apparently designed to breed doubts and excite suspicions. The well-informed reader is always at a loss to decide whether Mr. Dixon has been shamefully imposed upon, or has determined to impose upon others. The drawback of books of travel ingeniously planned in order to sell, is that they are apt to be regarded by the uninitiated as trustworthy merely because they happen to be entertaining. Sir Charles Dilke in his ' Greater Britain' writes very sensibly and fairly about the Mormons and their ways; but he deals with the subject only as an episode in his long and eventful journey.

In addition to divergences of statement and opinion, this volume is distinguished from previous ones by containing particulars, alike curious and

novel, relating to the aspect of Mormonism since
the Pacific Railway has rendered it easy to visit
and to get away from the City of the Saints.   The
new order of things in Utah has made it imperative
to return a speedy and definite answer to the old
inquiry: ' What shall be done with the Mormons?'
I have supplied material wherewith to frame the
reply which must be given, and I have indicated
the form in which I think the reply may most
appropriately be couched.

CONTENTS.

———◆◆———

WESTWARD BY RAIL.

—◆—

I.

FROM THE MERSEY TO THE HUDSON.

BEFORE ARRIVING at the station, it is sometimes necessary to pass through an ordeal as trying as any encountered during the course of an expedition by rail. The distance to be traversed, the character of the conveyance, the space of time within which to catch the train, are considerations which have all to be taken into account, and of which each may contribute something towards rendering the traveller anxious and uncomfortable. My preliminary journey was neither short nor easy. Prior to travelling ' Westward by Rail,' I had to traverse three thousand miles of a stormy ocean, and undergo the chances and changes incident to a voyage extending over ten weary days. By many persons a trip across the Atlantic is regarded as a commonplace and uninteresting excursion. According to them, it is as much a thing of everyday

occurrence as the passage of the Channel or a sail
up the Rhine. It is true that, with a memorable
and immortal exception, a narrative of a voyage to
America has ceased to inspire universal and abiding
interest. The unknown sea has been transformed
into the ocean highway. Yet to those who make
the voyage for the first time, the sensation is as
novel and impressive as it was to the daring
mariners who unveiled the mysteries of an unexplored deep, and dazzled mankind with the spectacle of a new world. In the hope of noting a few
particulars not wholly devoid of general interest, I
venture to repeat what is in the main an old and a
hackneyed tale.

About nine o'clock one Saturday morning, towards the end of August 1869, I formed one of a
group on the deck of the tender *Satellite*, which
was to convey the passengers for New York from
the Prince's Landing-stage to the Cunard steamer
China, lying at anchor in the Mersey. On another tender the luggage was being piled up without
delay. Porters, staggering under the weight of
huge trunks, portmanteaus, and leathern bags, followed each other in rapid succession. This was
no new sight, but it differed in one respect from
everything of the sort which I had witnessed elsewhere. Nearly every passenger seemed to be the

possessor of one of those cane-bottomed arm-chairs which are arranged so as to fold together till they are nearly flat. These chairs I had seen exposed for sale in several of the Liverpool shops, but I did not even imagine that they formed a necessary part of the outfit of those who sailed across the sea. Greatly to my surprise, I learned that those who failed to bring their own chairs could not expect to be comfortably seated on the deck of a well-found Cunarder. This piece of information diminished my respect for the company which boasts of never having lost a letter or a passenger, and which makes its reputation an apology for charging more than any other for a passage across the Atlantic.

Soon after stepping on board the *China*, I gained another item of knowledge, which would have been very useful, had it not been acquired too late. A rush was made to the saloon by those passengers who knew the importance of being the first to perform the simple ceremony of affixing their cards to the places at table which they wished to occupy during the voyage. Those who omitted to do this, or who were ignorant of the advantage of being ranked among the first comers, were doomed to the discomfort of sitting where the unpleasant effects caused by the rotation of the screw-propeller were even more to be dreaded than the motion of the steamer as she pitches, when the waves are dashing against her bows, or when she rolls heavily under the influence of cross seas. In this case, however, the law of compensation operated in a manner which afforded a grim pleasure to the disappointed. Those who had established a claim to the best seats did not always appear to occupy them. Circumstances over which they had no control frequently forced them to remain in their berths or on the deck while feasting and mirth prevailed in the saloon.

After the *China* had steamed a short distance down the river she was stopped, in order to allow a tender, bearing the latest despatches, to come alongside. Several persons who had embarked at Liverpool now went on shore in this tender. There were the usual painful scenes which occur when partings take place between those who cannot see each other for a long interval, or who are doubtful about meeting again. A demonstration, of a marked and unusual kind, made it evident that a passenger of note was on board. As he stepped forward to acknowledge the greetings of those about to depart, and lifted his hat to return them, the noble features of a great American poet were recognised by many persons, who congratulated themselves on the good fortune which had accidentally made them the fellow-travellers of Mr. Longfellow, on his return home, after a protracted sojourn in Europe.

The first evening at sea was unmarred by any of the discomforts which frequently attend those who go down to the sea in ships. Every one ate, drank, and made merry. There were many children on board the steamer. As they gambolled about the deck, much more to their own satisfaction than to that of their elders, the more cynical passengers remarked that the Irish Channel was almost too smooth and the breeze too light. The fineness of the weather enabled us to view the coast of Wales to great advantage. Places were pointed out where large ships had gone to pieces during the raging of the terrific storms of winter. For the present these dangerous headlands were gazed at with pleasure by those who delighted to view without risk the bold, rugged outlines of stupendous cliffs, which are generally the terror of the sailor, but were now objects to be admired. At an early hour on Sunday morning the steamer reached Queenstown, where, after a detention of ten hours, the last mails were embarked; and then the voyage across the ocean may be said to have really begun. Rounding the south coast of Ireland, the long Atlantic swell imparted to the steamer an amount

of motion which cast down the spirits of the bad
sailors whose hearts had beat high at the hope of a
voyage devoid of suffering, because made across a
sea as placid as a land-locked bay. Still, the movement was not sufficiently great to produce inconvenience to the most timid or sensitive. Never
have I witnessed a more beautiful spectacle than
that which was presented at nightfall. It was one
which no poet could adequately reproduce in words,
nor any painter in colours. The grand Atlantic
waves were slowly heaving with a long and measured motion; the full-orbed moon was set in a
serene and cloudless sky, and the wind was still.
The spray, raised by the steamer's prow swiftly
cleaving the dark blue water, fell back in a shower
of fire, or fitfully flashed along the steamer's sides
in a stream of dazzling light. As the moon's ivory
beams quivered upon the agitated water in the
vessel's track, and mingled with one of the phos-
phorescent flashes on the crests of tiny waves, the
combination of colours thus produced was magical
alike in variety and vividness. These effects, being
not continuous, but intermittent, a watchful eye
had to be kept for a glimpse of unexpected beauties.
Far on into the night did many passengers gaze on
the attractive and novel spectacle, and sate their
eyes with its loveliness. It was one which they

might never again behold during a passage across the Atlantic.

On the morrow the scene changed. The angry coursers of Neptune were careering over the deep, and spending their fury against the steamer's stout sides. Strong head-winds retarded her progress. By not a few, life on the ocean was found to be vexation of spirit, a burden too terrible to be borne without murmuring. The noisy children of the preceding day were now lying like logs in out-of-the-way corners; passengers who had been jubilant as to the prospects of the voyage now shook their heads and bemoaned their lot. The attendance at meals was agreeably select.

The state of things during the remainder of the voyage cannot be set forth more truthfully as regards the majority of the passengers than in the words which the late Lord Jeffrey wrote in his journal when crossing the Atlantic in 1813. According to him, the pleasures of a voyage were:— *Imprimis*: Oppression and intolerable sickness, coldness, loathing, and vertigo. *Secundo*: Great occasional fear of drowning, and penitence for the folly of having come voluntarily in the way of it. *Tertio*: There is the impossibility of taking any exercise, and the perpetual danger of breaking your limbs if you try to move from your chair to your bed, or even to sit still without holding. *Quarto*: An incessant and tremendous noise of the ship groaning and creaking, cracking and rattling—to say nothing of the hissing of the wind, and the boiling and bubbling of the sea. *Quinto*: The eternal contact of the whole crew, whom you hear, see, feel, and smell, by day as well as by night, without respite or possibility of escape; crying children, chattering Frenchmen, prosing captain, and foolish women, all with you for ever, and no means of getting out of their hearing. *Sexto*: The provoking uncertainty of your fate, now going 150 miles in one day on your way, and then taking seven days to 100; the agreeable doubt whether your voyage is to last three weeks or three months. *Septimo*: The horrid cooking, and the disgusting good appetites of those who are used to it. *Octavo*: The uniformity and narrowness of your view and its great ugliness.' Jeffrey adds, that there are twenty other items which might be mentioned, but these are enough.

Two of the distinguished contributors to the renowned 'Review' of which Jeffrey was the distinguished editor, were more fortunate than he, and they regarded a voyage not as an affliction to be dreaded, but as an opportunity for profitable reading and careful composition. When Sir James

Mackintosh went to India he learnt German, and pursued a regular course of study while on board ship; and on his return voyage he studied metaphysical problems, penned sketches of historical characters, and composed the introduction to his projected 'History of England.' Macaulay is said to have turned a similar opportunity to account by adding a thorough acquaintance with the works of St. Chrysostom to the vast stores of his miscellaneous knowledge.

Those among my fellow-passengers who were in good health seemed to care little about improving their minds. They smoked; played at cards; watched the heaving of the log; speculated as to the length of the run made during the twenty-four hours; were assiduous in eating all the five copious repasts provided between eight in the morning and nine at night, and were ready to initiate novices into the mysteries of 'cock-tails.' Some of them were able to communicate pieces of information much more curious than useful. The peculiarities of English custom had been carefully noted by an American gentleman, who plumed himself upon the accuracy and extent of his attainments. He expressed to me his surprise at the continued existence in England of relics of a more barbarous age. One monopoly he regarded as peculiarly obnoxious. This was the assumed necessity of a wedding-ring being stamped by the Goldsmiths' Company in order to render the marriage contract valid and binding. When I assured him that, not only was this notion a pure fiction, but that two persons could be legally married in England without a wedding-ring being used at all, he shook his head incredulously, and expressed his opinion that I was not well 'posted' as to the practices and laws of the country in which I lived.

The sceptics as to the utility of daily newspapers would change their views after they had been a week at sea. For the first day or two the several passengers have some personal topics about which to converse; but these are soon exhausted, and the dearth of ideas becomes painfully evident. Gloomy dulness characterises some, while a childish querulousness is manifested by others. Their minds being no longer occupied in discussing the rise and fall of stocks, the ins and outs of politics, the guilt or innocence of the last alleged criminal, are now concentrated on counting the hours which must elapse before they will again set foot on shore, or else busied in finding fault with every imaginable thing. As soon as the pilot brings newspapers on board, the scene changes. Tongues that had been still, or had been moved only to utter complaints, now wag cheerfully and pleasantly again. The alteration is so great as to be marvellous. If permanently deprived of newspapers, Englishmen and Americans would become as taciturn as Turks.

When the voyage was drawing to its end, a notice was posted up outside of the saloon, to the effect that the Government of the United States required every passenger to fill up a form with particulars as to age, occupation, last legal residence, purpose in visiting America, and as to whether, or not this was the first visit. Such an intimation took the majority by surprise. If it had emanated from the despotic Government of Russia, or from the Government of the police-ridden kingdom of Prussia, no surprise might have been exhibited. Despots are fond of asking impertinent questions, and are wont to act as if travellers ought to be placed in the same category as the plague, and treated accordingly. While the war lasted, the Government of the United States was justified in resorting to the obnoxious passport system, and treating every stranger as a foe or a spy in disguise. Happily, this excuse cannot be urged now that treason has been extinguished and the Union has triumphed. The Americans on board were as much puzzled and annoyed as the visitors to the land of freedom.

2

They used vigorous terms in characterising what was simply an indefensible demand. They were the more angry because they knew that a similar interference with liberty of action does not take place when a steamer nears the coast of the United Kingdom, and they disliked the comparison which could be drawn to the disadvantage of their own country.

The last day of the voyage being nearly as fine as the first, a large number of passengers mustered on deck and occupied seats at table. To all appearance, they had suffered severely. Their pale faces and tottering steps were unmistakable tokens of the bitterness of the ordeal through which they had passed. A newly-married pair, who had chosen to make a wedding-trip to America, instead of paying the customary visit to the continent of Europe, excited general commiseration. Their first ten days of matrimony had been the reverse of blissful and satisfactory. Of the two, the gentleman was the more thoroughly prostrated. He resembled one who, having been smitten with a malignant fever, had barely escaped with his life. An elderly American lady was in some respects a spectacle still more deplorable. From the moment that the steamer had begun to rock, she felt convinced that her death was imminent. Nearly every time that the vessel lurched and pitched she believed that a catastrophe was at hand. Her husband vainly tried to reassure her. He began by speaking soothing and inspiriting words, but without success. Appeals to her common sense were in like manner disregarded. Nor did strong and threatening language have any better result. In truth, the poor lady was thoroughly unnerved, and had temporarily ceased to be able to control herself. The sight of land gave her a certain relief, but her longing to be safely on shore again was intensified by the prospect.

The approach to New York by sea has been eulogised in glowing terms, yet nothing that has been said or written outstrips the reality. The most high-flown anticipations are gratified to the full. After Sandy Hook is passed, the panorama on either side is most beautiful. On the right, the shore of Long Island, with its white beach and rows of neat houses, may be perceived in the distance. On the left, the luxuriant foliage and the dark green vegetation remind the English traveller of the richest and most charming rising grounds in Kent. The water is studded with steamers and sailing vessels. In the distance are islands covered with verdure, and in the background are the masses of redbrick buildings which constitute the chief city of the Empire State. Conspicuous among the various structures is a towering edifice, imposing in outline and white in colour. I was told that this was the office of the *New York Herald*. There is something alike significant and appropriate in the fact that the office of one of the most enterprising among American newspapers should be the most conspicuous object beheld by the stranger who approaches New York from the sea.

The landing-stage of the Cunard steamers is at Jersey City, on the side of the river immediately opposite to New York. To pass his effects through the Custom House is the traveller's first task. This office is as dingy and uncomfortable a place as any one of the sort to be met with elsewhere. Thinking that the rules which were in force here resembled those of the Custom Houses of the Old World, I first hunted for my luggage, and then, having found it, waited patiently till an officer was disengaged. On appealing to one who was unemployed, I was told that, before the examination could take place, I should have to fill up and sign a paper describing the various articles I had with me. I went to the official who gave out and countersigned those papers. He was seated, quietly smoking a cigar, and indisposed to say much in response to those who plied him with questions and requests. He was addressed as 'Judge.' He certainly did not display any

interest in the proceedings, or show much concern for those who were most anxious to obey his
orders. After glancing at and countersigning my
paper, he returned it, and then I had little trouble
in getting the examination completed. Varying and
contradictory statements have been made about the
conduct of the American Custom House officers. I
was told that they were the most exacting, overbearing, and detestable of any upon earth. My
own experience did not bear out this opinion. They
seemed to be overworked. So many articles being
liable to duty, the search they make must necessarily be minute. The examination of my luggage
was most thorough; but of ill-manners, or of an
intentional desire to give annoyance, I could not
detect a trace. Indeed, a Prussian Custom House
officer would not only have given me more trouble,
but he would also have done his part in a way which
proved that he gloried in the opportunity to be
disagreeable and inquisitorial. Nor would he have
acted like his American brother, and helped to re-
fasten the articles which had been laboriously opened
for his inspection. If this officer expected to receive
a bribe for neglecting his duty, or a gratuity for
showing civility, his manner belied his thoughts. It
may be that these officials are corrupt, and that a
money present will cause them to be conveniently

shortsighted. But the persons who should share
the blame are those who tempt them to betray their
trust. Several of my fellow-passengers, who had
various effects on which duty was chargeable,
boasted of the immunity which they had purchased
for a sovereign. If a tithe of what I heard were
true, then the utmost vigilance of the officers is
required in order to circumvent the stratagems of
dishonest travellers. An English acquaintance, who
meant no harm, but whose manner was a little too
abrupt to please the officials of the Republic, had
some reason to complain of the treatment he received. He was a solicitor, of high standing and in
large practice, who had determined to improve his
holiday by paying a hurried visit to the United
States. He would as soon think of smuggling as
of committing the smallest breach of professional
etiquette. An officer, who was too astute by half,
fancied that this gentleman had resolved upon sur-
reptitiously importing watches into the Great Republic. Being sharply questioned as to whether or
not he had more than one watch in his possession,
my acquaintance, astonished at the query, replied
in a manner that seemed to confirm the suspicion
which his demeanour had excited. To his surprise
and annoyance, he was ordered to step into a room,
where he was subjected to a minute personal search.

The natural conclusion is that an American Custom House has its good and its bad side; that the officers are neither wholly immaculate nor uniformly unbearable; that the warning against being too precipitate ought to be carefully observed there; that patience and courtesy go a great way towards ensuring considerate treatment; that much depends on the temperament, the manners, and the appearance of the individual and not a little on the merest chance whether a traveller shall denounce all connected with it in the harshest terms of opprobrium, or speak of its officials as persons who discharge a difficult duty in a rational and defensible manner, and admit that they are neither much superior nor vastly inferior to Custom House officials all over the world.

There is nothing strange or foreign to English eyes in New York when beheld for the first time. The impression made on the traveller who, after having crossed the straits of Dover and landed at Boulogne or Calais, sees French soldiers in their national uniform, workmen in their blue blouses, servant girls in their neat white caps; who notices the peculiar arrangement of the shops, with prices marked in a foreign currency and signs printed in a foreign tongue; who hears the people on every side conversing in a language which he never heard

spoken before, is an impression far more startling
and lasting than that which his mind receives after
the long voyage of three thousand miles is over
and he alights in the streets of New York. If the
feeling be one of disappointment at the absence of
marked novelty in the spectacle, it is dispelled as
soon as he enters one of the monster hotels for which
America is famous. He then becomes conscious of
the fact that Liverpool and London, Edinburgh and
Dublin are indeed far away, and he discovers that
any experience he may have gained when travelling
through France, Germany, and Italy avails him
nothing. All the arrangements are new to him: he
is emphatically an ignorant and bewildered foreigner
in an English-speaking land. Fortunately, he has
not much trouble in learning the ways of the house.
The arrangements are as simple as they are complete. Many of them are admirable. They are
designed so as to combine the maximum of comfort
to the visitor with the minimum of labour on the
part of the servants. Grumblers who would stigmatise Paradise as a detestable place of abode if it
differed in petty details from the land of their birth,
have written bitter things about the hotels of New
York and have been far too successful in misleading and prejudicing the English readers of their
books. The truth is that in the Old World there

are royal palaces in which the occupants are less luxuriously housed and enjoy a smaller share of life's minor comforts than would be their lot if they sojourned in the splendid and well-appointed hotels which have been erected in the United States for the reception and use of the Sovereign People.

II.

NEW YORK TO SAN FRANCISCO: THE ROUTES TO THE WEST.

WHEN I first saw New York it did not appear to me a foreign city in the same sense as Paris, or Frankfort, or Milan. A closer and more leisurely examination produced a different impression. To walk along Broadway recalls a walk along Regent Street, but it also recalls a walk along the Rue de la Paix. What seems to be English is rivalled, if not outdone, by what is unmistakably French, while many things have neither a French, nor an English impress. The architectural effects are extraordinary in their variety. The want of simplicity and repose is as marked as the absence of a distinctively national style. Everyone has apparently followed the bent of his fancy, and the straining after originality has led to a confusion of ideas and a clashing of aims.

All nationalities seem to have sent their representatives to this city. Half the languages of Europe are spoken by the motley gathering. The

English tongue is in the ascendant; but the eye fails to see many figures or faces to match the hereditary language. The ladies are dressed after the latest French mode, yet the fashion of their apparel is the only thing they have borrowed from Paris. Their looks are native to the soil, and to call them good is not to speak of them in language sufficiently eulogistic. The men are dressed with a regard for appearances which is more common in Paris than in London. There is none of the uniformity in their attire which is akin to monotony. All do not seem to have been condemned, by a law which cannot be gainsaid, to wear the same hideous hat. The ' wideawake ' is as common as the ' chimney pot ' and the mixture of the two produces a pleasing effect.

The purity of the air is delicious. If a dwelling be built of marble, or brick, or stone, the beholder has no difficulty in pronouncing as to the nature of the material, and has the satisfaction of duly appreciating the whiteness of the delicate marble, the warmth of the brick, the solidity of the stone. The principal streets are broad : the principal squares are spacious. The several Avenues which run parallel to each other throughout the greater part of the city are so wide that the tramways which are laid in them do not in the slightest degree interfere with the traffic. For the passage of all conveyances there is room enough and to spare. At the upper end of the city is the Central Park. This public ground covers an area of more than 800 acres. It is laid out in a style resembling the Bois de Boulogne rather than Hyde Park and Kensington Gardens. Several years hence when the trees shall have attained their full height the Central Park will be second to no other place of the kind.

Quite as remarkable as the cosmopolitan aspect of New York streets is the contrast between the different portions of the city. The business quarter has a finished and substantial look; the offices seem as if they had been built for some time. Proceeding westward the several edifices are evidently built for show and are apparently of comparatively recent date. In the former case the buildings have a money-making impress upon them: in the latter the stamp of the successful millionaire is unmistakeable. From the fine mansions of the rich in a fashionable Avenue, the transition is rapid to the miserable shanty of the Irish squatter. At the one end gorgeous carriages roll along: at the other geese are feeding among the grass. Another contrast is that between the splendour of the buildings and the wretchedness of the pavement. The streets are filled with ruts. For this the City Fathers are

severely censured; but they can afford to brave the
indignation of their fellow-citizens so long as they
are permitted to hold office and to deal with the
funds at their disposal in the manner most pleasing
to themselves.

In my opinion scant justice has yet been done to
New York on the whole. It has its drawbacks, as
has every city on the face of the globe, but it possesses excellencies which more than outweigh them.
The man of business finds it as good a centre for
his operations as London. The pleasure-seeker
can amuse himself as well as in Paris, while men
of letters and students of art affirm that the prospects of New York becoming an honoured home
of literature and art grow brighter every day.

Before beginning my journey by rail from the
Atlantic coast to the Pacific slope, I had to ascertain various particulars as to the route. There was
no difficulty in purchasing a through ticket. In
most of the hotels and in numerous shops the
tickets of any railway in the United States can be
bought. Although the Pacific railway is constantly
spoken of as a line which actually runs between
New York and San Francisco, yet this is merely a
conventional way of stating the fact that there is
communication by rail between the two cities. A
traveller can journey in a railway carriage from

Dover to Inverness, but there is no such thing as a
Dover and Inverness Railway. He has the choice
of two lines of rail between Dover and London,
of three between London and Edinburgh and of
two over a part of the remainder of the route. If
a stranger to the country, he may be embarrassed
with this variety and be at a loss what selection to
make. So it is at New York. The stranger sees
innumerable advertisements in which Union Pacific
Railroad is conspicuous, but in which the names of
various lines are enumerated as being in connection
with it. He reads in one that the 'Allentown Line'
is the shortest and the best; in another that the
' Great Central Route' is indisputably without a
rival; he may even see the advantages of the ill-
fated Erie Railway extolled to the skies. As the
fare in all cases is the same the puzzle consists in
ascertaining the respective merits of the competing
lines. He learns that in any event he must first
reach Chicago. If, as is possible, the name of
Niagara has an attraction for him and if, as is very
natural, he is curious to become acquainted with
the far-famed ' Pullman's Cars,' he will probably
decide upon travelling by the ' Great Central
Route' and in doing so he will have no reason to
repent of his decision. Should time be no object,
he cannot do better than ascend the Hudson River

in a steamboat to Albany and enter the train there instead of at New York. The scenery of the Hudson has been highly lauded, but not over-praised. It is quite as romantic as that of the Rhine. In the autumn the aspect of the woods on the river's banks and heights clothed in the gor-geous tints of that season is a spectacle of wonder-ful beauty. The vine-clad hills between Coblentz and Bingen, when seen at their best, cannot match the Hudson in its most picturesque parts. Nature has done much for that river. One thing, however, is wanting to render it as famous as its European rival; the Hudson has not yet had its Byron. While no great poet has rendered it attractive by his inspired verse, a steamboat company has endea-voured to create an interest of a more prosaic and more practical kind. The steamers which ply between New York and Albany are marvels in their way. To call them 'floating palaces' is not the language of hyperbole, but is the simple truth.

Let me suppose that the 'Great Central Route' has been chosen and that the traveller bound for the Far West starts from New York in the evening by the Pacific Express. On the morning of the following day he arrives at Rochester, where 'Pullman's Palace Cars' are attached to the train; he gets a good view of Niagara Falls as the train slowly crosses the bridge over the boiling rapids, sees a large portion of the Western section of Canada, and then, after having passed two nights and one day in a railway carriage and traversed a distance of 900 miles, he arrives at Chicago.

The lines of Railway over which this train runs are the Hudson River, the New York Central, the Great Western of Canada, and the Michigan Central. The present was the first occasion on which I had travelled over the Great Western of Canada. By Canadians I heard this line very highly praised. Like the Grand Trunk it has been constructed with English capital and belongs to an English company. Its shareholders are much more fortunate than the investors in the Grand Trunk, inasmuch as, while the directors of the Great Western declare dividends, the directors of the Grand Trunk apologise year after year for their inability to do likewise. The reason is that the Great Western runs through a dividend-producing country and has enjoyed an immunity from the trials which have crippled the hands of the managers of the Grand Trunk.

The misfortune of the latter is, that, owing to various circumstances, it has been a bone of contention between opposing political parties. One side has upheld and assisted, while the other has denounced it. Having had to look to the Government for assistance, its managers have heretofore been compelled to keep on good terms with the Ministry of the day, and have more than once assented to propositions which, if wholly free agents, they might have declined. As a natural consequence, not only has the company had to make many sacrifices, but its efforts to give satisfaction have proved futile. Of late years the company has endeavoured to break away from an alliance which has proved the source of injury and discord. It would be an exaggeration to say that Canadians have ceased to revile the Grand Trunk; yet it is certain that the desire to give it fair play is more generally manifested now than at any former period in its history, while its prospects are brighter and more encouraging than they have ever been before. Its more fortunate competitor, the Great Western, has had no trials of an equally severe kind to endure. The losses occasioned by the depreciated American paper-money have been the chief drawbacks to its prosperity during the past few years. It is a dividend-paying line. Probably in consequence of this it is in many respects superior to others which have considerable difficulty in procuring the capital requisite for the purpose of keeping the permanent way in good repair and condition. The train whirls along the Great Western line not only at a rapid rate, but also without the immoderate jolting and oscillation which are common incidents on Canadian and American railways.

Hamilton is the first Canadian city of note at which a stoppage is made. Situated at the western extremity of Lake Ontario, and having communication by water and rail with the principal cities of Canada and with the capitals of the Eastern States of America, the city of Hamilton has many chances in its favour It has prospered hitherto, notwithstanding the mistakes made by those of its citizens who, in their eagerness to advance, incurred an amount of indebtedness which they found it difficult to discharge to the perfect satisfaction of many English bond-holders. However, the days of rash speculation are said to have passed away, and the lessons learned have been profitable. At Hamilton station the passengers dine, with the exception of those who are so fortunate as to have secured seats in the Hotel Car attached to the train. The occupants of this car take their meals ' on board.' I had heard much said in praise of ' Pullman's Palace Cars,' but I was unprepared for the reality. The first trip in one of these cars forms an epoch in a traveller's life. To one accustomed to English railway carriages

they are specially welcome.   The contrast between
the waggon in which Roderick Random journeyed
to London and a modern carriage is not much
greater than the contrast between life on the rail in
an English first-class carriage and in a Pullman's
car.   In order to form a fair notion of the character
of the latter it is but necessary to recall the descriptions of those luxurious saloon carriages which the
directors of our railways have had constructed for
the use of the Queen.   No Royal personage can be
more comfortably housed than the occupant of a
Pullman car, provided the car be an hotel one.
In the train by which I travelled, one out of the
three sleeping cars was of the latter description.
The Hotel Car is divided into sections, forming state
rooms, wherein parties of four can be accommodated.
Between these rooms are seats arranged in the
usual way.   At the rear is a kitchen, which, though
small, contains every appliance necessary for cooking purposes.   There are water tanks, in which is
stored a supply of water for washing and drinking
sufficient to last the journey.   A wine cellar contains the liquors which are likely to be in demand,
and an ice-house preserves ice for the gratification
of those who prefer cold beverages.   At stated
intervals the conductor walks round, taking the
passengers' orders, who make their selections from

the bill of fare. The choice is by no means small.
Five different kinds of bread, four sorts of cold
meat, six hot dishes, to say nothing of eggs cooked
in seven different ways, and all the seasonable vegetables and fruits, form a variety from which the most
dainty eater might easily find something to tickle
his palate, and the ravenous to satisfy his appetite.
The meal is served on a table temporarily fixed to
the side of the car, and removed when no longer
required. To breakfast, dine, and sup in this style
while the train is speeding along at the rate of
nearly thirty miles an hour, is a sensation of which
the novelty is not greater than the comfort. An
additional zest is given to the good things by the
thought that the passengers in the other cars must
rush out when the refreshment station is reached,
and hastily swallow an ill-cooked meal. It is proposed to construct dining cars which will be at the
service of all who travel by the train, and when
this is done, the limit to improvement will almost
have been reached. Yet it would be a mistake to
assign any bounds to the possibilities connected with
railway travel in the United States, and in the
Western States in particular. No prejudices exist
against novelties, nor are the directors of the several
companies able to scorn the demands of the travelling public for increased comforts and conveniences.

So many railways run between the same points that competition forces each company to outbid its rivals. In other countries reduction of the fares would be the course adopted under like circumstances. Here, the lowness of price is less considered than the amount of comfort obtainable on a particular line, as well as the shortness of the time occupied by the journey. Thus the rivalry has taken the form of providing cars resembling that described, and thus it is that railway travelling in America is assuming the form of luxury tempered by accidents. The wonder is that more accidents do not happen. Many of the railways are single lines, hence the risks are multiplied as the traffic increases. The probability of a wrecked train being ignited by the burning embers scattered from the stove adds another horror to the prospect. Still, when due allowance is made for all things, it must be admitted that the comparatively small number of railway accidents is very remarkable.

Meantime, the train has been speeding on its course towards Chicago. Paris has been left behind, a place of which the name alone recalls the capital of France. More familiar to an English ear is London, with its river Thames and its Middlesex. At last Windsor is reached. This is the frontier town of this part of Canada. The river Detroit separates the United States from the Dominion, and across it the train is transported on a large flat-bottomed steamer. From Detroit the journey is made on American soil through the State of Indiana and of Illinois. The country as seen from the window of the railway carriage is not prepossessing. The land may be very fertile, but it is certainly very swampy. Many of the farmhouses must be unhealthy places of abode. Contrary to Ricardo's theory of rent, the least valuable lands would appear to have been first brought under cultivation. When Lake Michigan comes in sight, the objects that arrest attention are the sand-hills, which, for a considerable distance, line its shore. These heaps and flats of sand give to the lake a maritime aspect, which the waves rolling shorewards tend to increase. Indeed, it is hardly possible to realise the fact of these huge sheets of water forming no part of the great ocean. The vessels which navigate them are to all appearance the same as the vessels which sail across the Atlantic, while the storms on these lakes are as terrific and disastrous as any which make the open sea the theatre of ruin and terror. Finally, the train runs in front of handsome dwellings, which not only represent Chicago, but which line one of its most fashionable avenues. A man appears who sells tickets to those who purpose going by omnibus to an hotel, the price being half a dollar. He also takes charge of the luggage checks. By taking a check from him in exchange for that procured at starting, the traveller finds his luggage safely deposited at any address he may give. In this way much subsequent confusion and inconvenience are saved. At the station, a notice in a conspicuous place arrests the attention of the traveller. It is a warning against lending money to strangers. This excites a suspicion adverse to the sharpness, and favourable to the generosity of the travelling public in America.

III.

THE GARDEN CITY.

IF the Michigan Central Railway express train arrives punctually at Chicago there is no difficulty in continuing the journey towards the Pacific. Seventy-five minutes are allowed for getting from the station of arrival to the station of departure. In my own case the times of the trains did not correspond; the one train had started an hour before the other arrived. This was not the only illustration in my experience of a want of punctuality on the part of American railway companies. My fellow-passengers took the disappointment very quietly, regarding the shortcoming as a matter of course. This failure involved a delay of twenty-four hours, as there is but one through train daily over the Pacific line. As I had intended to make a brief sojourn in Chicago, I was even more unconcerned than my philosophical fellow-travellers.

By the residents Chicago is often styled the 'Garden City.' Both its citizens and its admirers sometimes claim for it the still more dignified title of the ' Queen City of the West,' or the ' Queen City of the Lakes.' The pride they take in it is extreme, and the language in which they express their feelings is high-flown. This appears quite natural to the traveller who has journeyed from England to the United States in order to witness the marvels which human industry and energy have wrought on the surface of the vast American continent. Books and newspapers may have prepared him for an extraordinary spectacle, yet neither tables of statistics nor any printed statements can enable him to realise the grandeur of the impression produced by a stay, however short, in the modern city of Chicago. With a sensation of incredulity hardly to be repressed, he listens to the stories which tell of the city's foundation and history. Forty years have not yet elapsed since the site of palatial dwellings was distinguished from the surrounding wilderness by a log fort, in which two companies of soldiers were stationed for the protection of a few traders who collected furs from the Indians in exchange for trinkets. In those days civilized men regarded a visit to the shores of Lake Michigan much in the same light which many persons now regard a visit to the sources of the Nile. Those who made the journey had to brave the

3

attacks of ferocious animals; had to face the perils incident to an inhospitable and uncultivated region; had to live in constant dread of an attack from Indians more deliberately cruel than any beast, and more crafty than any other enemy in human shape. The wild men and wild animals have both disappeared. The land which once yielded a precarious subsistence to the hunter now repays the skilful farmer one hundred-fold. Where weeds formerly throve in rank profusion, peach trees are now heavy with precious fruit. A city of palaces has taken the place of a few miserable hovels. Similar transformations have occurred in other parts of the globe. Venice and Holland do not fall short of Chicago as evidences of what man can achieve in his struggle with rugged Nature and hostile elements. Yet the growth of either city was the work of many years, as well as of much toil; whereas Chicago has waxed great and famous within the memory of men still living, and not yet old. If another Queen Scheherazade were compelled to rehearse a tale of enchantment for the gratification of an exacting husband, she might find in the authentic story of the rise of Chicago materials which would produce a result as striking as that caused by a recital of the fabulous doings of Aladdin.

Although figures convey but an imperfect notion

of the wonders performed by the spirited and enterprising inhabitants of this city, yet, in default of a better medium through which to supply information, they must be employed.   In 1830 the population of Chicago was about 100 persons, of whom a small proportion was white, the majority being black men and half-breeds.   It was incorporated as a city in 1837, when the census was taken, and the number of inhabitants found to be 4,170.   Ten years later the number was doubled; twenty years after its incorporation it contained 100,000 citizens, and at this moment the estimated number is 300,000. Nor is there any prospect of a stoppage in the rate of increase.   In every quarter hundreds of workmen are labouring at the erection of new houses or the substitution of larger for smaller dwellings. Nor is the rapidity of the city's growth less extraordinary than the way in which natural obstacles to its progress have been confronted and overcome. Situated on a low-lying part of Lake Michigan's shore, it was found to be very unhealthy.   In order that neither damp foundations nor bad drainage should breed malaria in any of the houses, the entire business quarter of the city was elevated eight feet above its original level.   This was done without interference with domestic comfort, stoppage of traffic, or injury to trade.   While houses and shops were rising upwards, families slept securely in their beds, sat at ease in their rooms, took their meals as if the even tenour of their lives was undisturbed, while merchants conducted their daily business, and the public made their daily purchases. For some years complaints had been made about the lack of good water for drinking purposes. The water supply obtained from the Lake was adequate in quantity, but was by no means wholesome. This was owing to the place from which it came being near the shore, and, in consequence of this, being contaminated with the sewage and refuse accumulated not far off. It was resolved in 1864 to remedy this defect by means of a tunnel carried under the water for a distance of two miles, and open at its farther extremity to the pure water of the Lake. Three years afterwards the new waterworks were in active operation, and they are capable of supplying 57,000,000 of gallons daily. Even this is hardly sufficient, and it is proposed to build a second tunnel. In addition to the supply from this source there is a large quantity of pure water obtained from two Artesian wells, one of which is 700 and the other 1,100 feet deep. Another great work is the Washington-street Tunnel, an undertaking quite as noteworthy as the tunnel under the Thames, which used to excite the admi-

ration of country cousins and intelligent foreigners.
Finding that the amount of traffic in the Chicago
river seriously impeded traffic over the bridges,
which had to be opened whilst vessels were passing,
it was determined to construct a tunnel under the
river, and a short time after the project had been
mooted the work was executed.

The rapidity with which Chicago has attained to
the commanding position now held by it in the estimation of Americans is due to the way in which
opportunities have been turned to account quite as
much as to any natural advantages it has enjoyed.
The situation is certainly a most favourable one.
There is communication by water from this city
to the Gulf of Mexico and to the mouth of the
St. Lawrence. The lines of rail which centre here
embrace fifteen trunk lines, and they run to every
part of the Union. Agriculture flourishes in the
vicinity, and the farmer finds in Chicago both a
market where his grain always commands a price,
and a storehouse, whence he draws whatever he requires for the purposes of husbandry or for the
comfort of his home. There is thus a continuous
current of produce streaming through Chicago on
its way to the consumer in the Eastern States or in
Great Britain. How speedily the trade in grain
has been converted from an insignificant industry

into an industry of unprecedented importance, let the following facts bear witness. In 1838 the shipments of grain were 78 bushels; in 1848 they were 3,001,714 bushels; in 1858 they were 20,035,166 bushels; in 1868 they were 67,896,760 bushels. If these figures did not appear in official returns of unquestioned correctness, they would be read with incredulity. As it is, they excite wonder, and this is intensified when it is found that in other departments of commerce, such as the trade in cattle and lumber, the like progress has been made. Not long ago Cincinnati took the lead of every city in the Union as the place where the largest numbers of pigs were slaughtered, salted, and packed for exportation. On this account, the city was commonly known by the name of Porkopolis. But, if the statements of the citizens of Chicago are to be accepted, the glory of Cincinnati has passed away, and the Garden City must henceforth be regarded as the one which lovers of bacon and ham are bound to honour.

The abundance, excellent quality, and moderate price of peaches, apples, and other fruit sold here in the autumn excites the admiration of the visitor. In some streets the pavement is encumbered with boxes of fresh peaches. I learned that these are produced in the southern part of the State of

Illinois. The soil and climate of that locality render fruit-growing as profitable there as it is in the southern parts of Germany. During the strawberry season five cars filled with strawberries arrive at Chicago daily. When the peaches are ripe the supply sent to market every morning fills twenty cars, each carrying five hundred boxes of peaches. Egyptian Illinois is the name of this prolific fruit-bearing region. Intersected by railways, the market is within easy reach of the cultivator's door. It is seldom that a crop fails, the climate being equable and temperate. Thousands of acres are still to be had by the settler. When I add that this land may be purchased for less than 2*l.* the acre, I have said enough, I think, to excite the desire of many to possess and cultivate it.

Material prosperity and rapidity of growth have made Chicago a city of note, yet other things have made it a city of influence. Its newspapers are quite as remarkable and worthy of praise as its splendid streets and magnificent buildings, its extended commerce and public works. Among the magnificent edifices which, in different parts of the United States, are monuments of successful journalism, the office of the *Chicago Tribune* commands admiration. Situated at the corner of one of the principal thoroughfares, it impresses the beholder by the effectiveness of its architectural design, and this impression is not weakened by the fact that it is built of white marble. As a newspaper, the *Chicago Tribune* exercises a vast and beneficent authority throughout the West. Its columns are singularly free from those offensive personalities which, in the United States, are too frequently considered the lawful weapons of the journalist. Its articles are at once pointed in tone and scholarly in style. A supporter of the Republican party, the *Tribune* is at the same time an energetic and astute upholder of free trade. It is the ablest representative in the press of that large and compact body of shrewd Western agriculturists which calls in question the justice of taxing the people at large in order to give the manufacturers of Pennsylvania and Massachusetts exceptional facilities for doing business on a large scale, and accumulating fortunes with unprecedented speed. The *Chicago Times* is the democratic organ. Like its political rival, it is ably edited and well written. The *Chicago Evening Journal* is another of the more important newspapers. An attempt has recently been made to add a monthly magazine to the periodical literature of the Western States. The *Western Monthly* is well supported both by men of letters and the reading public. The founders of this magazine said that their design was to develope ' Western Intellect and Enterprise' and to enable the people of the West to keep pace with those of the East in ' the great literary race of the Age.' They saw no reason why their literature as well as their grain should not be shipped to points across the Atlantic. As yet the grain is the better appreciated of the two, but the day may come when the literature will be more heartily welcomed than it now is. Judging from one point of view, it might be thought that in their feverish chase after wealth the citizens of Chicago had become indifferent to religious observances. Their favourite journals appear on Sundays as well as on the other days of the week. This is opposed to the practice not only of England, but of the Eastern States of America also. In the principal cities there are Sunday newspapers, but as a rule the daily journals are not published on Sunday. Here, on the contrary, the Sunday copies of the *Tribune* and the *Times* are much sought after, and contain an extra quantity of attractive matter. Yet while newspapers are in demand, the churches are not deserted. As a church-going people the citizens of Chicago will bear favourable comparison with the inhabitants of any city wherein the forms of religion are rigidly observed. The churches are very numerous. Some of them are fine specimens of modern ecclesiastical architecture.

What a traveller values most in a strange city are good hotels, fine buildings, well stored shops, and well kept streets. In Chicago he will find all these things. The Sherman and the Tremont House are the principal hotels, and both are equal to the best hotels of the East. They both are on a par with other American hotels as regards the difficulty experienced by the passing traveller in getting a bed. Throughout the United States and Canada the demand for hotel accommodation is one which seems to be insatiable and perpetual. On inquiry, the weary and astonished traveller learns that the state of things which gives him so much annoyance is the rule, that the revolving seasons exercise no influence on the huge and anxious crowd hurrying from one hotel and from one railway-station to another. At certain periods of the year an increase in the number of visitors to any American city of importance is perfectly natural. In the autumn it is customary for each State to hold its annual fair. These fairs, unlike those of the Old Country, have for their object the exhibition of the industrial products of the several States. The annual conventions, held for social and political purposes, likewise contribute to swell the throng of those who desire hotel accommodation. Another and exceptional gathering made the Chicago hotels crowded with visitors during my stay. A large party then stopped here on its way from California to the States of the East. This party was no ordinary collection of excursionists bent upon enjoying a holiday and seeing sights. It was composed of persons taking to themselves the credit of being the pioneers of civilization in California. Each one had gone to the Pacific coast in 1849, with a view to better his condition, and each boasted of having made California one of the richest States and brightest stars in the Union. The reception of this party was enthusiastic. The party itself was an illustration of the benefits conferred by the gigantic undertaking which supplied the link required to unite the Pacific and Atlantic with an iron highway. A printed list of the names and occupations of the excursionists gives evidence of their representative character. They had come not only from cities of note like San Francisco and Sacramento, but also from others less known to fame, such as Benecia and Stockton, Colfax and Elko. Men of every position in the social scale had associated together to testify that they had laboured for a common purpose in bygone days. Newspaper editors, mechanics, farmers, carpenters, state senators, hotel-keepers, miners, policemen, druggists, shepherds, bricklayers, undertakers, merchants, and one artist, composed the motley gathering. The occasion was a memorable one, for it was the first on which the people of the Pacific had been brought into formal and fraternal contact with their brethren in other and remote parts of the Continent.

The way in which the streets are kept is creditable to the city authorities. There is still room for improvement; yet, when the condition of those in New York is borne in mind, the streets of Chicago seem very good. Special and praiseworthy attention is shown to the safety of the foot passengers who cross over crowded thoroughfares. Policemen are stationed to see that the street is not monopolised by conveyances, to the danger and annoyance of pedestrians. These guardians of public order discharge their duty with an impartiality which merits praise. It is too often the custom, and in New York it is the rule, for policemen to be attentive to young and gaily dressed ladies, and to suffer all others to shift for themselves. To quacks selling nostrums the police are not a terror. These charlatans ply their trade on the footpath in complete security, and with a success which is only too great. Among the crowd of poor labourers surrounding them they find credulous listeners and an easy prey.

I saw one of these impostors doing an enormous business within a stone's throw of a leading hotel. His dress was that of a gentleman, and his manners and language were far superior to those of an itinerant vendor of the London streets. He had a pill which would annihilate every known malady, and an oil which would assuage every pain. As an inducement to buy the pills and the oil he presented the purchasers of either with an infallible cure for corns and bunions. This seemed to give satisfaction to his audience, for numbers exchanged their greenbacks for his rubbish. Another branch of imposture flourishes here in the evening. In one street large numbers of mock auctions are publicly held. The business of many auctioneers appeared to be the same, that is, to sell watches and tell lies. Their energy and boldness could hardly be surpassed. Some used phrases which sounded new and strange to my ears. One made a point of assuring his hearers that the particular watch he had to sell was 'Equal to anything on the top of God's Kingdom Come.' Another, whose appearance and accent proclaimed the Yankee, and who failed to attract persons into his room, assured the spectators at the door, that whatever money he got after that hour he would distribute in charity. Dutch auctions were also going on, but, as far as I could judge, with less success than the others. Many of the articles for which twenty dollars were asked had to be laid aside for lack of a bidder at four.

As the chief halting place between New York and San Francisco, the future of Chicago promises to be even more brilliant and extraordinary than its marvellous past. Its traders have already secured many new customers; its merchants have found new spheres in which to transact a lucrative business. To its markets additional supplies of valuable produce are now brought over the Pacific Railway. Thus the wealth of its citizens will increase with multiplied rapidity. Certainly, those who live here must have much money at their command if they would enjoy the ordinary comforts, to say nothing of the luxuries of life. House rent is very high; clothing is very expensive. A married couple, whose income is 1,000*l.*, would hardly be numbered among the well-to-do citizens of this community. But, while the cost of living is great, the opportunities for growing rich are exceedingly numerous. None but the idle starve: none but the stupid die poor. The Garden City is the paradise of the modern man of business. Compared with the bustle of Chicago, the bustle of New York seems stagnation.

IV.

ACROSS THE PRAIRIE.

FROM CHICAGO, on Lake Michigan, to Omaha, on the Missouri River, the distance across the Prairie is about 500 miles. This journey has to be made in order to reach the Eastern terminus of the Union Pacific Railway. The question which perplexes the traveller is 'which of the several routes shall he select?' He has three lines of rail from which to choose. There is, first, the Chicago and North Western; second, the Chicago and Rock Island; and third, a composite route passing over the Chicago, Burlington and Quincy, and other lines. In advertisements, it is said that the first is much more direct than the lower route, that the second is a hundred miles shorter than the lower route, thus leaving the third at the bottom of the list. Indeed, that anyone would voluntarily and knowingly travel by the third is absurd. A glance at the map suffices to show that it runs out of the direct course. However, the ticket agents often succeed in persuading the unwary passenger to buy a

ticket which answers their purpose rather than
suits the passenger's convenience.   I met more
than one passenger who had been imposed upon in
this respect.   As a matter of fact the Chicago and
North Western is the shortest line.   Its rival, the
Chicago and Rock Island, holds out the inducement that, 'this company build and run their own
elegant sleeping coaches and palace day cars, and
have no worn out rails to run over.'   Moreover, the
Chicago and Rock Island station in Chicago is one
of the handsomest and most commodious buildings
of the kind in the United States.   I mention these
things so that those who wish to form an opinion
for themselves may do so.   For my own part I
preferred a seat in a Pullman's palace car on the
North Western.   I have already given a description of his hotel car.   Before leaving this city,
which is the headquarters of Pullman's Palace Car
Company, a few additional particulars may appropriately be furnished.

About six years ago, Mr. Pullman first constructed one of the cars which have made his name
famous throughout the Union.   Before that time
he had made experiments on a small scale, and of
an imperfect character.   Their success emboldened
him to fresh efforts.   Instead of confining himself,

as at first, to providing sleeping accommodation for
night trains, he devised an arrangement which
combined comfortable sleeping berths at night with
luxurious seats by day. He appealed to the eye as
well as to the sense of comfort, furnishing his cars
with artistic and costly materials. As much care
was spent in decorating them as is expended in
decorating the dwellings of the rich. Nor were
any of the appliances omitted which could render a
railway journey agreeable. The perfected car was
a combined drawing-room, dining-room, and bed-
room on wheels. That no expense was spared is
proved by the fact that the cost of a single car
exceeded 5,000l. sterling. But it was not enough
to lessen the tedium and misery of a long railway
journey by merely providing softly-cushioned seats
by day, clean and most comfortable beds at night,
and well-cooked meals for those who chose to
order them. The Western railroads over which
these cars were destined to run had sometimes
been constructed far too hastily to be smooth. In
England, and in America also, the smoothness with
which the train speeds along is in proportion to
the care with which the rails have been laid, and
to the completeness of the permanent way. The
problem for Mr. Pullman was how to diminish
jolting on rough roads. He solved the problem by

giving more attention to the wheels and springs of his cars than the engineers had given to the rails, the joints, and the sleepers. The springs of a Pullman's car are so well adjusted that the oscillation, which would be unbearable if the springs were imperfect or badly contrived, is reduced to a minimum. By employing double windows, constructed so as to render rattling impossible, noise is prevented, while dust and cold air are excluded. Arrangements of a very satisfactory kind have been made for heating and ventilation. These cars are run over the several railways on terms agreed to between the companies and the proprietors of the cars. The passengers pay an extra fare for a seat in one of them. The result has been profitable to both, while the risk of loss to the companies is infinitesimal. The business having grown too large for Mr. Pullman to manage alone, he transferred it to a Joint Stock Company in 1867. He is both president and general manager of the company. The shareholders have no reason to complain of their investment. They receive a monthly dividend of 1 per cent., while the reserve fund is increased by a like amount. When the citizens of Chicago shall desire to devote a small portion of their enormous fortunes to commemorate the services of their distinguished men, they would act wisely in subscribing liberally to erect a monument to Mr. Pullman. If an Englishman would earn the gratitude of the large body of railway travellers let him emulate Mr. Pullman's career. He would thus revolutionize railway travelling in England, and at the same enrich himself beyond the dreams of avarice.

Once a day the through train for the Pacific coast starts from Chicago. The advertisements announce the starting of two trains; but the traveller who rashly starts by the evening one finds that he must spend a night at Omaha. Let it be supposed that, having taken his ticket by the Chicago and North Western Railway, he arrives at the station in time to get his luggage 'checked' and to take his place in a Pullman's palace car at 10.15 in the morning. The bustle and confusion are greatly in excess of what would occur at a well-managed European railway station. Labour is very scarce here, consequently the services of a multitude of porters are dispensed with. The passenger must do for himself what porters do for him elsewhere. If he be experienced he will have no more luggage than he can move unassisted. This implies that he has no incumbrances to whom he must be polite and attentive. On such an occasion as this the solitary and compassionate man has good reason to rejoice in his loneliness, and to pity those who are accompanied by ladies. When the struggle to get the luggage 'checked' is crowned with success, the traveller who has engaged and paid the extra charge for a seat in a palace car takes possession of it. This seat he retains throughout the journey. It is absolutely reserved for him. At night the seat is folded down on either side, blankets, and clean sheets, and pillows are arranged in due order, a curtain is drawn in front and a sleeping berth is thus formed. The berths in the cabins of many fine steamers are less comfortable than the berths in these cars.

When the moment for departure arrives, the conductor calls out 'All aboard.' The engine gives a low and not unmelodious whistle, the ear-piercing screech of our engines being happily unknown in America, and the train starts for the journey across the Prairie. It may be useful to give some hints as to the terms employed by travellers on American railways. In the United States as in other countries, fluency in speaking the language of the people is an art to be acquired if possible. If he would avoid being singular, the English traveller will say ' railroad ' instead of railway, ' track ' instead of line, ' car ' instead of car-

riage, ' depot,' 'freight-train,' ' baggage car' instead
of station, goods train, and luggage van. Luggage
consists of so many ' pieces '; it is not registered
but ' checked.' If a portmanteau forms part of it,
the portmanteau must be spoken of as a ' valise.'
Nor must luggage be asked for, or referred to under
any other name than that of ' baggage.' Over the
blunders made by Englishmen, who use the word
luggage, I once heard an American gentleman
make merry in the presence of his countrywomen.
He told them how, when in England, he had been
surprised at the ignorance of the railway porters,
because they asked him if he had any luggage.
In France, on the contrary, he considered that
their standard of education was far higher. By
them the word ' baggage ' was always employed.
He explained that the French had borrowed the
word from the Americans. Probably he would
have some difficulty in meeting with a Frenchman
who would agree with him in so thinking.

The arrangement of the seats in a Pullman's car
is such as tempts the several occupants to become
acquainted. As a rule the Americans are not a
loquacious people when travelling by rail. But in
their case, as in that of persons of other nationalities, the fact of being closely associated together
for a long journey tends to encourage good fellow-

ship. Towards Englishmen they are disposed to
be very reticent. The following reason is assigned
for this. A notion is prevalent that the majority
of English travellers visit America solely in order
to accumulate materials wherewith to fill volumes
with sneers and abuse. That such a belief is base-
less cannot be maintained by anyone moderately
well versed in the English literature of travels in
America. More than one of my travelling companions had a story to tell of unpleasant personal
experience of the John Bullism which is so offensive
to foreigners. One of them related how, having paid
all the attention in his power to an English fellow-
passenger, he naturally expected to hear an expression of admiration for some of the sights pointed
out. But he had laboured in vain. Everything was
pronounced good in its way, but far inferior to
what might be seen in England. In the hope of
succeeding at last, he remarked that the moon,
which shone so brightly that small print could be
read by its light, must rival that of the Old
Country. The reply was that the moon was not
at all bad for America, yet that the spectacle was
far inferior to what is beheld on a moonlight night
in England. This is but one of many stories of
a like kind told to me by those who seemed as
much surprised as gratified at my disposition to

admire what was really praiseworthy in the country, the scenery, and the people. I protested, not without success, against the notion of regarding every traveller as a paragon of cultivated taste and refined manners, as a man whose opinion ought to be accepted without hesitation or challenge and as one who truly typified his countrymen. Nor was it difficult to turn the tables by representing the doings of some American travellers in Europe. Having seen notorious members of the ' Petroleum' and ' Shoddy' aristocracy of the United States excite the amazement of Frenchmen and Germans by their lavish expenditure, their bejewelled persons, their coarse talk, and their overbearing demeanour, I was in a position to ask whether it would be fair to judge all Americans by the standard of these personages, and pass sentence of condemnation accordingly.

Among the passengers occupying the car in which I had a seat were two or three well qualified to speak with authority on matters relating to parts of the Union widely separated by distance, and differing greatly through the operation of natural or accidental circumstances. One was a large manufacturer of machinery in Philadelphia. The firm of which he was a member had supplied locomotives to nearly all the railway companies in the land. He

avowed himself a strenuous upholder of the law
which, by imposing protective duties, enriches the
manufacturer at the expense of the farmer. It was
curious to find in him, as the employer of two
thousand artificers, the counterpart of many Englishmen who boast of the number of ' hands ' in their
pay. To him, as to them, the dreaded and intolerable bugbear was trade-unionism. But in his case
the grievance assumed a new aspect. Between him
and his workmen the bone of contention had been,
not the rate of wages, but the employment of English
labour. He told me that he had been coerced into
dismissing Englishmen with whom no other fault
could be found than the cardinal and inherent defect
of their nationality. He was one of the very few
Americans I met who had a harsh word to say
against the Patent Laws. Like certain English
manufacturers he longed for their abolition, on the
ground that these laws tied his hands and fettered
his actions too tightly, conferring on poorer men
rights which they sometimes used to the detriment
of their richer brethren, who were ready to turn the
workmen's inventions to their personal advantage,
and treat the ingenious poor as convenient and
serviceable tools. Another passenger, who resided
in Alabama, and who in days not long gone by had
treated his darker fellow-man as a chattel, was

in many respects a more genuine liberal than the
wealthy manufacturer of Philadelphia. This gentleman was a planter who had fought in the rebel
army, and had suffered severely in person and estate.
About the result he manifested no bitterness. The
issues of the war he frankly and unreservedly accepted. In his opinion the question alike of seces-
sion and of slavery had been finally settled against
the South. His chief desire was to cultivate cotton
again, and his hope lay in the labour of Chinamen.
More prescient than his fellow-planters, this gentleman had purchased ten thousand acres of land in
Nebraska prior to the outbreak of hostilities between North and South. He was now on his way
to inspect and deal with this property. A third
passenger was a merchant in Omaha. He had
intense faith in the future of the young city, which
but yesterday was an outpost in the wilderness, and
is now the mart of an increasing trade. Two ladies,
travelling alone, were members of the friendly group
formed in the car by the accident of neighbourhood.
The one was going to rejoin her husband at Omaha;
the other was bound for San Francisco on the same
errand. At nightfall this little party produced
materials for a pleasant supper out of its joint resources. Patriotic and complimentary toasts were
drunk in excellent Californian wine. Loyal and

rebel songs were sung, and the merriment was continued till the conductor interfered on behalf of the other passengers, who, having retired for the night, did not wish their rest disturbed.

In order to give clearness to the narrative of this trip it is necessary to return to the starting point and ask the reader to imagine the train speeding along, after having left the Chicago Station behind. For many miles westward the line traverses the plains of Illinois. On either side the eye rests upon neat farmhouses, embosomed in trees which the settler had planted at the time he built his habitation. Not far from Chicago an Artesian well is pointed out, and a story is told respecting its discovery which the believers in Spiritualism would accept as testimony in favour of their views, and the disbelievers would cite as condemnatory of them. A short time ago a Spiritualist had a communication to the effect that if he sank a well in a particular locality he would ' strike oil.' Full of faith in the message, he set to work, heedless of the scoffs of his neighbours. Foot after foot he bored downwards, but without achieving the promised end. Yet he did not despair of success, and he boldly expended what money he had in the prosecution of the undertaking. Still there was no sign of oil. At last, however, a stream of liquid rushed to the surface, and his hope of success waxed strong. A reaction took place in his mind as soon as the liquid was tested, for it proved to be pure water. Instead of discovering a spring of oil, the explorer had sunk an Artesian well, and thus, although he had not wasted his substance in vain, yet he had performed no marvellous feat. It is possible to sink an Artesian well without the intervention of the spirits. Farther west, and on the other side of the line, I saw what appeared to be a nursery garden devoted to the growth of young trees. The young plants were in ordered rows, and disposed with a special view to regularity. A fellow-traveller who knew the country and its customs, told me that my supposition was erroneous. The spot was the chosen site of a future city. It is thus that speculators plan out and prepare the way for the settlement of uninhabited tracts of suitable land. Not only do they plant the trees destined to overshadow the footpaths on which unborn children will play, but they also give names to the streets, and even set apart sites for imaginary buildings. All these things are carefully noted in a map which is shown to the seekers after new abodes. They buy lots where their fancy dictates, and sometimes find on arriving to take possession that they are the first and the only inhabitants. The trick is not a new one. It was played upon Martin Chuzzlewit when he determined to make his home in what he thought was a new and rising city, but which proved to be an old and dismal swamp.

Five hours after leaving Chicago, the train reaches the bridge which crosses the Mississippi. This bridge is nearly a mile in length, and is constructed partly of wood and partly of iron. The structure has a very unsubstantial appearance, and, as it creaks and sways while the train passes over it, the contingency of an unwelcome descent into the deep and rapid stream beneath is one which flashes over the mind. Once across the bridge, the Westward-bound traveller enters the young, yet flourishing State of Iowa, a State in which countless settlers may find pleasant homes on its rolling prairies. On either side, as far as the horizon, a few farmhouses alone serve to break the monotony of the prospect. To these vast tracts the epithet which Homer affixed to the sea may not inaptly be applied. They are literally 'unharvested,' awaiting the touch of industry to yield up their teeming treasures. The long, rank grass which waves on their surface, rots for lack of a mower to gather it in, or is converted into dust and ashes when the spark falling from the passing locomotive, or thrown by the heedless wanderer, kindles the flame which no human power can extinguish. The spectacle of a prairie on fire is one of infinite grandeur. For miles on every side the air is heavy with volumes of stifling smoke, and the ground reddened with hissing and rushing fire. The beholder can with difficulty apprehend the possibility of the mass of flame being quenched till the entire country had become a barren and blackened waste. Much depends upon the strength of the wind as well as the quarter from which it blows. A lull will stay the conflagration, while a sudden change, by reversing the direction of the fiery waves, will sweep them back over the tract which they have devastated, and thus lead to their own extinction. A scene less impressive, but far more enjoyable, is that of the moon flooding the silent prairie with silvery light. The smallest object then stands forth in bold relief and fixes the attention. Innumerable wild flowers perfume the air. The senses are at once quickened and overpowered by the impression of illimitable space. As the mind is awakened to the thought that those who people these vast tracts of fertile land will enjoy a freedom hardly less complete, while far better ordered than that of the wanton breeze, balmy with perfume, it is not difficult to understand the proneness to exaggeration, which is the characteristic of the Americans of the West, and to sympathise with their opinions of countries in which an untrodden wilderness is an impossibility, and every acre is cultivated like a garden. Nor is it unpatriotic to feel a longing that the thousands who earn precarious livelihoods in the United Kingdom by tilling the soil, of which their taskmasters are the lords, could be transported to a locality where the strength of their arms would not only win for them a comfortable subsistence, but would also enable them to become possessors in their own right of the soil which yields them their daily bread. If the Dorsetshire labourer, who hardly knows what it is to taste butcher's meat, or the Irish peasant, whose ambition is to possess a bit of land, could be convinced of the lot which he might enjoy as a settler on the prairies of Iowa, the former would soon cease to serve and reverence the squire, and the latter would turn his face to the setting sun with the feeling which the Mahommedan cherishes for the city of Mecca.

The picture is a bright one, but it would be unnatural were it unrelieved by shade. The State of Iowa has its drawbacks, in the shape of swamps, as well as its treasures, in the form of rolling prairies. Fortunately the prairie predominates over the swamp. From east to west this State extends 287 miles, and it is 210 miles in breadth. At its western extremity the line of the Chicago and North Western Railway passes through one of the worst swamps in the whole State. A few days previous to my journey the rain had swollen the waters, and the rails were inundated. The train went along at a snail's pace. It was a puzzle to comprehend how the rails kept their places and the sleepers upheld their burden. The latter were resting upon what appeared to be liquid mud. It was well that they remained unbroken. Had they given way, the consequences would have been disastrous. When asked by an anxious and timid passenger what would happen were the road-bed to sink altogether, the conductor answered, 'Guess the cars would go to hell's bottom.' These swamps are veritable quicksands. Whatever enters them is engulphed for ever. As it happened, the only serious mischief was a detention of the train. Since then I have learned that the company has profited by the warning, and has renewed the line at this part in such a way as to render a recurrence of the danger almost an impossibility. Several miles before Council Bluffs, the station on the eastern bank of the Missouri, is reached, a fine view is had of Omaha, on the western bank. The prospect is

deceitful, as is not unfrequently the case when
cities are viewed from a distance. Situated on a
rising ground, Omaha appears to be a city with
fine streets and stately buildings. Seen more
closely, the streets are found to be straggling and
the buildings common-place, with but few exceptions. One of the disenchantments for which the
traveller by this line must be prepared, occurs when
he has to be transported across the Missouri from
Council Bluffs to Omaha. The accounts he may
have read of palace cars running through from
New York to San Francisco must have led him to
underrate the discomforts to be faced and borne.
One of these is changing from car to car and rail
to rail. A short time ago I read in the *New
York Tribune* a glowing account of the luxurious
way in which a party had travelled without change
of cars from Sacramento to New York. That
this was the rare exception I learned before leaving
Chicago; but I did not know that the arrangements were still incomplete for transporting passengers in comfort across the Missouri River, and
my ignorance was shared by many of my fellow-
passengers. On arriving at Council Bluffs, we
found omnibuses in waiting at the station. The
morning was cold and raw. But a small proportion
of the passengers could get inside seats, the re-

mainder having the option of either sitting on the
roof among the luggage, or else being left behind.
In itself the seat on the roof was not objectionable,
provided the time occupied were brief. As nearly
an hour was thus spent, the feeling of satisfaction
at having got a seat at all was supplanted by a
feeling of annoyance at the treatment received.
Through deep ruts in the mud the omnibus was
slowly drawn by four horses to the river's bank,
and thence on to the deck of a flat-bottomed
steamer. Seated there, a good view was had of
the Missouri. It has been called mighty, which it
doubtless is, considered as a stream, yet the appellation of 'Big Muddy,' which is current here, is the
one which more truthfully characterises it. The
banks are masses of dark mud, resembling the
heights which line the sea coast at Cromer, in
Norfolk, and just as every high tide undermines
and crumbles away the latter, so does the river's
current sweep away portions of the former. The
peculiarity of the Missouri is the shifting character
of its current. Now and then it suddenly abandons
its old bed, scooping out a new one an hundred
yards distant. A fellow-traveller who had seen
it a month previously said that since then the river
had shifted its course, and that what was now a
vast bed of mud had then formed the river's

channel. The erratic career of this river is giving
sad trouble to the railway company. There is no
certainty that any particular spot chosen for the
landing-stage will continue available for the purpose from hour to hour and from day to day.
There is a plan for erecting a bridge over the Missouri, but the difficulty of finding a solid foundation has hitherto proved insurmountable. The bed
and banks of the river are quicksands of great
depth. These physical obstacles will probably be
overcome, but the cost of success must assuredly
be heavy. Moreover, the question of labour is one
which adds an element of complication to the
problem. It is proposed to bring Chinamen from
California in order to build the bridge. To this
the Irishmen already employed make vigorous objections, threatening terrible things should their
protests be unheeded. There is too much reason to
fear that when the unoffending Chinamen arrive
they will be the victims of dastardly outrages.

The first thing which catches the eye on reaching the western bank of the river is a small shanty
in which liquors are sold. On the one side are
the words, 'First Chance;' on the other, 'Last
Chance.' Regardless of the risk of getting some
vile compound bearing the name of whisky, many
rushed to avail themselves of the opportunity, and

the enterprising proprietor had reason to congratulate himself on having founded his bar on Missouri mud. Through this mud the omnibus laboured slowly, the outside passengers being advised by the driver to move about from one side of the roof to another, in order to guard against upsetting the overladen vehicle. A general feeling of relief was manifested when the station of the Union Pacific Railway was reached. From this point the traveller really begins his trip over the great railway which Americans justly class among the grandest and most wonderful achievements of modern times.

V.

OVER THE ROCKY MOUNTAINS.

OMAHA is one of those American cities which seem
to spring up, flourish, and wax great in the twinkling
of an eye. Its history dates from 1854. In that
year a few squatters fixed their residence in this
section of what was then the Territory of Nebraska,
which was regarded as in the heart of the Far West.
Situated on the bank of the Missouri River, at a
point almost equidistant between the Atlantic and
Pacific Oceans, Omaha had many natural advantages, and these have been turned to profitable
account since the Pacific Railway has furnished the
opportunity. Certain it is that the city's prospects
are bright. In 1860 the population did not exceed
1,883; now the number of inhabitants is estimated
at 20,000. There are many manufactories within
its bounds, one distillery, and several breweries. In
the year 1868–9 the sales of the merchants were upwards of a million and a quarter sterling. Like most
American cities it possesses two daily newspapers,

the one the Republican the other the Democratic organ. Four other journals are published at longer intervals. Of schools, both public and private, there is abundance. The churches are fifteen in number. There are eleven hotels, of which one or two are first-class establishments. That this progress should have been made within the space of a few short years is not only marvellous, but inspires hope that the city's future will be a great and an enviable one. Although the chief city, Omaha is not now the capital of the State of Nebraska. When it was the capital, its enterprising citizens built an imposing State House, a structure which can be seen for many miles on all sides, and one which is an ornament to the city. However, for reasons unknown to me, Lincoln city, a place of far less note and importance, was made the capital in 1868. A story is told of the postmaster which illustrates the changes made here during the past few years. Mr. Jones, one of the first squatters, was appointed to the office of postmaster in the autumn of 1854. At that time there was no office, while letters were rarities. The letters which did come were kept by the postmaster in the crown of his hat till he met their owners, or till their owners claimed them. Those who expected letters had to look sharply after this official, and had sometimes to go long distances over the prairie in order to make the necessary inquiries of him. Only fifteen years have elapsed since this primitive state of things was the rule, and the post-office has expanded from a hat into an office wherein six clerks are employed.

The early history of the Pacific Railway is surrounded with obscurity, and is the subject of controversy. The claimants for the honour of having first mooted the project and of having the most materially furthered its progress are very numerous. It cannot be disputed, however, that John Plumbe a Welshman by birth and a naturalised American, began a vigorous agitation in 1836 in favour of carrying a railway across the Continent. He lived till after the gold discoveries had been made in California, and he used them as additional arguments in support of his pet scheme. As the tide of emigration flowed towards the Pacific slope and as States and Territories of vast importance were being founded beyond the Rocky Mountains, it became a national necessity to obtain easy means of communication between the East and the West. That many men of weight and ability should have advocated the construction of a railway is merely what might have been expected under circumstances such as these.

In 1853, Congress voted funds wherewith to conduct a survey in order to ascertain which was the best route. Two routes were traced out and the particulars concerning each were detailed in reports which fill thirteen large volumes. The greatest difficulty consisted in agreeing as to whether the more northerly or the more southerly was the preferable one. The representatives of the Northern and Eastern States supported the former, while the representatives of the South preferred the latter. The result was a discussion which promised to be interminable. Had it not been for the outbreak of the war this great undertaking might still have remained a project. But the war, which was destined to settle several controversies in a decisive way, brought this one to a summary close. The isolation of California was percived to involve a peril to the Union. To construct the transcontinental railway was regarded as a strategic move. Those who had favoured the extreme southerly route were no longer able to take part in the debates of Congress, nor was Congress then in a position to decree the construction of a railway through the southern part of the States. Hence, when in 1862 the scheme came up for practical settlement the present route was approved of on the ground that, despite some drawbacks it was on the whole the most feasible one which could then be selected.

Two Companies were empowered by Congress to undertake the work, subject to certain conditions and in return for certain advantages. The Union Pacific Company was to begin at Omaha and proceed Westwards, the Central Pacific Company was to begin at Sacramento and proceed Eastwards and both were to continue operations till a junction was effected. The estimated cost was one hundred millions of dollars, or about 20,000,000*l.* In aid of the undertaking subsidies of bonds, on which the interest was guaranteed, and grants of land along the line were awarded by Congress. The bond subsidy was divided into three sections. For the most level portion the rate was sixteen thousand dollars per mile; for the portion more precipitous, thirty-two thousand dollars, and for the mountainous portion forty-eight thousand dollars, per mile. The total subsidies of this character have been fifty-eight million eight hundred and forty thousand dollars. Interest on bonds to a like amount has also been guaranteed. The land grants consist of every alternate section for twenty miles on each side of the line, that is at the rate of 12,800 acres per mile. It is calculated that of these grants the Union Pacific has become entitled to an aggregate of

13,875,200 acres, and the Central Pacific to 8,832,000. Much of this land is valueless, but a large proportion is of excellent quality. The time may come when by the sale of the land the Companies will realise an amount sufficient to recoup them for the greater part of their outlay, and thus the shareholders will have acquired a most lucrative property for an almost nominal sum. But the individual advantages which may hereafter be reaped no one should grudge. The prospective gain to the Companies is a mere trifle when compared with the immediate and tangible benefit which has already been conferred on the country. Less wise than some of the other provisions was one inserted in the charters in furtherance of the policy of Protection which was rampant at the time when Congress legislated for this railway. It was provided, under the penalty of forfeiture of all the privileges conferred, that every pound of manufactured iron used in the construction of the line should be of home make. This was done at the instigation and for the personal enrichment of the iron-masters of Pennsylvania. Several American gentlemen with whom I conversed on the subject censured this arrangement in stronger terms than I care to reproduce. The bargain was unfair to the nation. The result of it has been to add at least twenty million of dollars to the cost of construction. Nor is this lavish and needless expenditure the worst part of the arrangement. The iron is admitted to be at once more costly and less perfect than that which the Companies might have imported from Europe had their charters permitted them the free exercise of their discretion.

Quite as noteworthy as the fact of the line having been constructed at all, is the speed with which it was completed. On the 5th November, 1865, the first sod of the Union Pacific Railway was turned near the Missouri River, and within a short distance of Omaha. In less than four years afterwards the line was completed, the ceremony of driving the last spike having taken place on the 10th May, 1869. When it is considered that the length of one portion is 1,084 miles, the rapidity of construction almost staggers the most credulous. It is true that the line is a single one, that the stations are temporary structures, and that the bridges are built of wood, yet this does not render the enterprise the less extraordinary.

Passing from statistics about the Union Pacific to an account of personal experience of the railway, let it be supposed that the forenoon train is about to start on its long journey of more than

1,000 miles from the terminus at Omaha to the station at Promontory, which is the eastern terminus of the Central Pacific. Confusion reigns supreme here, as at most American railway stations. Excited passengers are rushing about in quest of the luggage which, despite the system of ' checking,' is often going astray or getting out of sight. Frantic efforts are made to attract the attention of the baggage clerk, and to induce him to attach the necessary check to the trunk or portmanteau, which has at length been discovered. Those who get this part of their business over proceed to the office in order to secure berths in Pullman's sleeping car. The number of these berths is limited and bitter is the disappointment of those who fail in obtaining one. The prospect of spending several nights in an ordinary car is enough to depress the mind and daunt the courage of the hardiest traveller. Having had the good fortune to be among those who had secured berths by telegraph, I was able to hear the exclamations of the disappointed with pleasant equanimity. As a class, the passengers differed greatly from those with whom I journeyed to Omaha from Chicago. Some were old Californians returning home after a visit to their birthplaces in the Eastern States. Others were taking the overland route to San Francisco, in order to compare its comforts with those of the route across the Isthmus of Panama. A considerable proportion consisted of adventurers bound for California to seek their fortunes, and a very few were travelling for their pleasure. To nearly every one the journey is a new one, partaking of the character of a daring enterprise. Some who profess to be well informed mis-spend their time in endeavours to excite the fears of the timid and the apprehensions of the excitable. They enlarge on the dangers incident to a line constructed too hurriedly. They draw ghastly pictures of perils to be faced in the event of the wild Indians putting obstructions in the way of the train, and attacking the passengers. It is possible that these tales promoted the sale of insurance tickets. An agent of a railway insurance company walked through the train before it left the station, and vigorously canvassed the passengers. Many of them had already made this provision for accidents. Indeed, the Americans are too shrewd a people to omit making arrangements in view of the consequences of a railway accident. In ' Appleton's Handbook of American Travel ' the last piece of advice given in the introduction is, ' Having laid in your necessary supplies, it only remains for you to insure yourself against accident by sea or land.' The reader of this is not unnaturally induced to ask himself whether, if pleasure travelling in the United States be regarded as fraught with so much danger it is not wiser to stay at home.

Four miles after leaving Omaha, the first stoppage is made. The journey is now fairly begun and every one is on the look out for new scenery and strange adventures. As mile after mile is left behind, the remark is very generally made that the surrounding country, instead of being wild and desolate, is rich and filled with settlers. Farm houses and tilled fields are seen on both sides of the line, and this spectacle is a common one throughout a large tract of the State of Nebraska. The Platte river is the first object of interest which breaks the monotony of the plains. Along the south bank of this river runs the old emigrant road for many miles. The train of white-covered waggons, called ' Prairie Schooners,' drawn by teams of oxen, might in former days be seen stretching as far as the eye could reach. At long intervals the sight of one or two of these waggons recalls the bygone times, when a trip across the plains took as many months as it now takes days, and was seldom accomplished without the loss of several cattle, and of a few human lives. The magnitude of the trade carried on over the plains may be understood from the fact that nearly 7,000 men regularly earned their living as teamsters. Glad though the drivers of these teams were to keep near the Platte River as long as possible, they were by no means pleased with the river itself. Its channel is continually shifting, and its bed is treacherous sand. Looked at, the river seems one of those noble streams destined by nature to bear heavily laden vessels on its bosom. In breadth it averages three-quarters of a mile. The water is turbid, and its depth seldom exceeds six inches. But while it has these drawbacks, it is nevertheless the silent agent of innumerable blessings to this section of the country. The valley through which it flows is fertilised by its waters. Luxuriant vegetation and clumps of trees attest the course of the stream. Without this river the valley would be a waste; with the river the valley only awaits the hand of man to be transformed into a garden.

The first real sensation is obtained at Jackson, a small station an hundred miles west of Omaha. Here many of the passengers see genuine Indians for the first time—that is, men who live by hunting, and who glory in getting scalps. They are Pawnees. We are told that they are friendly Indians, being supporters of the United States Government. They may be friendly at heart, but they are bloodthirsty in appearance.   They probably consider themselves civilised, for each carries a revolver in a belt strapped round his waist.   That they are staunch adherents to old traditions is proved by an inspection of their encampment.   Outside the tents are poles stuck into the ground.   From the tops of these poles, wisps of hair flutter in the breeze.   The seeker after knowledge naturally asks the meaning of these things.   His belief in the friendliness of the Pawnees is not strengthened when he is informed that the wisps of hair are trophies of victory which have been cut from the heads of vanquished foes.   The Indians, whose advance in civilisation is manifested by the addition of the revolver to the scalping-knife, are not persons for whom it is possible to entertain great admiration.   Their acquaintance is more to be avoided than courted. Seen at a distance they are picturesque additions to the landscape; when met by the defenceless traveller they prove to be brutal monsters.   The chief testimony given in favour of the Pawnees is that they are better than the Sioux, and that they are always ready to demonstrate their loyalty to the Union by murdering the Sioux without mercy. How to deal with the Indians is one of the most complex among the problems with which the Government of the United States has to deal.   The

desire is to treat them with perfect fairness, and to
strain many points in their favour. But the conduct of the Indians themselves is the frequent bar
to a uniform adherence to a policy of gentleness.
The stories of Indian outrages, which are told by
the settlers on the plains, excite indignation and
inspire revenge in the breasts of the most humane.
It is true, on the other hand, that the settlers have
been guilty of many barbarities. They maintain,
however, that if they slaughter Indians it is always
in self-defence, or in retaliation for some intolerable
and unpardonable outrage. The Indians, they say,
not content with slaying white men in cold blood,
must needs torture their victims with every refine-
ment of savage brutality. Were it a mere question
of shooting the men with whom they came into
contact, or against whom they had a grudge, the
white men would have less complaints to make.
It is the practice of torture, rather than the commission of murder, which displeases and provokes
them. Certainly, if but one half of the stories be
true, the hatred borne by the white men against
the Indians is not without excuse. It would be
well, however, before coming to a decision, to learn
the Indian version of the case.

At Grand Island station the train stops, and the
passengers are allowed half an hour for supper.

On leaving this place the traveller is told that if of
a religious turn of mind he may bid good-bye to
schools and churches, and keep ' his eye peeled ' for
buffalo. The next two hundred miles run through
the tract crossed by the buffalo herds on their mi-
grations from South to North. However, the ex-
pectation of getting a sight of these denizens of the
plains is one which is more frequently excited than
gratified. Since the opening of the railway the
buffaloes have shunned this district. They may
return to it again, as it is not uncommon for them
to leave a particular spot and then revisit it after
the lapse of two or three years. Still, the days
of buffalo-hunting are numbered. As the country
becomes settled, the bunch grass, which is the
favourite food of the buffalo, gives place to the corn
plant. Already the newspapers of these districts
are protesting against the wholesale slaughter of
buffaloes by sportsmen. When the time arrives
for preserving wild animals, the moment of their
extinction is not distant. To the passengers by
this train the presence or absence of buffalo herds
mattered little, seeing that the favourite feeding-
grounds of these animals were passed during the
night. The event of the succeeding morning was
halting at Cheyenne city for breakfast. This is
one of the towns which sprang up during the con-

5

struction of the railway. In July, 1867, there was but one house here. At present there are 3,000 inhabitants in Cheyenne. The population has been as large as 6,000. It was what is here styled a 'rough place,' that is to say a miniature hell upon earth. Thieves and gamblers, murderers and prostitutes, were numbered among its 'prominent citizens.' But the day of its orgies is passed away; the scum of the population has moved off to other pastures, and the streets of Cheyenne are as quiet as the streets of other Western cities in which law has conquered license. The breakfast supplied at the railway-station deserves a word of praise. It was a plain but wholesome meal, and it had the charm of novelty in the shape of antelope steaks. The flesh of the antelope is most palatable, the flavour being something between the flavour of venison and beef. The animal is a hardy one, and it might easily be acclimatised in England.

The scenery from this point onwards is tame and uninteresting. In every direction the limitless plains extend to the horizon. Here and there a tuft of wild flowers relieves the monotony of the grass flats. A herd of antelopes bounding along is a sight most welcome to the fatigued eye, while the rare spectacle of two Rocky Mountain sheep, with wild aspect and long twisted horns, excites speculation as to how they had wandered so far from their native haunts. Dead oxen by the wayside bear witness to the passage of an emigrant train, and to losses sustained by its members. At Hazard, a station beyond Cheyenne, is a little mountain tarn. A few miles farther on, small patches of white in the crevices of the rocks cause the statement to be made that the country of alkali dust has been reached at last. This, however, is contradicted. The patches in question prove to be traces of snow. It is true that the sun shines brightly overhead, and that the winter has not yet begun. Nevertheless, the intense coldness of the air excites general remark. The explanation is simple. We are nearing the highest point of the line. Since leaving Omaha the ascent has been gradual, but continuous. We have ascended nearly 8,000 feet above the sea level, and the height gained is amidst the peaks of the Rocky Mountains on which snow always rests, and where not a day throughout the year passes without the fall of a larger or smaller quantity of snow. The purity of the air is extreme. Objects many miles distant seem as if they were but as many feet removed from the spectator. With difficulty do the lungs become fully inflated, so great is the rarity of the air. As mile after mile is traversed the ground is more steep. Cuttings

through the rocks have been made to reduce the
incline. The strain on the engine becomes greater;
the speed of the train is diminished, until the ascent
is. finally made, and the train halts at Sherman,
a railway . station of which the elevation exceeds
that of any in the world, it being situated 8,235
feet above the level of the sea.

V.

THE ROCKY MOUNTAINS TO THE GREAT SALT LAKE.

SHERMAN STATION, the highest point on the
Pacific Railway, is in the Territory of Wyoming,
the youngest among the Territories of the United
States. It was named after the Valley in Pennsylvania which is known in history as the scene of
a horrible massacre and which lives in poetry as
the abode of Campbell's 'Gertrude.' Wyoming
Territory has already attracted the attention of the
world on account of the social and political reforms
of which it has been the theatre. Here the enfran-
chisement of women has not only been conceded, but
the logical results have been accepted. Women have
been empanelled as jurors, and even entrusted with
the discharge of judicial functions.

Some writers strongly advise the traveller to
make a halt at Sherman station. The inducements
held out to him are mountain scenery, invigorating
air, fishing, and hunting. A sojourn among the
peaks of the Rocky Mountains has the attraction of

novelty to recommend it. Life there must be, in every sense of the word, a new sensation. But some sensations are undesirable notwithstanding their undoubted freshness. That splendid trout swarm in the streams near Sherman admits of no dispute. Yet the disciple of Isaac Walton should not be tempted to indulge rashly in his harmless and charming sport. It is delightful to hook large fish; but it is less agreeable to be pierced through by arrows. Now, the latter contingency is among the probabilities which must be taken into consideration. A few weeks prior to my journey, one of the conductors of the train by which I travelled learned, by practical experience, that fishing amid the Rocky Mountains has palpable and painful drawbacks. Having taken a few days' holiday, he went forth, fishing-rod in hand, to amuse himself. While whipping the stream in the innocence of his heart, he was startled to find himself made the target for arrows shot by wild Indians. He sought safety in flight, and recovered from his wounds to the surprise as much as to the gratification of his friends. His story did not render me desirous of sharing his fate. The trout-fisher might employ his leisure to greater advantage elsewhere than in the Territory of Wyoming. The sportsman runs fewer risks and would fare much better. If he sallied forth to shoot antelopes, elk, or deer, he might return unpierced by arrows and laden with game. The Indians are bold and forward enough in presence of a man carrying a fishing-rod, but they keep at a very respectful distance from him who is armed with a repeating rifle. The accommodation at Sherman is not luxurious. It is a place consisting of a few buildings erected for the use of the railway officials.

The scenery around Sherman is bleak and wild. Several famous peaks are said to be perceptible in the far distance. I have read a statement to the effect that Long's Peak, one of the principal mountains of Colorado, 75 miles to the South-west, and Pike's Peak, 165 miles to the South are ' both plainly visible.' To the North, Elk Mountain is ' another noted landmark,' about 100 miles distant. It is possible that these mountain tops may have been discerned in a vision by the compilers of guide books. To the eye of the ordinary and unimaginative traveller they are invisible. What he does see to the left of the line looking westward is the snow-capped range of the Wahsatch mountains. On the right are rough and irregular elevations dotted over with dark pines. These are the Black Hills of Wyoming. A huge mass of red rock stands forth here and there on the solitary plains. Most welcome to eyes wearied with the savage grandeur of the scene, are the patches of purple and yellow wild flowers which flourish amidst the short brown grass. It is with a feeling of relief that Sherman station is left behind. The train descends by its own weight the rapid incline which leads to the Laramie Plains. Three miles westward of Sherman the line crosses Dale Creek on one of those wooden bridges which appear so unsubstantial, yet are said to be so strong. It is 650 feet long and 126 feet high. The trestle work of which it consists resembles the scaffolding erected for the purpose of painting the outside of a London house. An enthusiastic writer terms this bridge 'the grandest feature of the road,' and commends it for its 'light, airy, and graceful appearance.' The contractors are said to boast of having erected it in the short space of thirty days. It is not stated how many days the bridge will bear the strain almost hourly put upon it. More than one passenger who would rather lose a fine sight than risk a broken neck breathes more freely, and gives audible expression to his satisfaction, once the cars have passed in safety over this remarkable wooden structure. Downwards speeds the train, at a pace which makes one shudder at the consequences of an accident. In twenty miles the descent of a thousand feet is accomplished. No steam power is employed. On the contrary, the brakes are tightly screwed down alike on the locomotive and the cars. At Laramie City a halt of thirty minutes is made, and a good meal is provided for the hungry passengers. We are now in the midst of the Laramie plains, reputed to be the finest grazing land in this part of the Continent. Here thousands of buffaloes used to feed and wax fat. With the exception of Texas, no place can be found where cattle may be fattened at a less cost. As we proceed onwards the plains widen on either side, and the mountain ranges recede into the distance. We are again on the rolling prairie, but not such a prairie as is to be found in the States of Illinois and Iowa. The sage-brush plant begins to show itself. This constitutes the sole vegetation of the arid and desolate tract which is known by the name of the Great American Desert. The only thing alleged in favour of the sage-brush is that, when used as a medicine, it is a specific for ague. If the malady were as common as the plant is plentiful hardly a human being would escape a seizure. Millions of acres are covered with sage-brush. On the right of the line is a small sheet of water, to which the name of Como Lake has been given. In nothing but the name does it recall the famous Italian Lake, yet the prospect is a pleasing relief to the monotony of the surrounding waste. Carbon station is one very important in reality, though apparently insignificant. Here the company's workmen made a discovery which has helped to fill the company's coffers. During the construction of the line a seam of coal was cut through. This was literally a godsend. It had been feared that all the fuel used along the line would have to be transported from the remote East. In this locality wood is very scarce, and the carriage of coal would have been costly. However, the discovery of a coal-field at Carbon settled the fuel question at once and for ever. The quality of the coal is first-class, and the quantity is practically unlimited. Two hundred tons a day are extracted with ease. Not only is the coal burned in the locomotives, but it is also supplied to the stations along the line, being sent as far eastwards as Omaha. Nor is this the only coalfield which has been discovered and worked at a profit. In other parts of the Territory large fields of coal have been proved to exist, while iron ore of the richest kind abounds in the vicinity of the coal. Thus the Black Hills which have been regarded as yielding nothing but dark pine and have been more notable heretofore for their picturesqueness than their mineral treasures, may hereafter become the centre of an industry in coal and iron as important as any upon this Continent. From this point the line passes through elevated land on either side, till a wild gorge is entered a few miles to the east of Fort Steele. The mountains which stretch away from the mouth of the gorge seem designed to guard its entrance They have the look of battlements carefully wrought and prepared to withstand a siege. The beholder naturally expects to see sentinels keeping watch on the top, and cannon protruding over the sides. It is difficult to believe that these escarpments have been cut by no mortal hand, but are due to the action of the warring elements on the friable red rock. At Fort Steele there is a garrison of four companies. All around is barrenness and desolation. Nothing but sage-brush covers the ground. The pools of water are bitter with alkali. Great enthusiasm or a high sense of duty can alone render life here other than a perpetual burden. At Rawlings Springs a stoppage is made for supper, and a few miles farther on the backbone of the Continent is reached and crossed. This point is 191 miles west of Sherman, and 1,034 miles distant from Sacramento. The height above the level of the sea is more than 1,000 feet less than at Sherman, yet the configuration of the country is such as to constitute this the watershed, whence the stream which runs

East falls into the Atlantic, and the stream which runs West falls into the Pacific.

At an early hour the following morning the passengers are roused to take breakfast at Wahsatch. This place has a bad reputation. I was told that ' out of twenty-four graves here, but one held the remains of a person who had died a natural death, and that was a prostitute who had poisoned herself.' I give the statement in the words of my informant. It was evidently his opinion that suicide was perfectly natural under the circumstances; and possibly he was right. The line is now in Utah Territory; the land we now see is the land of the Mormons, and the people are Saints in name. Moreover, this part is the most striking and picturesque of any on the Union Pacific Railway, for the line runs along Echo and Weber Canyons,* passing by the Devil's Slide, passing through the Devil's Gate. It was in

---

* As the word ' Canyon' will occur several times, I may now explain its meaning and defend the form of spelling which I have adopted. The word which is a Spanish one, and as such is spelled *Cañon*, signifies a ravine. Here it is always used to denote those sudden depressions in the ground, the sides of which descend sheer down to the depth of from two to six thousand feet, which are common in Colorado, Utah, Nevada, and California. Some persons write the word in its Spanish form; others spell it ' Kanyon,' while the most general method of spelling it is Canyon. I have thought it best to spell the word in the way which renders its correct pronunciation easy, and to conform, at the same time, to the practice of the majority.

Echo Canyon that the Mormons determined to make a stand against the army commanded by General Johnson, which President Buchanan sent to subdue them in 1857. They fortified the pass on the system which barbarous tribes adopt to withstand the passage of regular troops through mountainous countries. At the height of a thousand feet above the bed of the Canyon, huge rocks were heaped up in readiness to be hurled down upon the soldiers toiling along below. But the experiment was not tried. General Johnson negotiated instead of fighting, assented to the Mormon demands instead of insisting upon the acceptance by them of the terms he was sent to enforce. This was the beginning of the temporising policy which, since then, has characterised the dealings of the United States Government with the Mormons.

While passing through these Canyons the passengers are eagerly watching the points of interest which abound. The platform of an American railroad car is well adapted for the sight-seer. Although passengers are forbidden to stand on the platform, yet the rule is one to which the exceptions are numerous enough for the convenience of all who choose to run a little risk. Adequately to depict the spectacle is hardly possible. It is pre-eminently a grand one. It recalls the magni-

ficent sight to be witnessed between Botzen and
Verona when the railway passes near to the gigantic piles of rock which have been fitly entitled
The Gateways of the Alps.   Beneath our feet the
Weber river rushes along in turbulent might.   At
one moment the line skirts the margin of deep,
dark pools.   At another a bend removes the river
into the distance, and then the attention is fixed
on some huge chasm in the rugged mountain side.
Where the pass narrows stands a solitary pine
bearing the name of the 1,000 mile tree.   It was
so named because it was the first tree of any size
which the constructors of the railway met with
while they were carrying the line westward from
Omaha.   High up on the distant mountain slopes
are beautiful tufts of a red shrub, and in the clefts
of the rocks are a few stunted trees, but with
these exceptions the whole scene is wild and barren.
Not far from the tree just mentioned is the Devil's
Slide.   This resembles the wooden structures, down
which the trees cut on mountain heights are shot
to the river below, only this slide is fashioned by
Nature's hand out of solid rock.   Swiftly does
the train speed along the Canyon, until emerging
from the narrow space between the sundered rocks
which is called the Devil's Gate, the Great Salt
Lake is discerned in the distance, and the view of

a luxuriant valley is in pleasing contrast to the frowning rock and foaming river. The train stops at Uintah. Here Mormon lads sells peaches and Mormon women tempt the ladies in the train to purchase gloves which they have tastefully embroidered.

VII.

VISIT TO THE MORMONS : THE CITY OF THE SAINTS.

THE Pacific Railway runs through Utah Territory
and skirts the northern end of the Great Salt
Lake. From the nearest railway station to the
City of the Saints the distance is about forty miles.
A branch line, called the Utah Central Railroad,
has now brought Salt Lake City into communication by rail with the principal American cities of
the East and West. When I made the journey,
the visitor to the capital of Mormondom had to
leave the Union Pacific at Uintah station, and to
take a seat in one of the stage coaches of Wells,
Fargo, & Co. The coach which meets the train is
what is styled a ' Concord Coach.' It has seats
for nine persons inside and for at least five on the
roof. The inside seat for three is placed crosswise
between the two doors. Those who occupy it are
not only cramped, but are exposed to disagreeable
pressure from the knees of the passengers behind,
as well as to inconvenience from the feet and legs
of those facing them. To suffer this during five

hours, the time occupied by the journey, is bad
enough, yet this is not the worst. The road itself
is unique of its kind. To rival it would be difficult; to surpass it impossible. In badness it is
pre-eminent. Execrable is the strongest epithet
in the language for a road having no redeeming
points. This word, however, serves but feebly and
inadequately to describe and stigmatise the road
between Uintah station and Salt Lake City.
There are innumerable ruts and depressions in it.
Huge stones interpose obstacles to the smooth
passage of a vehicle. If the occurrence of the
ruts were more uniform, and the arrangement of
the stones more regular, less complaint might with
justice be made. But the perverse combination of
the two is utterly unbearable. On one side, at
short distances apart, is a rut a foot deep, on the
opposite side is a row of stones a foot high. As
the four horses harnessed to the coach draw it
rapidly over those rough places, the effect is that
of a sudden lurch and stunning blow produced
simultaneously. The swing to the one side, which
follows the sinking of the wheels, bumps the passengers against the sides and against each other,
while the jar of the other wheels against the stones,
throws their heads against the roof or their backs
against the front or rear of the coach. Thus they

learn, in a way alike practical and unpleasant, the import of the threat to beat a man into a jelly or to break every bone in his body. On reaching their destination the passengers have good grounds for charging the company with a species of assault and battery. That no steps have yet been taken with a view to obtain redress for physical injuries sustained during the drive is probably due to the fact that every one who has survived the ordeal must be so thankful that he has escaped with his life as to have no disposition to foster vindictive feelings against his fellows. It is a standing miracle that the driver sticks to his post. Judging from the one who drove the coach when I was among the passengers, I should say that the risks run and the jolting undergone had a souring effect on the temper, and a saddening influence on the mind. A more surly, ill-conditioned, and taciturn driver I never met before. The chief point in his favour was his determination to keep his cattle going at full speed. When we halted to change horses, and were detained a few minutes beyond the allotted time, he told the outside passengers to hold on firmly, as he meant 'to go ahead like greased lightning.' As the road before us looked even worse than that behind, this intimation seemed equivalent to a threat of extra sufferings about to be inflicted. On the other hand, the warning was accepted with gratitude. It was better to have one's misery shortened in time, even if intensified in degree, than to have it protracted as well as extreme. To this hour, I am amazed that the wheels and the framework of the coach remained unbroken and unstrained.

The trials by the way did not hinder my admiring the surrounding scenery. The road runs along the mountain valley which stretches from the outlet of Weber Canyon to the Wahsatch Mountains, southward of Salt Lake City. The ground on the right is a continuation of the great valley, and in the distance the vast Lake glitters under the rays of the bright sunlight. Around our path to right and left were hundreds of stunted shrubs, among which dwarf oaks had the leading place. Among the scanty herbage were numerous anthills, rising to the height of at least three feet and having the ground at their base carefully cleared for several inches. On the mountain slopes were masses of a dwarf maple. As the maple leaves were brilliant with the autumnal tints, the appearance of the variegated mass was at once picturesque and charming. Several farms are visible from the road, and the fields give distinct token of careful cultivation. Everywhere is to be seen evidence that the people of these parts are hard-working and energetic. The first meal eaten within sight of Salt Lake was got at a little roadside station. This erection is of a rude and temporary character, being one half wooden hut and one half canvas tent. More noticeable than the dwelling in which we sat, and the food set before us, was the multitude of house-flies which seemed to have taken possession of every spot. The tablecloth was black with them. They swarmed over every dish as soon as the cover was removed, nor did they confine their attentions to meat, or milk, or sugar. They justified Mr. Ruskin's remark that house-flies are black incarnations of caprice, by settling upon and seeming to enjoy pickles as much as a lump of sugar, or the fresh face of a stranger. Never before could I realise the terror which must have overspread the land of Egypt when the plague of flies was sent to soften the hard heart of Pharaoh. It added to the discomfort of the moment to learn that the visitation was not exceptional, that the flies were quite as numerous and tormenting in the city to which I was hastening. After the lapse of about five hours and when the heat, and dust, and flies, and jolting had maddened and exhausted the passengers, a sudden turning in the road brought relief to every mind, for in the distance could be seen the gardens and dwellings of the capital of Mormondom.   The aspect of the city from this point is that of a large country village.   No building, except the Tabernacle, stands forth to give an air of importance to the cluster of houses, and the Tabernacle, when viewed from afar, cannot be called imposing.   In appearance it resembles a gigantic dish cover.   Besides, the number of houses is not large enough to adequately fill up the foreground of the extensive landscape.   The valley in which the city lies is on a huge scale, and the range of snowy peaks in the background rivets the eye more forcibly than the handful of white houses embosomed in trees.   On nearer approach the first impression is deepened.   The width and length of the streets are disproportioned to the buildings which line their sides.   In Main-street are some handsome structures, but these are the rare exceptions.

The thought now predominating over all others is one of thankfulness that the moment of release from the torments of the stage coach is at hand. Seldom has a hotel seemed so truly a place of refuge as did the 'Townsend House,' in which my travelling acquaintances and myself found accommodation.   This is a Mormon hotel, the landlord rejoicing, or the reverse, in the possession of three wives. It has the reputation of being one of the best houses in the city, but this reputation is based less on its intrinsic merits than on the circumstance that it is kept by a Mormon, and that, consequently, it affords the inquisitive stranger an opportunity of learning something as to the practical working of the peculiar institution in which Mormons glory. Without enlarging on a topic to which I have already referred, a topic, too, of which the interest is happily local, let me here simply mention that if any reader has an enemy whom he would like to torture in the most refined yet cruel way, he can attain his object by persuading him to go to the Townsend House in the autumn. The flies will worry him to death in the course of a few weeks. They render the enjoyment of a meal wholly impossible. Every dish is seasoned with dead flies; the hands, heads, and faces of the visitors are covered over with living ones. The landlord is the gainer, for many persons prefer to leave the table long before their appetites are stayed, rather than sit through a meal to be the sport and the victims of the flies. The flies do for the traveller what the physician did for Sancho Panza.

The plan of Salt Lake City is that on which nearly every American city is built. There is a

main street, with which others run parallel, and
from which side streets branch off at right angles.
The majority of the shops and stores are in the
principal street. On many of the stores is a sign-
board, with the following inscription. At the top
are the words, 'Holiness to the Lord,' underneath
is painted the All-seeing Eye, and then follows
the announcement, 'Zion's Co-operative Mercantile
Institution.'   These stores were opened several
months ago for the purpose of keeping the business
of the place exclusively in the hands of the Saints.
The device is one of the many expedients of Brigham Young for retaining his hold over the Mormons, and for driving away the Gentiles. Among
the latter are included the Jews, of whom several
are engaged in business here and who are numbered among the Gentiles, while the Saints are
classed with the sinners. At the northern end of
this street are the Tabernacle, the Tithing-office,
the Endowment House and the residence of President Young. Within the enclosure of the present
Tabernacle are the foundations of the structure
destined to be the Tabernacle of the future. The
stone employed is a beautiful grey granite, and
every part has been planned with a view to solidity.
But the progress is very slow, and no one professes
to expect that the building will be speedily, if ever,

finished. The existing Tabernacle is an oblong or egg-shaped structure, devoid of ornament, and wholly destitute of beauty either in proportion or outline. It is said to have accommodation for 8,000 persons. This is an exaggeration. A friend who carefully estimated the available space assured me that there is not room for more than 5,000 sitters. At the one end is a very large organ, now in course of construction; on a raised platform at that end are benches for the elders and rulers of the Church, the President and his twelve apostles having places in the centre. In front of their pew are barrels containing water. After the water has been blessed, it is handed about in tin cans to every person in the congregation. A sip of this water and a morsel of bread constitutes the ceremony of taking the sacrament according to Mormon rites. Alongside of the Tabernacle is a small structure similar in shape and arrangement, wherein service is generally held. The Tithing-office and the house, or rather houses, of Brigham Young, are in no respect remarkable. Indeed, very little can be seen of them, as they are surrounded and shut in by a high wall. The official room of the President is small and simply furnished. On the walls within the entrance are portraits in oil of the twelve Apostles. As likenesses they may be good; as works of art they are hideous. In appearance, the President of the Saints is not prepossessing. He is above the middle height, is portly in person, has a large head, and a visage which betokens the man of firmness rather than of intellect. His large mouth, heavy lower features, and sensual expression proclaim in unmistakable signs his fondness for a ritual which, by consecrating polygamy, gives free scope for indulging in every whim and freak of passion. He has the look of a determined man, and the character of being an obstinate one. According to the saying of an admirer, 'all hell could not turn him,' once he had made up his mind. About the secrets of his harem I have nothing to reveal. Many of his children and some of his wives I have seen, but I am unable to say how many of both he claims as his own. Nor do I believe all the tales about Brigham Young and his harem which have been published for the edification of English readers. Even if accurate particulars could be obtained, it does not follow that they should be communicated to the public. What passes in the privacy of the domestic circle should never be disclosed for the gratification of vulgar curiosity; and this rule, which has the sanction of public opinion when a man has one wife and a few children, should be as uniformly observed and as rigorously

6

enforced when the man's wives are many and his children numberless. To pander to a morbid love for scandal is nearly as unpardonable as are the worst practices of the most heartless polygamist.

Next in importance to the Tabernacle, if it be not an adjunct to it, is the theatre. This is a stone building which would do credit to many cities of greater importance. It will hold at least 1,500 spectators. Were it lit up with gas, the house would present a striking spectacle on a crowded night. But as the lighting is accomplished by means of petroleum lamps, it has a gloomy appearance. This may be remedied hereafter, as there is a project to establish gas-works here. The pit is divided into family boxes, or rather benches, in which a Mormon may surround himself with his wives and children. Whether the arrangement be intentional or accidental I know not, but the custom seems to prevail for one or two out of the several wives who accompanied most of the men to wear 'poke bonnets,' resembling those which Quaker ladies wore in former days. The wearers of those bonnets are either elderly, or else ill-favoured in features. The younger and comelier wives have fashionable hats on their heads. It is worthy of note that female beauty which is the rule throughout the United States is the exception in Salt Lake City. Some of the girls have charming faces, but the wives of the Saints are not over-burdened with good looks. In a long box at one side of the theatre were seated many girls of different ages, and they were said to be the President's daughters. Brigham Young himself occupied a stage box, his last wife keeping him company. The others could look up from the pit and envy their preferred rival. About the performance I witnessed, I shall say but little. The occasion was a special one, it being a 'Grand complimentary benefit tendered by the citizens of Salt Lake to the Great Tragedian Neil Warner.' This actor was described in the advertisements as a 'great English tragedian.' In what part of England he acquired his fame I am ignorant, yet I must admit that his physical power was extraordinary. He roared and gesticulated through the part of Sir Giles Over-reach with a robust vigour and fire altogether exceptional, and he performed a death scene in a manner which perfectly exemplified the difficulty of dying naturally upon the stage. When recalled after the fall of the curtain, he apologised for not making a lengthened speech, on the ground that no man could be expected to have much breath or any voice left after exertions like those through which he had gone. None of the regular members of the company, some of whom acted in a way that was truly praiseworthy, were summoned before the curtain. Although the audience testified by loud and prolonged applause their admiration for the strength of Mr. Warner's lungs and for the vehemence of his gestures, yet I overheard remarks made by individuals which were not wholly complimentary to him, and these remarks led me to think that a few Mormons are judges of good acting. The newspaper critics were as greatly pleased with the performance as modern dramatic critics are with theatrical performances of a sensational type. In the *Salt Lake Daily Telegraph* of the following morning it was said that Neil Warner 'is the greatest actor we have ever seen and a splendid career awaits him.' The *Deseret Evening News* wrote that the delineation of the part of Sir Giles Overreach 'was a perfect triumph, and we think could not possibly be excelled.' It seems clear, then, that Salt Lake City is a blissful abode for English actors with powerful lungs and boundless pretensions.

When the moon does not shine, the streets of Salt Lake City are wrapt in darkness, street lamps being unknown luxuries there. It is the boast of the Mormons that, in the streets of their capital, the scandalous sights of other cities are never witnessed; that drunken Mormons never stagger along the pavement, and that the female harpies, of whom drunkards are the natural victims, are unknown curses. There are four bars at which liquor is sold, and of these the Gentiles are said to be the patrons. Temperance is enjoined by President Young, and he has the credit of practising what he preaches. He can do this the more easily, if report speak truly. Avarice and lust are the vices which master him to the exclusion of all others. It is not surprising, then, if he has no love for strong drinks. But I cannot give his followers credit for being as abstemious as himself. Not all of them are over-mastered by avarice and lust. Neither is it credible that all the persons daily fined for drunkenness, are ostracised and calumniated Gentiles. It is not strange that, apart from other considerations, in a city destitute of lamps, nocturnal vice should not flaunt in the streets. Put out the lights in the Haymarket or in Broadway, and the leprosy of great cities would be concealed, though not extir-pated. On the other hand, the darkness which prevails in Salt Lake City by night furnishes a convenient cloak for the enforcement of what the Mormon leaders eulogise as righteous retribution and the horrified Gentiles denounce as brutal murder.

I neither accept without reservation all the harsh things said by the Mormons and the Gentiles respecting each other, nor do I doubt that there may be some foundation for their mutual dislike and recrimination. The eagerness of the Mormons to extort praise from the visitors to their Zion is very noteworthy. They are ready to trumpet forth their own merits, and to charge all alleged, or demonstrated shortcomings upon the Gentiles. The Gentiles, in turn, do not hesitate to sing their own praises. Which of the two is in the right constitutes the problem that has been the subject of warm controversy, and of which the desired solution has not yet been discovered.

VIII.

THE MORMONS AT HOME.

THE MORMONS have been highly praised for their
industry and skill in converting the desolate Salt
Lake Valley into a region of fruit trees and corn-
fields. This praise is subject to qualification. It
is true that they have planted trees and sown grain
where rank herbage seemed the natural product of
the soil; that their peaches and apples are well fla-
voured; that their corn is excellent in quality. But
it is likewise true that the soil and climate of Salt
Lake Valley combine to render gardening and farming easy and profitable occupations. Irrigation is
the one thing needful, and to irrigate the thirsty land
is here the merest child's play. The country is intersected with streams of fresh water descending from
their sources among the mountains to fill the lakes in
the lower ground. On the borders of these streams
a vegetation far more luxuriant than that of the
parched plains indicates the course to be adopted by
him who would till the soil in the hope of reaping a
harvest. Of these hints the first settlers took full

advantage, and the result is seen to-day in the acacias which line the streets of the city, and the orchards which surround the houses. No miracle has been wrought here. They only will marvel at the spectacle who are unaware of the simplicity of the process. Yet there is a valid excuse for the exaggerated eulogiums which certain visitors to Salt Lake have passed upon Mormon intelligence, foresight, and perseverance. Before the railway made the journey comparatively easy, the visitor who crossed the plains underwent so many hardships and passed through a country so sterile in appearance that, on reaching Salt Lake City, he overrated the achievements of the Saints, because he argued that the country with which they had to deal resembled in reality, as well as in look, that through which he had toiled. Hence it was, that when the Saints bound for their terrestrial Zion arrived at Emigrant's Gap, from which they saw the neat houses of their brethren in the faith on the slope at their feet, and beheld the Great Lake towards which hundreds of streams meandered through the pleasant fields, they were so overcome with the unwonted sight as to fall on their knees in an ecstacy of admiration and shed tears of joy. I have not heard of one among the thousands who have arrived here since the opening of the Pacific Railway, and who have entered the city by the road which I have described, manifesting a particle of the like enthusiasm. The first impression made by any city depends altogether on the point of view. Now that Salt Lake City can be seen under a new aspect, it is less fascinating in appearance, and is far less remarkable as an example of a great work accomplished under difficulties, than when it was the haven of the dispirited emigrant and wearied traveller. Thousands who never heard of Joseph Smith, and who would scout the pretensions of Brigham Young, have overcome quite as many obstacles, and performed as great feats of courage and endurance when founding and erecting cities in the Western States and Territories of the American Union, as the enthusiasts who have made for themselves homes in this splendid and fruitful Valley. The history and progress of Chicago and San Francisco approach the miraculous far more closely than the building of Salt Lake City.

It has suited the purposes of the Mormon leaders to make the most of the persecution to which they have been subjected, and of the triumphs they have achieved. By magnifying their work they have instilled into the minds of their ignorant followers a confidence in their power to vanquish any dangers which may again menace the Church of the Latter

Day Saints, or bode ruin to the social organization of which Brigham Young is the founder and the head. In this respect, the writings of some travellers have been of great service to them. Taking the people at their own valuation, these writers have contributed to increase the confidence of the people in their own resources. The extent to which they are self-deluded is almost incredible. Speaking to more than one Mormon as to what would happen were the United States Government to put down polygamy with a strong hand, I always received the reply that if the contingency occurred the Mormon army would fight to the death in support of the cornerstone of the Mormon faith. Pressing the question home, and asking what a few thousands could possibly do against the force which would be arrayed on the other side, I was assured, with a confidence of tone and manner which denoted implicit belief in the assertion, that the Lord would indubitably arise to the help of his servants in their hour of need, just as he had done in former days when their very existence as a community was in extreme jeopardy. It will facilitate the understanding of what I am convinced is the true state of the case if I indicate what I believe to be the conclusion arrived at by recent travellers in Mormondom, by whom works of undoubted attraction have been written for the enlightenment and amusement of readers in the United Kingdom and the United States.

The impression left on the readers of these volumes must have been that Salt Lake City is a place which cannot well be matched for beauty of site and amenity of climate; that it carries off the palm from all other cities as the abode of a united, peaceful, and prosperous people; that the industry of its inhabitants bears fruit in the material comforts which they enjoy; that their devotion to their spiritual leaders amounts to a passion; that their belief in their eccentric creed knows neither doubt nor shadow of turning; that they stand shoulder to shoulder against those who question the veracity of their Prophet, and deny the inspiration of their sacred books; that, living as they do, they enjoy an amount of happiness greater than what falls to the share of other dwellers on the earth, and that they feel and express a confidence in securing an incalculable amount of happiness in the world to come, such as few mortals cherish, and a still smaller number venture to avow. At one time all this may have been said with a semblance of truth. Indeed, I have been assured that had I been here a few years sooner, I should have held opinions similar to those expressed by earlier visitors. This is another way of saying that the golden age of Mormonism has passed away. Whenever persons begin to talk of a happier past, they are unable to weigh existing facts with impartiality, and to argue questions of the moment with perfect coolness. For my own part, I am sceptical as to the harmony which is said to have prevailed among the Mormons. I have conversed with some who have been excommunicated, and with some who have left the Church in disgust, as well as with firm believers and good Mormons. The doubters having proved rebellious, were summarily dealt with. In their case rebellion meant a disinclination to submit to the arbitrary sway of Brigham Young. The latter is at once despot and high priest. He interprets the law as written in the Book of Mormon, and he compels the acceptance of his interpretation. To Mormons, freedom of thought or of action is as impossible as to idiots or slaves. Their whole duty consists in thinking as they are enjoined, and doing as they are told. When the Mormon Gospel is preached in Europe, little is said about dogmas, and much is said about farms. The believers arrive at Salt Lake in the hope that they will soon attain independence by the sweat of their brows. A piece of land is made over to them on conditions which they deem light. The price is to be repaid in instalments; and one tenth of their earnings is to be handed over to the Church. Assistance is afforded them to build a house of wood or of sun-dried brick, here called 'adobe,' and to stock and cultivate their land. For all this they have to pay in money or in kind. If things go well with them, they soon succeed in placing themselves in a position of comparative comfort. They can live on the produce of their land; possibly, they may be able to take unto themselves several wives and to maintain a numerous family without apprehending bankruptcy or the workhouse. Yet, despite all this, they do not grow rich. Of food they may have abundance while continuing destitute of money. Here it is that the shoe pinches. The arrangements of Brigham Young are admirably adapted for keeping the majority of his followers obedient to his will. So long as they can neither buy nor sell, but must supply their wants through the primitive agency of barter, it is hard for them to become strong enough to challenge his claims. The payments he makes are calculated in dollars; but instead of paying his creditors in cash, he hands them orders on the Tithing-office, where grain, firewood, flour, or other necessaries of life, can be had at the option of the holders. Some payments are made in Salt Lake notes, which are current in the Territory only. Men who nominally receive so much a day for their labour have told me that the very sight of United States money is a rare one to them. They get wherewith to sustain life, but they cannot lay up that store against a rainy day which the thrifty labourer loves to accumulate. These persons are virtual prisoners in Utah Territory. Without money they cannot escape from the house of bondage, and of money they are almost bereft. Now and then one of the dissatisfied class does that which leads to his excommunication and the practical confiscation of his property. As soon as he is cast out of the Church or voluntarily secedes, the whole power of the Church is exerted to crush him. Good Mormons are forbidden to give him shelter, to associate with him, to trade with him. The great object is to expel him from Utah. Should this end be attained, then the outcast is obliged to begin life again, after his hopes have been blighted, with his labour expended in vain, and his experience gained to no good purpose.

If there be one point on which Americans and Englishmen are thoroughly agreed, and about which they are justly entitled to boast, it is that their homes are sanctuaries, and their houses castles; sanctuaries into which no stranger can enter unbidden; castles into which no stranger can demand admission. To the true Mormon, this notion of home is foreign. I do not now allude to his domestic arrangements, nor shall I allege that happiness is wholly impossible where polygamy is the rule, or maintain that filial duty and parental love are virtues which never flourish where several wives contend for a husband's affection, and flocks of children have claims on his tenderness. How these matters are managed, and what is the actual result, a stranger may imagine, but cannot discover. As far as he can ascertain, a Mormon household is in no respect exceptional; the wives appear to him the same as the ladies who preside over the household of a Gentile, while the children are as great torments or as great pets as the children whom he has seen elsewhere. The fallacy to which several writers have succumbed consists in supposing that, because nothing in such a household grossly offends the eye or shocks the senses, therefore the system of polygamy is unobjectionable, and that the Saint whose ' creed is singular and whose wives are plural,' is a personage worthy of unstinted praise. As well might the inference be drawn that, because man and wife usually say smooth things to each other in the presence of third parties, and because children sometimes conduct themselves with propriety in the presence of strangers, the former have no private differences of opinion, and the latter are never unruly and disobedient. Frankly admitting the domestic affairs of the Mormons to be mysteries which none but the initiated can fathom and into which strangers have no right to pry, let me confine myself to that part of their social arrangements with which all the world may become acquainted, and let me repeat that a home, in the English and American sense of the word, has no existence among the Saints of the Great Salt Lake. For example, should a Bishop or other person in authority knock at the door of a Mormon house in his diocese, he must be admitted without question, and his orders must be obeyed without hesitation, under a heavy penalty. Should he think that the floor ought to be scrubbed, or the kettle polished, or any alteration made in household arrangements, he has but to give the order, and the command is obeyed. The despotism of Mormonism, as taught by Brigham Young, is temporal as well as spiritual. Nothing is left to the free will of the people. Everything is done in obedience to a decree. The phrase 'Thus saith the Lord' is always uttered by the leaders when they desire to impose their decisions on their credulous followers. Marriage itself is not always an affair of choice and inclination. If it be thought expedient that a man should add to the number of his wives, he is advised to take another, and advice of this kind cannot be disregarded with impunity. President Young tolerates no differences of opinion between himself and his flock. He has been elected by them, and he considers it his prerogative to govern them with a rod of iron. Universal suffrage, exercised by the ignorant, has placed him where he is, and he interprets universal suffrage, as others have done in Europe, to mean the prerogative to act without scruple in pursuance of his personal ends.

With the Mormons, Sunday is emphatically a day of rest. Every shop is closed. The Tabernacle is filled with worshippers. There is a morning and an afternoon service, and in the evening each ward has its meeting, over which the ward Bishop presides. The service begins with a hymn, sung by the choir with an organ accompaniment. In the singing the congregation does not join. The majority turn in their seats and stare at the singers. A prayer is then offered up. The prayers which I heard consisted of the invocation of blessings upon the Mormons, their rulers, their homes, their fields, and their families. A special blessing was invoked on behalf of Brigham Young and other Mormons in authority. Not a word was said on behalf of the Government and the President of the United

States. I heard two sermons, both of which were harangues about things in general; the only special doctrines enunciated and enforced by repetition, not by argument, being that the Mormons were God's chosen people, and that Polygamy was a divine institution. Mormonism has now entirely resolved itself into preaching that polygamy is the one thing required in these latter days to regenerate and sanctify a world steeped in wickedness. If the Mormons are in the right, then none but the followers of Mahomet and Brigham Young deserve the title of civilized beings, and enjoy the privilege of counting upon entering and reigning in Heaven. It must be allowed that their religion is a bold attempt to make the best of both worlds.

On the same day that I heard religion preached according to Brigham Young, I also heard an exposition of the doctrines of pure Mormonism as revealed to Joseph Smith, proclaimed by him to the people, and now upheld and inculcated by his sons. David and Alexander Smith are here on a mission to rescue the Mormons of Salt Lake City from the hands of President Young. They stated openly in a crowded hall that the doctrines of the latter are 'foul, false, and corrupt.' They denounced him as an impostor; they charged him with usurpation. No Gentile has ever uttered more

stinging phrases against the chosen leader of the
Saints than were given vent to in the course of an
hour by these two men. Moreover, they cited
authentic documents in support of their statements.
They proved, from the accepted Mormon books
that polygamy, instead of being enjoined as a duty,
was formally condemned as a crime. While Joseph
Smith was yet alive certificates to that effect were
signed by men and women of influence in the
Church. Some of these men and women are now
among Brigham Young's staunchest adherents.
Judging from remarks openly made by some of the
Mormons present, it appeared that these facts were
alike new and puzzling to them. They were evidently at a loss what to think and whom to trust.

In a conversation which I had with one of Joseph
Smith's sons, the following was the explanation
furnished of the apparent contradiction. Nothing
in the Mormon Scriptures can be interpreted as
sanctioning polygamy. The assertion that Joseph
Smith had more wives than one is a calumny propagated by those who wish to have a religious
sanction for the gratification of their lusts. Emma
Smith, who was the Prophet's wife, stoutly denies
that she ever had any rival in her husband's love.
In opposition to this, Brigham Young offers to
prove that the murdered Prophet had several wives.

Furthermore, he cites a revelation made to Joseph Smith on celestial marriage, which certainly characterises a plurality of wives as the great privilege of the Saints. But, then, dense obscurity surrounds the transmission of this important document. Joseph Smith may have received it from Heaven; but how did Brigham Young get it from Joseph Smith? It is said that the paper on which the Prophet inscribed the revelation was snatched from him and burnt, but that Brigham Young was so fortunate as to have procured a transcript of it prior to its destruction. Be it noted that President Young makes no formal pretensions to the office of prophet. He is too much occupied with other matters, to have any leisure for prophesying. Besides, some experiments he once made as a prophet proved very disastrous. He has benefited by the lesson. What he now preaches is preached on the authority of Joseph Smith. The responsibility is thus shifted on to the shoulders of the deceased. It is obvious that the living priest has a great advantage over the dead prophet; because, while the latter printed his doctrines, the former claims to have been the recipient of other doctrines to be spread abroad at a convenient season. Several years after the Prophet's murder, Brigham Young thought that the convenient season had arrived for proclaiming polygamy a dogma of the Church of the Latter Day Saints. Accordingly, in 1852 he told the people that he had in his custody a revelation sanctioning plural marriage. The statement was accepted with satisfaction, and from that date uncompromising Mormons have regarded polygamy as the basis of their creed and the best part of their system.

I anticipate the query: 'How can liberty of speech be pronounced impossible throughout the Territory of Utah when two sons of Joseph Smith are thus permitted to beard President Young in his stronghold, to repudiate his doctrines, to denounce his conduct?' The answer I return is that which I have received from more Mormons than one. By Brigham Young, the sons of Joseph Smith are intensely hated. He would rejoice if they could be removed out of his path. He has refused to allow them to officiate in the Tabernacle, while according this privilege to the preachers of every other religious denomination. Indeed, one of the brothers told me that on the very Sunday when the pulpit of the Tabernacle was formally closed against both of them, it was occupied by a Methodist minister to whom free scope was accorded as an expounder of the Christian Gospel. Others, far less obnoxious than these two men, have disappeared in a mysterious way, or have been found shot to death by bullets, or beaten to death by clubs. Mormons are pointed out to whose charge these murders have been publicly laid, but no one has ever been brought to justice, nor is it believed that the culprits will ever receive the punishment they deserve so long as crimes committed at the instigation of Mormon leaders, and in furtherance of the Mormon cause, are regarded as highly meritorious. But the Destroying Angels dare not serve David and Alexander Smith as they served Dr. Robinson. As the sons of their revered Prophet, the people look upon them with respect, and listen to them with attention. That these men should go about unmolested, and preach undisturbed, is the only proof I have discovered of the existence of a public opinion in Utah. This discovery would have been far more welcome and valuable had the manifestation of opinion given token of a latent love of fair play and free speech, instead of proving the existence of an undercurrent of superstition in the uncultured and fanatical Mormon mind.

IX.

In few American cities are the nationalities of England and Wales so largely represented as in the city of the Great Salt Lake. The English visitor who makes the acquaintance of Mormon bankers, merchants, journalists, and hotel-keepers is surprised to find them well versed in the domestic affairs of the Old Country, and he learns with increased surprise that by birth they are his countrymen. Nor are his countrywomen less numerous, if far less fortunate. When questions are asked about the wives of distinguished and polygamous Saints, one of the answers is that most of them are Englishwomen. Of other European nationalities there are several representatives, those from Denmark and Norway being in the majority. Out of the 150,000 citizens of Utah Territory at least three-fourths have emigrated from Europe. As many as 4,000 European Latter Day Saints are said to cross the Atlantic yearly in order to cast in their lot with their brethren beyond the Rocky Mountains. In no country has the success of the Mormon missionaries been so great as in England, because in no other country has the like liberty of action been accorded to them. Elsewhere, they have fared badly on account of the obstacles put in their way by intolerant mobs, or despotic Governments. The record of their missionary enterprise is a chequered story of struggle and failure.

Regarded as a whole, the labours of the Mormons to win proselytes supply the strongest proofs which can be desired of their indomitable energy and steadfast endurance. No sooner had the Church of the Latter Day Saints been established in the United States than missionaries were despatched to make converts to the new religion. England was the earliest field wherein Mormon missionaries laboured, and is the one in which they have reaped the richest harvests. In 1837, no less than eight Mormon Elders went forth to preach to the English people. They began at Preston, in Lancashire. Before many months had elapsed, they had disseminated their views throughout the United Kingdom, the result being that 1,500 persons were baptized into the community of the Saints. Three years afterwards, others, of whom Brigham Young was one, took part in advancing the mission on English soil. They preached for upwards of a year and founded branches of the Mormon Church in all the more important cities from London to Edinburgh; they set up a printing press; they established an emigration agency; they published the Book of Mormon, the Book of Doctrines and Covenants; they issued 60,000 pamphlets and the first volume of the *Millenial Star*.

The next experiment of a like kind was an attempt to bring the Children of Israel within the fold of the Church of the Saints. With a view to effect this, a mission was despatched to Jerusalem, but it had to be abandoned in despair. The Isles of the Pacific were next selected as the theatre of a missionary crusade. Upwards of 1,200 natives of the Society Islands were baptized in 1843 and the prospects were hopeful, till the French assumed the Protectorate over these Islands. In 1851, not only were the Mormon Elders expelled and forbidden to return, but the French also ' compelled the native converts to discontinue their worship.' The Sandwich Islanders are said to have been as tractable converts and firmer adherents; yet, as no statistics are given, the actual results in their case must be left to conjecture. Among the French, the work of conversion received a check from the police. The Elder who went to Paris in 1849

7

complained that his hands were tied owing to the
stringency of the laws.   Eventually, the Prefect
of Police forbade the preaching of the Mormon
gospel.   Nor was Germany a land in which the
Elders received a welcome.   One of them was
'expelled by the authorities of the Free City of
Hamburg.'   In Prussia, the missionaries fared very
badly.   Two of them, who arrived at Berlin in 1853,
'found that it was impossible to preach or publish
the truth of the Latter Day Work in consequence
of religious intoleration.   These Elders wrote to
the King's Minister of Public Worship for per-
mission to preach, but were immediately summoned
before the police court and catechised as to the
object of their mission.   They were ordered to leave
the kingdom next morning, under penalty of trans-
portation.'   The opposition in Austria was equally
bitter.   After spending some months in learning
the German tongue Elders Pratt and Ritter had
to relinquish their undertaking and leave Vienna,
because they found themselves unable, 'in consequence of religious intolerance,' 'to open the door
for the proclamation of the Gospel' in Austria.
In Denmark, a missionary was more fortunate; but
one who 'proceeded to Sweden, and endeavoured
to introduce the work there' 'was summarily
banished.'   The Swiss looked askance at Mor-

monism. The Elders were non-plussed by a twofold
hindrance to their progress in Switzerland. ' Some
of the cantons would not allow publishing, but
allowed preaching ; others prohibited preaching,
but would allow publishing, and some would no
allow either.'   Only one attempt was made to
convert the inhabitants of South America from the
errors of their accustomed ways to the errors of
the Mormon creed.   Two Elders went to Chili in
1851, ' where they remained several months, not
having the opportunity of even teaching in private,
except in violation of the most rigid laws.'   Being
obliged to return to California, one of them remained there for some time and, with a result which,
as it is unrecorded, cannot have been wholly satisfactory, ' continued to preach and teach until he
returned to Utah.'   The Chinese were appealed to
in April, 1853.   The Mormon missionaries to
China did not get farther than Hong Kong.   They
decided that, as a civil war was raging, it would
be unwise to undertake a journey into the interior.
Moreover, the Chinese with whom they conversed
did not appear to be a promising people on whom
to expend their energies.   ' The inhabitants told
them that they had not time to " talka " religion.
The way soon opened for them to return to San
Francisco, which they did in August.'

Very interesting and not a little instructive is the tale of the attempts made in the colonies and dependencies of Great Britain to gather in converts to the Mormon fold. In South Australia, New South Wales, Tasmania and New Zealand the success seems to have been most complete. On the other hand, the missionaries met with palpable rebuffs in Hindostan, Ceylon, South Africa, and the West Indies. They went up the Ganges, visited Simla, laboured in Bombay and the adjacent country, but without effect. The zeal they displayed failed to produce the expected impression. Their explanation runs thus: ' Finding the Hindostanees destitute of honesty and integrity, insomuch that when converted and baptized they would for a few pice join any other religion, and finding the Europeans so aristocratic that they were hardly approachable, they left the country, after having travelled to all the principal stations of India, where frequently they were ordered out of cantonments and had to sleep in the open air, exposed to that sickly climate, to poisonous reptiles and to wild beasts.' In Ceylon they suffered severely not only through the unwillingness of the people to hearken to them, but also because the people and the priests refused to open their doors, or give them food, unless they were well paid. At Cape Town, rioters broke up their meetings, but in the country districts 'they obtained a foothold and commenced to baptize.' What they endured in Jamaica cannot be better told than in their own words: ' They called upon the American Consul, Mr. Harrison, who advised them to hire a hall and announce public preaching, as the laws extended toleration to all sects, which they accordingly did; but a mob numbering one hundred and fifty persons, gathered around the building and threatened to tear it down were these Polygamists, as they termed the Elders, permitted to preach therein. Unless the Elders could give security for the price of the hall the landlord objected to their holding meeting. The Elders informed him that they were not there to enforce their principles upon the people—to quell mobs, nor to protect property, but to preach the Gospel of Jesus Christ to those who were willing to hear. The Elders got away from the Island safely, though while they remained they had to run the gauntlet, and two of them were shot at by a negro.' Two missionaries to British Guiana were quite as hardly dealt with, for they were refused passages by the shipping agents and had to return to the United States without even setting foot on the shore which they desired to reach. The authorities at Gibraltar treated the Elders as if they were persons of bad character, and summoned them to appear in the police court as soon as they landed on the Rock. Elder Stevenson who had been born there maintained his right to remain; Elder Porter, however, was ordered to leave. The Governor prohibited Elder Stevenson from preaching Mormonism. ' He, however, remained over a year and baptized several amidst threats, prohibitions and constant opposition. He also endeavoured to open up the work in Spain, but was not permitted by the authorities.' In no British possession does the success of the missionaries seem to have been greater than in Malta. What the Mormons say about their doings in that Island has a special interest for English readers. As the official account is not long, I shall give it unabridged:—' In 1853, Elder James F. Bell was sent from England to Malta, where several were baptized. Upon the breaking out of the Crimean war, the interest in the work was broken off, still a few of the soldiers in the British regiments that landed there obeyed the Gospel. There originated from this mission three branches of the Church, viz.: one in Florianna, Malta; a second, called the "floating branch," in the Mediterranean, which consisted of sailors belonging to her British Majesty's ships the *Bellerophon*, *Trafalgar*, *Vengeance* and *Britannia*; a

third, the expeditionary force branch, in the Crimea;
the latter consisted of brethren belonging to the
30th, 41st, 93rd and 95th British regiments.   A
few of the members of these branches lost their
lives in the Crimean war.' *

The great success of the Mormon missionaries in
England and Wales is partly due to the fact that
the people to whom they appealed were for the most
part grossly illiterate or fanatical. While the success
they have had is not a matter for national congra-
tulation, yet the toleration which was afforded to
them, standing out as it does in contrast to the intolerance and inhumanity of which the missionaries
were the victims in nearly every other land, is an
honour to this sea-girt home of free thought and
free speech. The Elders enjoyed fair play in England. The result has been that their zeal prevailed,
and converts were multiplied. If the consequence
is distasteful, the fault lies on the shoulders of those
who have neglected the paramount duty of edu-
cating the people. Owing to the large number of
converts who have gone from England and Wales

---

* These details explaining the missions of Mormondom have not,
as far as I know, been previously published in England. They have
the merit of being authentic as well as novel. I have compiled the
account from that contained in a pamphlet published in July 1869
at Salt Lake City. Its author is President George A. Smith, the
Official Historian of the Church.

to their earthly Zion beyond the Rocky Mountains, Salt Lake City bears a close resemblance to an English settlement in America. Those who have been instrumental in gathering together this multitude of English men and women are all native-born Americans. New England is the mother of Joseph Smith: President Brigham Young is a genuine Yankee; both being natives of the State of Vermont. The ablest and most trusted colleagues of the President are his fellow-countrymen. Indeed, not the least extraordinary among the mysteries of the Mormons is the circumstance that, while the native-born Americans are in the minority, and the people elect their leaders, the men certain to be elected, and as certain of re-election, are nearly always Americans by birth. While several of the Mormons are emphatically strangers and foreigners in this land of freedom, yet it is indisputable that in its inception and its growth, its organisation and its energy, Mormonism is thoroughly and entirely American. If the very existence of Mormonism be a cause of grief to England, its wider spread and increasing strength imperil principles dear to every patriotic citizen of the United States. In its present form it is a despotism. Brigham Young is the embodiment of that 'one man power' which Americans view with the deepest aversion and consider as utterly antagonistic to the principles of genuine Republicanism. Yet a fear of persecuting men for what they allege to be their religion makes many hesitate and hang back who would otherwise be swift to act. On the other hand, it must be difficult for American statesmen to sit unmoved at the spectacle of the laws made by Congress openly violated, wilfully derided, and treated as utterly impotent within the Territory of Utah. As a subtle and triumphant conspiracy against the harmony of the Union and the supremacy of Congress, Mormonism is an evil too momentous to be regarded with indifference or neglected altogether.

X.

MORMONISM ON ITS TRIAL

Two attempts, differing in character and aim, have been made to control and temper the intolerance of dominant Mormonism. Seven years ago the United States Government established a military post within a few miles of the city, and in a position well suited as a base for offensive operations. It was hoped that the presence of soldiers at Camp Douglas would tend to inspire confidence among the dissatisfied and timid inhabitants of the Valley, while acting as a check upon the conduct of the Mormon leaders. These expectations have not been fulfilled. The leaders themselves make merry over the policy of the Government. They say that the camp does no harm to them, but that, on the contrary, they make money by supplying the troops with stores on most remunerative terms. The other attempt was made about three years ago by a missionary society connected with the Episcopal Church in America. A mission was established in Salt Lake City. The missionaries were deputed to labour among both the Gentiles and Mormons resident there.

The Rev. Mr. Foote, who was charged with missionary duty, has worked with great vigour and in the teeth of great odds, to disseminate the tidings of the gospel of peace among a people prone to manifest hatred towards all who think differently from themselves, and who regard with unfeigned aversion all efforts made to substitute the tenderness of Jesus for the terrors of Jehovah. Not a few Mormons have voluntarily joined the Episcopal Church. As a rule, however, those persons who can no longer believe in the revelation proclaimed by Joseph Smith, or submit to the tyranny of Brigham Young, cease to entertain any religious belief whatever and relapse into unreasoning infidelity. In addition to holding the regular services of his church, the Rev. Mr. Foote has established a school for the education of the children growing up without any care being taken for their instruction. When this school was opened, two years and a half ago, the number of pupils was sixteen. When I visited it the number on the roll was one hundred and thirty. Of these children a small proportion has been sent by Mormons who have the rare courage to think and act for themselves. But this is done in opposition to the commands of the Mormon chiefs. They threaten the parents with the pains and penalties which the Church has in store for the chastisement of her disobedient members. As may be supposed, they are very anxious to let the Rev. Mr. Foote feel the weight of their displeasure for coming amongst them and converting their followers. Nothing is more remarkable about Mormonism than the wrath of its professors against those who induce Mormons seriously to reconsider their opinions. While nearly every Mormon is a pervert from some other religion, and while the Saints number among their trials the hindrances put in the way of their proselytising, they are bigoted opponents of any attempts to preach another religion to their own people. It is true that the pulpit of the Tabernacle is professedly thrown open to the clergymen of all sects. Several have availed themselves of the opportunity to address the congregation, and give their version of the Scriptures. But the result has been the reverse of edifying and satisfactory. I heard Mormons relate with great glee how a clergyman of the Church of England had accepted Brigham Young's invitation to preach, had appeared in his surplice and Oxford hood, and how, at the succeeding service, the President having taken a white table cover, placed it over his shoulders, and burlesqued the clergyman amid the hearty laughter of his flock. As the head of the Mormon Church always has the last word, the advantage gained by preaching to his congregation is not on the side of the recognised opponents of Mormonism. The liberty of preaching in the Tabernacle means simply license to become a laughing-stock.

Neither the presence of soldiers at Camp Douglas, nor the pastoral efforts of the Rev. Mr. Foote, can be considered adequate to counteract the disregard of law and the denial of justice to which the Saints are addicted. As general statements seldom convey a clear impression of the nature of abuses, let me cite two cases in support of my allegations. One of these is the case of Dr. Robinson. He had become the proprietor of a piece of land, a mile to the north of the city, on which were hot sulphur springs. These springs were reputed to be of great medicinal value. It was thought that their curative powers would attract invalids, and that whoever had the control over them would grow rich. Desiring to occupy this position, the city authorities laid claim to them, on the ground that the land in question was within the city's boundary. Dr. Robinson resisted this demand. Appeal was made to the law courts, and the decision was favourable to Dr. Robinson. He was warned that persistence on his part would prove dangerous; but these hints did not intimidate him. One night after he had gone to bed a knock summoned him to his door, where he was addressed by two or three men, who begged him to come to the help of a man who had fallen and broken his leg. He went forth, taking a revolver with him, as was his wont. A few hours afterwards he was found lying a few yards from his own house covered with wounds, and with a large gash on his head caused by the blow of a blunted weapon. The attack had been sudden and unexpected, for his loaded revolver was in his pocket. The object of the assassins was not plunder, for his valuables were untouched. A Gentile who helped to remove the dead body from the place where it was found to the house of the deceased, told me that Mormons who recognised the features refused to lend any assistance. They knew that the murdered man was highly obnoxious to the Church Authorities and they seemed to look upon his death by violence as the natural consequence of his conduct. A large reward was offered for the apprehension of the murderers. They are still at large. It is the general belief that the suspected murderers are living in Salt Lake City, and that they would be brought to justice if there were a tribunal before which they could be indicted with the certainty of the law being enforced. As it is, a Mormon jury never convicts a Mormon who had sinned in the interests of his Church.   But, if slow to punish a Mormon, the courts of Utah are ready to punish an erring Gentile.   A soldier who had become entitled to his discharge when at Camp Douglas, and had a right to the piece of land promised by the Government of the United States to those who had served their country during the war, elected to settle at Salt Lake, and received from the United States authorities the land which he had earned.   Not long after taking possession and building himself a small dwelling, the city authorities began to survey his land preparatory to selling it in small lots, alleging that the whole of it was city property. The discharged soldier threatened to assert his rights and to punish intruders.   No heed was paid to his protests.   Unfortunately for himself, he broke a law of the Territory forbidding the sale of spirits without a licence.   For this offence he was immediately prosecuted.   There being no doubt as to his guilt, the amount of fine to be inflicted was the only matter for consideration.   It had been customary in similar cases to fine the offenders twenty-five dollars.   In his case the penalty imposed was five hundred dollars, with the alternative of six months' imprisonment.   As the culprit could not pay this crushing fine, and did not wish to languish in prison, he assented to an official proposal to suspend legal proceedings on condition of his leaving the city within four and twenty hours. Thus the authorities rid themselves of a man who was an obstacle to their projects. They sold his land in lots of five acres. Perhaps the day may come when the purchasers of these lots will find that a title from the authorities of Salt Lake City is worthless in presence of a prior and perfect title from the Government of the United States.

The Territory of Utah is a scandal to America, because the impartial administration of justice does not prevail within its limits. The Government ought to tell the Mormons—'Believe what you please, retain whatever religious convictions you have formed, consider polygamy the cornerstone of your system, and teach that doctrine to your children, but do not break and despise the laws of which you disapprove. We do not mean to wound your consciences, or to trench on matters of a purely religious character, yet we purpose enforcing the Acts which Congress has passed for the well-being of all American citizens.' What the answer of the Mormons would be to this simple enuncia-tion of a just policy can be inferred from their own writings. In the *Salt Lake Daily Telegraph* for October 17, 1869, the question is discussed, and a reply is made beforehand to the arguments which may be used in Congress. The writer says that 'The right or wrong, the morality or immorality of polygamy is, in our opinion, no question for Congress to deal with, it cannot deal with it. The only question is, what are the rights of a people under a Republican form of government? Shall Columbia be the home of the Turk, the Parsee, the Japanese, the Chinese, and the inhabitants of the Eastern Hemisphere, as well as those of the Northern Hemisphere? Let the citizens of the whole world come to this glorious land, and let them worship whom they choose, and how they may. Let their faith be undisturbed—they are accountable only to their Maker, and not to man.' It is possible that the Mormons themselves would object to the logical application of these principles. If any Thugs, escaping from the exterminating hand of Colonel Sleeman, had emigrated from their Indian jungles to the Utah valleys, there to fit themselves for Heaven by strangling defenceless travellers, the deeds of violence committed by them would hardly be pardoned by the Mormon leaders even if justified on the ground that their religious creed enjoined the commission of murder in order to win Heaven. Nor is it necessary, even for the sake of argument, to conjure up the shadows of a bloodthirsty tribe which was once the scourge and terror of Hindostan. The Mormons have at their own doors examples of the crimes men may commit in the name of religion. The Savage who supposes that he will be a 'big Indian' in the happy hunting ground beyond the grave, if he only succeed in stealing many horses and collecting many scalps, acts on the supposition that religion consists in being a wholesale thief and murderer. He is half a Mormon in one respect. To increase the number of his wives is, in his eyes, a bounden duty. But there is no subterfuge about his inclinations in this matter. What he does is performed for reasons which are at least straightforward and intelligible. He honestly avows that in adding squaw to squaw he is indulging his inordinate lust and at the same time multiplying the number of his docile servants. He never pretends that religious zeal is a defence of plural matrimony. The Saints who uphold polygamy on religious grounds, would act wisely in imitating the candour and consistency of the wild Indians. The Mormons are selfish, as well as very illogical. They will not extend to others the privileges which they claim for themselves. They assert the right to worship God after their own fashion, yet do their best to exclude from Utah all who reject the Book of Mormon. They demand to be let alone just as the Southern slaveholders did.

Their treatment of a Gentile, who prefers the same request to them, resembles the treatment accorded to the Abolitionist who formerly upheld the right of free speech at the South. What the Mormons desire at present is the admission of Utah into the Union. They have several times petitioned Congress to that effect, but in vain. If raised to the dignity of a State, Utah would be more than ever under the domination of the Mormon leaders. So long as it continues a Territory, Congress is entitled to legislate for it, and many desire that this power should be exercised. It is within the jurisdiction of Congress to alter the boundaries of Territories and to create new ones. Thus the present State of Nevada was carved out of the Territory of Utah in 1861. In like manner, the Territory of Colorado comprises a portion of what once belonged to Utah. This process of division and subdivision might be continued with advantage until Utah were absorbed altogether. As citizens of a new Territory or of an adjacent State, the Mormons would be unable to overpower the Gentile majority arrayed against their illegal practices and disloyal acts. If treated in this manner Brigham Young would be more effectually checkmated than if brought face to face with the overwhelming military organization of the United States.

It is commonly supposed that the opening of the Pacific Railway or the death of Brigham Young will speedily lead to the annihilation of Mormonism. The visitor to Salt Lake City, who makes the necessary inquiries, must pronounce these expectations to have a very unsubstantial basis. By the Mormons themselves, the railway is not regarded with dread. It may be that, as the *New York Herald* has pithily remarked, 'Railroad communications corrupt good Mormons;' but this has yet to be demonstrated. According to Brigham Young the facilities for intercommunication by rail are certain to prove advantageous to the Church. He has informed his flock that he encouraged the construction of the Pacific Railway in order that the Gentiles might be the more easily converted. That he spoke seriously when he said this cannot readily be credited. Yet it is worthy of note, that in 1852 the Legislature of Utah sent a memorial to Congress, signed by Brigham Young as Governor, praying that a railway might be constructed across the Continent, and assigning many very forcible reasons in support of the proposal. In the number of the *Salt Lake Daily Telegraph*, from which I have already quoted, it is said:—'The opening up of this mountainous country, by the Pacific Railroad running through it, was expected to bring in a

great multitude of strangers, and by their settling
down in the country and mixing with the Mormons,
it was presumed that the question of polygamy
would be quietly disposed of by the force of Christian example and the election ballot box.   Since
the opening of the railroad there has been a large
influx of visitors to the city; but we have not
heard of a single Gentile family that has come to
reside among us, and, from the general current of
information that reaches us, we think the opposite
is the disposition.   Some who have resided here
have left the Territory, and more are preparing to
leave as early as they can dispose of their business
and property.'   The writer of the foregoing lines
is quite correct in saying that there is no probability of Gentiles occupying the Mormon Territory
to the exclusion of the Saints.   The arrangements
for rendering this impossible are too complete to be
upset by the railway or any similar agency.   That
a sudden change will follow the decease of Brigham
Young is doubtful.   When Cromwell died, the immediate dissolution of the Commonwealth which had
been expected as a thing of course was delayed for
some months.   The chances are in favour of the
place of President Young being occupied by a suc-
cessor quite as skilful, unscrupulous, and powerful as
himself.   He is the leading spirit of to-day, but his

counsellors are men not inferior to him in boldness
and executive ability. More than one of them
could at any moment step forward and fill the post
he might vacate. The hold which these men have
over their followers is the true source of their
supremacy. The ignorance of these followers cannot be paralleled save in the cases of the French
peasantry. Their fanaticism is proportioned to
their ignorance. To wait till they are neither
ignorant nor fanatic is as foolish as was the conduct
of the Roman rustic who waited for the stream to
exhaust itself by running.

XI.

DURING my visit to Salt Lake City the Saints were thrown into consternation by the announcement in the Tabernacle that some of the most notable among their number had been suspended from the enjoyment of Church privileges. This is the preliminary to excommunication. One of these erring brethren was Mr. Stenhouse, the editor of the *Salt Lake Daily Telegraph*. Born at Dalkeith, near Edinburgh, and a convert from Presbyterianism to Mormonism, he had given strong proofs of his devotion to the religion propounded by Joseph Smith. He was one of the enthusiasts who, on foot, had made the terrible journey across the plains from the Missouri to Salt Lake, drawing a handcart containing all his worldly possessions. He had gone as a missionary to Switzerland and to England, and gained many proselytes. As the husband of three wives, he had committed himself to the version of Mormonism promulgated and upheld by Brigham Young. He is supposed to have offended

by not being as ardent a supporter of the President's temporal power as of his spiritual pretensions. Another of the suspended brethren was Mr. Godbe, a Londoner by birth, the proprietor of a large ' store ' in Salt Lake City, and a man of re puted wealth. He had devoted a considerable portion of his substance to founding the *Utah Magazine*. In this publication the infallibility of the President has more than once been disputed by implication, and its conductors have even had the temerity to call in question the wisdom of his policy. Mr. Harrison, one of the editors of the magazine, was included among the number of the censured. Mr. Stenhouse submitted to the rebuke, and has made his peace with the Church. This can be done by making an unqualified admission of error, recanting the condemned doctrines, and preferring a humble request for pardon. The Mormons have borrowed some formulas from a Church more ancient than their own, and, like it, advancing claims to collective infallibility. Mr. Godbe and Mr. Harrison, remaining stubborn, have been formally excommunicated. As the Bull of Excommunication is not a lengthy document, and as it is certainly a curious one, I shall quote it entire :—
' To whom it may concern.—This certifies that William S. Godbe, E. L. T. Harrison, and Eli B.

Kelsey were cut off from the Church of Latter Day Saints on Monday, the 25th day of October, 1869, for harbouring and spreading the spirit of apostacy.—William Dunford, Clerk of Council.'

The following official explanation and warning was issued contemporaneously with the decree of excommunication :—' To the Latter Day Saints : Our attention has been called of late to several articles which have appeared in the *Utah Magazine*, a weekly periodical published in this city. An examination of them has convinced us that they are erroneous, opposed to the spirit of the Gospel, and calculated to do injury. According to the practice in the Church, teachers were sent to labour with the editor and publisher, to point out to them the evil results that would follow a persistence in the course they were pursuing. This did not have the desired effect, and they have since been tried before the High Council, and after a thorough and patient investigation of the case, it was found that they had imbibed the spirit of apostacy to that degree that they could not any longer be fellowshipped, and they were cut off from the Church.

' The *Utah Magazine* is a periodical that, in its spirit and teachings, is directly opposed to the Work of God. Instead of building up Zion and

8

uniting the people, its teachings, if carried out, would destroy Zion, divide the people asunder, and drive the Holy Priesthood from the earth. Therefore, we say to our brethren and sisters in every place, the *Utah Magazine* is not a periodical suitable for circulation among or perusal by them, and should not be sustained by Latter Day Saints.

' We hope this will be sufficient, without ever having to refer to it again.

' Brigham Young, George A. Smith, Daniel H. Wells, Orson Pratt, Wilford Woodruff, George Q. Cannon, Joseph F. Smith.'

I have not yet said anything about Eli B. Kelsey, who is among the excommunicated. He was one of the High Council by which the heretics were tried and sentenced. When the votes were taken it was found that he alone was in the minority. For having thus hindered the Council from coming to a unanimous vote he was summarily dealt with as one who had harboured ' the spirit of apostacy.' Such is the Mormon notion of free discussion and fair play.

The result has been that the schismatics have founded a new church under the name of the Church of Zion. The leaders of the movement allege that they are directly inspired from above, that they have been incited to action by communications from departed spirits. At a public meeting called to hear their programme, Mr. Harrison averred that 'Heber C. Kimball, Joseph Smith (whose identity was vouched for by the angels), Peter, James and John, and Jesus himself had come and talked with them; they did not see the faces, but they saw the heavenly light and distinctly heard voices, and during a long series of those direct and celestial visitations they had had revealed to them not only a grand system of theology, which will be developed in due course, but all the great principles connected with this globe from the beginning to the time when it shall become celestialized.' To the statements made by the founders of the Church of Zion a short and simple answer was returned by the leaders of the Church of the Latter Day Saints. In their opinion the Devil had done it all. The revelations of which Messrs. Harrison and Godbe were the recipients had proceeded directly from the Author of Evil. In a sermon delivered by Orson Pratt in the Tabernacle, the whole matter was discussed for the edification of the orthodox and the confusion of the spiritual rebels. The preacher explained that at first the revelation made to Joseph Smith was scoffed at, and then the Prophet was persecuted and murdered. But, the Saints still continuing to increase in numbers and in power, 'the Devil found that they could not be put down by persecution, he took another turn and said "I will show them that the world can have revelation enough."' Thus it was that what are called Spiritual Manifestations were produced. He was the more certain about the complicity of Satan in the movement, because some of the revelations said to have been made to Messrs. Harrison and Godbe by King Solomon were at variance with statements in the Book of Mormon. Whether the Devil had or had not any hand in the schism is a matter about which the public in England and America will doubtless manifest contemptuous indifference. Some may console themselves with the contemplation of the consequences which are said to ensue upon the falling out of rogues. Yet they will all note with satisfaction the confession made by Mr. Tullidge, one of the editors of the *Utah Magazine* and an adherent of the new sect. He states in a printed document that 'our leaders have reduced the people to an absolute temporal bondage, and the genius of a prophetic and spiritual work has died out of their administration' and that 'the Saints in Utah for nearly twenty years have been entire strangers to their former spiritual power.' As the leaders and supporters of this movement are polygamists either in fact or theory, the limit of the change for the better, which they are likely to effect, will soon be reached. Most significant of all is the aversion manifested by them for the temporal authority of Brigham Young. They have felt that they must either become the bond slaves of the President, or else must assert their right to individual action. It may be anticipated that after emancipating themselves from the personal tyranny under which they have groaned, they will not long remain in subjection to the spiritual supremacy of their former head. The 'spirits' with whom they hold communication may tell them that 'plural marriage' is an invention of the Devil, and then the real struggle between the men who think that to advance is imperative and those who maintain that adherence to the old formulas is a duty, will begin in earnest and may end in revolutionizing Mormonism.

This schism is the more ominous on account of the willingness displayed by its leaders to make common cause with the Gentiles in matters of a secular kind. Unfortunately, the combined forces make but a poor display of strength. It is clear that Brigham Young has an overwhelming majority at his back, and that the yearly additions to the number of the Saints contribute to swell his majority.

Fanaticism is the mainspring of nearly all those who leave Europe for Utah. In the eyes of these persons Brigham Young is a model ruler. They are unfriendly to smooth courses and conciliatory action and they have natural affinities with those who adopt a policy of intolerance and extermination. Having the fanatical and the ignorant obedient to his will and feeling sure that the annual immigration of 4,000 persons will add to the ranks of his followers more recruits than are required to fill up the vacancies made by deserters, Brigham Young has still a warrant for regarding the new schism with comparative equanimity and some reason for believing that he has not yet ceased to be master of the situation.

XII.

UTAH SCENERY.

FROM the petty squabbles of discordant and rabid Mormons it is a relief to turn and gaze upon the panorama of natural beauties which, from dawn to sunset, is provided for the enjoyment of the dweller in Salt Lake City. Some of the noteworthy characteristics of the city are by no means unique. The streams of sparkling water which flow through the streets, the trees which shade the pathways and the ample gardens in which the houses stand are not more bright, abundant, and attractive than those of the Pyrenean town of Bagnères de Bigorre. But with this exception, comparison is hardly possible. The site as a whole is incomparable.

The elevation is 4,000 feet above the sea level. If not absolutely rainless, the region is one in which the rainfall is scanty. Hence the air is almost free from floating vapour, and the sky is seldom obscured by masses of cloud. The extreme purity of the atmosphere renders the new-comer inexpert at calculating distances. The mountain slopes, which seem as if they were but a few yards from the city, are in reality several miles distant. But, if this miscalculation is sometimes disappointing, other effects due to the same cause are all the more impressive. The outlines of the far-off peaks and ridges, declivities and clefts are distinctly visible in every line of rugged contour or soft undulation.

Turning from the range of snow-crested mountains on the east of the city, another range is discernible across the valley beyond the western shore of the Great Salt Lake. The valley is more than forty miles broad. It is intersected by the Jordan which runs from Utah Lake several miles to the South and is absorbed in that inland sea of salt water, from which there is no outlet and in which there is no life. The valley appears to be wholly covered by the sage-brush which is worthless as food or fodder. Where this plant is abundant the chances are that nothing else will flourish in the bitter earth wherein it thrives. Here, however, the rich and nutritive bunch-grass is found also. Thus these plains are excellent grazing land for cattle.

By accident I learned that this valley had a special attraction for the archæologist. Indian burial mounds of great antiquity are situated in its midst. These mounds contain the relics of tribes which are now extinct, having been driven away or exterminated by the Indians who, in their turn, have had to give place to the Mormons. An English friend, a visitor like myself to this city and, unlike me, a well skilled archæologist, heard the tidings with delight, and made instant arrangements for a visit to the mounds. On enquiry, we learned that few persons knew their names, far less their history, and that hardly one cared a straw about them. The driver of a conveyance between the hotel and the city baths, professed to know where they were situated; he told us that the distance to them was eight miles and that his fare for the journey would be about one pound sterling. Closing with his terms, we started off on our quest. Taking the road which runs west, and crossing the Jordan, we then proceeded in a south-westerly direction. On our way we saw the half-finished canal which was undertaken at the command of Brigham Young with a view to repress discontent by finding employment for idle hands, and was also designed by him to prove that the age of miracles had not departed. If the canal had been finished and had served the intended purpose of bringing water from the Jordan to the city, then a miracle would indeed have been wrought, for the water of the Jordan would have run uphill!

After being driven about in different directions across the plains, the driver told us that the mounds had changed their position. Certainly, no trace of them could be perceived. We questioned men who were tending cattle, and got some hints for our guidance. They had never seen Indian mounds, but they had heard of sand-hills. As these were the mounds in question, we ascertained where they were situated, and at last, we reached them. It was evident that they were not natural formations. The labour of a few hours proved to us that they were in reality the places of sepulture of an ancient Indian tribe. Flint spear heads, flint arrow-heads, stone implements and fragments of rude potteryware, we disinterred from the sand. As the means at our disposal for making a thorough search were very imperfect and as the time in which to conduct it was very short, the total number of articles discovered was but small. All of them were found in the larger of the three mounds. It was something, though not much, to have satisfied ourselves as to the fact that in the Valley of the Great Salt Lake there are monuments of the buried past, and that the extinct Indians who once were the masters of this region have left behind them lasting records of their customs and their character.

The Indians who once lived here first passed away; others of fiercer manners and greater spirit occupied their places; the latter being now forced to acknowledge the superiority of a still more valiant and powerful race, have become the dependents of the white men, and are themselves gradually disappearing from the earth. The Mormons have annexed Utah to the Territory of the pale faces; they have instituted a form of government according to their fancies; to all appearance, their wills are law here, nevertheless an authority stronger than their own is the actual lord of this place. Two miles to the east of the city, the stronghold of the real, though quiescent superior over this Territory is situated. On a plateau, to which the ascent is gradual but continuous, the troops of the United States are encamped, and the artillery of the United States is in position. The ' sconce' which Dugald Dalgetty persistently advised Sir Duncan Campbell to erect ' upon the round hill called Drumsnab' could not have been placed in a more commanding position than Camp Douglas is for the purpose it was designed to subserve. Behind it is a mountain chain rising to a great height, before and below it is the capital of

Mormondom. The city could be shelled so as to become a heap of ruins in an hour; while the camp could be defended by a small force against the largest attacking party which is ever likely to be led against it. For any other purpose than that of a permanent and significant demonstration this camp has never been employed. Much tyranny and injustice may still be perpetrated under the shadow of the flag which is the symbol of liberty and equal rights, yet excesses such as once prevailed have been impossible since the United States troops have been encamped here. The Mormon leaders sneer at the folly of those who formed and garrisoned Camp Douglas, but while doing so they also hesitate to give the signal for deeds of bloody retribution to the Destroying Angels whom they once employed to murder in the name of the Lord for the consolidation of the Church.

The Gentiles who reside in Salt Lake City and the stranger who temporarily sojourns there, enjoy a sense of security while within the lines of the camp which they never feel within the city's boundaries. Looking down from this place of vantage upon the dwellings of the Saints, they can with difficulty give credence to the best authenticated stories of the acts of violence with which the Mormons are charged. Even if no camp were there the spectacle would absorb them to the exclusion of any other thought. The view of the distant Pyrenees from the Place Royale at Pau and the view of the Alpine range from the pinnacle of Milan Cathedral are among the most justly famed of European prospects. Neither is superior to that from this spot. In the foreground is the city with its houses and orchards; in the middle distance is the broad valley through which the Jordan winds to the Lake, while in the background is the large sheet of water with a bold range of mountains rising from its farthest shore till their summits mingle with the clouds. When the sun, sloping slowly to the West, sinks down behind these mountains the sight resembles a dream of fairyland. Mountain, Lake, and Valley are decked in a gorgeous robe of purple and gold. The Lake with its clusters of small islands resembles a glowing sheet of burnished steel, studded over with precious stones. These ineffable glories of sky, and earth, and water are visible but for a brief space, vanishing almost as soon as seen. The long English twilight is unknown here. For a few minutes after the sun 'has reached the horizon, a delicate rosy tint suffuses the sky; then the expiring day suddenly darkens into night, and the firmament is ablaze with stars.

Descending the mountain slope towards the city,

I forgot for the moment the reputation it bore. That man could be vile where Nature was so lovely appeared impossible. But the reality soon became apparent. Meeting and conversing with an acquaintance in the streets, observing him nervously glancing from side to side in order to see if we were watched and being told by him not to speak loudly lest eavesdroppers were within earshot, I was forcibly impressed with the fact that the Mormon system was inquisitorial as well as despotic. Nor was this opinion modified when, on arriving at the hotel, I recognised the hang-dog features of one whose duty, as I was credibly informed, consisted in following the footsteps of strangers and spying out their doings. I could not help thinking that the scenery of Utah was defective in one particular. In some parts of the Rocky Mountains, where villains congregate, justice is vindicated in a summary manner by hanging the detected criminal from a branch of the nearest tree. Photographs of these executions are labelled ' Rocky Mountain Scenery.' If criminals met with their deserts in Utah, opportunities would soon be furnished for taking similar photographs from life.

XIII.

THE PAST AND THE FUTURE OF MORMONISM.

INGENIOUS THEORIES have been advanced to explain
the origin and success of Mormonism. Attractive
pictures have been limned of Mormon society, and
plausible reasons put forth in defence of the most
reprehensible of Mormon practices. A sweeping
condemnation has, in like manner, been passed upon
the Saints: it has been denied that they possess
a single good quality, or that they are at all
better than the savages whom they have displaced.
If the best that has been said about them be true, it
does not entitle them to universal esteem. If the
worst be well founded, if they are indeed hypocrites
and rogues, sour fanatics and intolerant bigots, the
blame lies at the doors of those who, by unjustly
and cruelly persecuting them, laboured to make
them what they are. Had not Joseph Smith won
the crown of martyrdom, Brigham Young might
never have governed as a despot.

When the Angel Moroni disclosed to Joseph Smith
the reputed secrets which the Prophet communicated to the world in the Book of Mormon, the
minds of the younger men in America were pre-

pared to hearken to a revelation. Almost contemporaneously with the prophetic utterances of the first high-priest of the Latter Day Saints, Mr. Owen proclaimed to the citizens of the United States his scheme for achieving universal happiness by grouping mankind in parallelograms. The excitement which this proposal occasioned was due to the avidity of the public for any hints which might clear the way for the regeneration of the world. A like eagerness to experiment with the theories of Fourier was afterwards manifested. Joseph Smith had this enormous superiority over other speculators that, in addition to indicating the path towards a more perfect state, he provided a new religion as a solace for those who, having been buffeted by the waves of doubt, could find no anchorage for their faith. Moreover, his religion had the merit of being a complement to that which was generally accepted, giving precision to what was questionable, widening the boundaries of what was narrow. The heaven which he pictured was a heaven which human beings desired all the more strongly because it was but another and a more perfect representation of the world in which they lived. To the believers in him was afforded the supreme satisfaction of an immediate display of spiritual powers and a present experience of spiritual beings. They were convinced that the Deity had returned to earth and exhibited himself anew on their behalf.

Desiring to profit by the privileges accorded to the Saints, thousands enrolled themselves under the banner of Joseph Smith, patiently submitting themselves to his command in the hope of winning the rewards promised to the faithful and the obedient. When these votaries accompanied him to the Far West and there formed themselves into a Society under the name of the Latter Day Saints, they merely did what others performed when they constituted themselves into 'Communities,' and settled on lands purchased with a view to afford them scope for carrying out in practice the social theories which they had accepted as panaceas for all the ills of which society was the prey. That nearly all these communities were soon dissolved was directly due to bankruptcy and was indirectly caused by the absence of a tie sufficiently strong and lasting to bind them together. Their religion saved the Latter Day Saints from sharing the fate of Owen's 'New Harmony;' of the many phalanxes in which Fourier's speculations were reduced to practice; of Brook Farm where the transcendentalists of New England made a vigorous but futile attempt to demonstrate the right manner in which to purge the world of corruption preparatory to ushering in the

Golden Age. A deplorable combination of ignorance and fanaticism was brought to bear against the infant Church and the newly formed association of which Joseph Smith was the head and the originator. The rough dwellers in Missouri arrayed themselves against him and compelled his followers to abandon their settlement. Fleeing to Illinois they were there treated with a barbarity equally gross and blameworthy. The law proved to the Prophet not a protection, but a snare. Again and again he was imprisoned on paltry pretexts, but his persecutors would not believe in his innocence even when repeatedly proclaimed by a Court of Justice. The prison in which he was last immured pending the progress of another trial was broken open by armed men and he was foully slain in cold blood. His followers, instead of immediately dispersing in dismay, banded themselves together with increased ardour, having resolved to dare and endure everything in the defence of a faith which they regarded with the stronger admiration on account of the hatred it inspired in the breasts of lawless, depraved, and cruel men. The desperate resolve to seek safety in an unexplored part of the country can be paralleled by nothing but the lofty courage which moved the Dutch to resolve upon submerging their entire country and to take ship for the Indian Archipelago rather than submit to the debasing bondage which would have been their lot had the King of France become master of Holland.

Having arrived at the Valley of the Great Salt Lake and assured themselves that the parched desert and the towering mountain were insuperable barriers against the inhumanity and intolerance of their foes, they began to live in the way which seemed the best according to their lights.

If the Mormons had never learned what it was to battle with difficulties almost superhuman and to obtain a triumph almost miraculous, they might have speedily cooled in their devotion for the creed they had adopted, or interpreted the accepted doctrines in diverse ways. But the fires of persecution had strengthened their faith. They not only believed implicitly in the divinity of their martyred Prophet, but they were disposed to interpret his revelations in the manner most consonant with their personal experience. They considered themselves as the Chosen People with whom God was ever present and against whose enemies God was always ready to fight. Just as the Puritans smarting under the atrocious discipline of the Star Chamber readily adopted as their own the fulminations of the Old Testament against the wicked in authority, and were only too ready, when opportunity offered, to smite with the sword of Gideon, and consider the reeking battlefield, on which their foes weltered in blood, as a pleasing sight in the eyes of the Almighty, so did the Mormons incline to give effect to all the harsh threatenings of the Bible and to regard as of no account the admonitions to be slow to wrath and abounding in mercy.

The spirit with which they were ready to resist attack from without was displayed in the works that were requisite in order to render their position secure and their existence easy. They laboured at their daily tasks as if they were vindicating their sincerity and demonstrating their piety. Under the double incentive of religious enthusiasm and individual requirements they built houses, planted fruit trees, tilled fields and reaped harvests. Even if no ignoble ambition animated their souls, the circumstances in which they were placed furnished an irresistible stimulus to exertion. For none of them was any way of escape from the Valley open, and, unless all toiled to the uttermost of their powers, to none was subsistence certain. What was effected under these conditions, all Utah bears witness.

With comparative security and unlooked for prosperity came a longing for compensation as a reward for their patience under privations, bravery

in the face of obstacles, victory over great odds.
No longer apprehending the attacks of declared
enemies, they desired to evince that they were a
peculiar and an exceptional people working out
an intricate problem in a new sphere. In their
eyes the Old Testament had gradually become an
authority of great weight: its statements had commended themselves to their minds; when, then, it
was proposed to adopt as their own the rules of
the Patriarchs respecting marriage the proposition
met with general acceptance, because it chimed in
with the prevailing sentiment. Whether Brigham
Young had really received from Joseph Smith the
' Revelation on Celestial Marriage ' which he promulgated in 1852 was not a circumstance scanned
too closely by those to whom the revelation was
addressed. To be different in all things from the
Gentiles was dear to the hearts of the persecuted
Latter Day Saints. The indignation which the
Gentiles have displayed towards those who openly
practised Polygamy has tended more than anything
else to confirm the Mormons in their notion as to
the divinity of plural marriage.

Mormon principles have triumphed all along the
line; yet, in the thoroughness of the victory, lurks
the greatest peril to the cause. The high-handed
measures which commanded cheerful assent while

the danger lasted, have been regarded with aversion and have excited antipathy since the time has arrived for enjoying the fruits of conquest. To the vigour and foresight of Brigham Young, and to the daring and devotion of colleagues not inferior to him in ability, the Mormons are almost wholly indebted for their prosperity. But, even while acknowledging this, they hesitate to yield uniform respect and implicit obedience to those who originally guided their footsteps and sustained their efforts. They see that the leaders have had their reward in the form of positions of honour and of large possessions. These leaders cling to the authority which they have acquired or usurped. They will not relinquish it save under compulsion. Hundreds refuse to submit to its exercise. Those who have stood forth and challenged the claims of Brigham Young, who point out his shortcomings, who contest his right to demand that he shall be blindly obeyed, and who ridicule his pretensions to be infallible, elicit sympathy and aid from among the mass; and the warfare which once was waged by the Gentiles against the Mormons promises to be succeeded by an embittered strife between Mormonism and Brigham Youngdom.

Under these circumstances what should be the course of Congress, what the attitude of the Government of the United States? Interference with Mormonism as a system of religion is above all things to be deprecated. It does not follow, however, that everything which assumes the cloak of religion should be connived at, tolerated, or approved. If a minority were to contend that a divine revelation authorised them to pick pockets and cut throats, the majority would rightly reply that they were empowered by law to imprison thieves and hang murderers. The same argument applies to such a case as that of the Mormons as far as Polygamy is concerned. To marry several wives is alleged to be a part of the Mormon religion. The majority may retort that their religion pronounces Polygamy illegal and, in a country like the United States, where the supreme law is the will of the majority, the Mormons must either convert the majority to their views, or else suffer the penalty provided for law-breakers. No American citizen is entitled to complain of persecution when the law is impartially administered.

To be just and fear not; to enforce the law which is no respecter of persons; to treat the erring Mormons as citizens of the United States who have no royal claim for exemption from the penalties which other wrongdoers must pay, but whom, at the same time, it would be iniquitous to single out and sacrifice on the unhallowed altar of religious fanaticism, is the sacred duty incumbent on Congress, is the imperative mandate of the executive authorities. The original and crying grievance of the Mormons was that justice had invariably and intentionally been denied them. They were exiled from Missouri, they were expelled from Illinois because an unjustifiable prejudice had been excited to their detriment. No Act of Congress had they infringed, nor had they denied the supremacy of the law of the land. In turn they have become violators of statutes and ruthless persecutors; the Gentiles have suffered at their hands indignities quite as unbearable and injuries nearly as unpardonable as those which they underwent at the hands of the Gentiles. The fountain of justice is tainted in Utah: the juries and judges are corrupt or biassed. A righteous policy requires that these gross abuses should be extirpated and that in the eye of the law Mormon and Gentile should be absolutely equal. To accomplish this should be the endeavour and aim of American statesmen and rulers. That more than this should be undertaken or achieved, no right-thinking man will desire.

If Salt Lake Valley were to become the home of a really free people, it would be one of the glories of the American Union. Its situation is unrivalled in this part of the Continent. A temperate climate blesses the inhabitants with good health; a fruitful soil yields them food in abundance. The surrounding mountains are rich in minerals; the multitudinous streams are alive with fish. Nature has designed this valley to be a terrestrial paradise: hitherto, the doings of man have frustrated, rather than forwarded the designs of Nature.

My statement of actual facts will probably produce an impression very different from that made by the brilliant but misleading pictures with which preceding visitors to the mountain home of the Mormons have delighted the public. As no two persons ever see the same thing in precisely the same light, so any two travellers may widely differ in their estimate of an institution or their opinion of a people. It is quite true, as several writers have averred, that President Brigham Young inculcates on his flock as a paramount duty that of labouring with their hands, and he does this with the greater success, inasmuch as it is certain that those who will not work must starve. So far, I agree with certain other visitors to Utah. Rather than note the points of disagreement in detail let me give by way of conclusion the summarised

9

results of my own observation. I found the Mormons as a body, very backward and ignorant when compared with the other dwellers on the American continent.* I found them reluctant to embody their thoughts in words, afraid to speak their minds lest they should be punished for giving utterance to what was obnoxious to those in high places. The leaders and rulers of the Mormons are, for the most part, shrewd and determined Yankees who exercise a control over the multitude as grind-

* Mr. Horace White, one of the most distinguished members of the American Press, gives as the result of his enquiry into the working of Mormonism an opinion similar to mine, and supports it with examples which, I think, merit quotation:—'I happen to know a Norwegian settlement in Wisconsin, whose original constituents were as ignorant and desperately poor as any Mormon immigrants from Wales or Denmark, and who have been in occupation of the soil about the same length of time as the Utah Mormons. They are o-day more than seventy-five per cent. in advance of the Mormons in point of intelligence, wealth, culture, and everything which goes under the name of civilization, and they have neither gambling shops nor grog shops, nor houses of prostitution licensed, or unlicensed, among them. They had no better start in America than the Mormons. They have no better market for their crops. If they had a rather richer soil to begin with, it was not so good in the long run, for while the crops in Wisconsin are subject to constant vicissitudes of climate, those of Utah are unfailing and enormous in their yield.' 'Returning to my Norwegian friends on Jefferson Prairie, Wisconsin (and I might point with equal force to the Swedish settlement at Galva, Illinois, or to the Hollanders of Iowa), we find that Mormonism, so far from advancing the physical condition of the common people, has kept them from making the advancement to which the bountiful earth and sky have constantly invited them.'— *The Chicago Tribune,* 16th July, 1869.

ing and despotic as that of the worst tyrants in history. Neither Jew nor Christian can safely and easily establish himself in Utah, either for the sake of pleasure or for the purposes of trade. All non-Mormons are subjected to a system of persecution skilfully organised and conducted with a view to their expulsion from the Valley of the Great Salt Lake. In the Territory of Utah I found a parody on the religion of the Bible and of the Koran, sanctioning and prescribing the treatment of women, not as intellectual human beings, but as mere human toys. Having had this experience, I am unable to accept, as a reply to all objections and a counter-balance to all drawbacks, the incontestable facts that President Young preaches the gospel of labour, and that Mormon orchards yield annually many thousand bushels of large ripe peaches and rosy-cheeked apples.

XIV.

THE GREAT SALT LAKE TO THE GREAT AMERICAN DESERT.

To ENTER the cars of the Union Pacific Railway after having paid a visit to Salt Lake City is
like setting foot on one's native soil after sojourning
among a strange people in a foreign land. The
habits and modes of thought of the Mormons and
the social atmosphere in which they live are alien
to the visitor who has neither special sympathy with
their creed, nor is predisposed to admire their
customs. Seated in the cars again, he feels himself
free to speak his mind without dread of being mis-
understood and without danger of giving offence.

After leaving Uintah and proceeding Westward,
Corinne is the next station of note. Passengers
bound for the Territory of Montana, which lies to
the north of Utah, leave the train here and take
the stage coach. Montana has the reputation of
being a second California. Although a Mormon
town and almost exclusively subjected to Mormon
influences, yet in Corinne a most vigorous and un-

relenting warfare against the Saints is waged by Mr. J. H. Beadle, the editor of the *Utah Daily Reporter*. In Salt Lake City this could not be done. The Mormon leaders would soon find means for silencing a declared foe to their system and scoffer at their pretensions. Certainly they would be justified in protesting against the virulent language of their critic. In a leading article, the Mormons in authority are likened to men 'who would rob their grandmothers of their spectacles and sell their frames for silver.' The principal Saints whom the mass of the ignorant people of Utah almost worship, are represented as 'a lot of New England Yankees out on a speculation with not the least speck of moral or honest sentiment in their whole composition. They are out here lording it over a lot of foreign converts who are here made peasants and slaves to these Yankee masters. With such men to obtain absolute sway over an ignorant and bigoted people, can we expect anything else than that these leaders should be what they are—crafty swindlers and licentious monsters?' When the editor leaves Corinne for other parts of the settlement he does so at the risk of his life. He has more than once experienced harsh treatment at the hands of exasperated Mormons. It is possible that his voice will one day be silenced by

such irresistible and congenial Mormon arguments
as bullets from a revolver or blows from a club.

After passing Corinne, around which the country
is fertile and well-cultivated, the line runs through
a barren tract, skirts the shore of the Great Salt
Lake, and ascends the side of Promontory Mountain. The gradients here are very steep, and the
cuttings in the rock must have been made with
much expenditure of toil and money. Two trestle
bridges are crossed, a sharp curve is rounded, and
the station of Promontory is reached. This is the
Western terminus of the Union Pacific, and the
Eastern terminus of the Central Pacific Railway.
Here it was that the ceremony of uniting the two
sides of the Continent by rail was performed on the
10th of May, 1869. The point of junction was
then the subject of controversy, and has not yet
been finally settled. The present arrangement is
the result of a compromise. The two companies in
their anxiety to earn as much as possible of the
Government subsidy, carried their respective lines
as far as an hundred miles to the east and west of
Promontory. These unfinished roadways are still
to be seen side by side with the completed line.
As one result of the disagreement, there are few
through trains. In general the passengers have to
change carriages, secure fresh sleeping berths, and

get their luggage moved from one train to the other. Two hours are allowed for this, as well as for taking a meal. There is usually ample time to stroll through the town and see the sights. The town is built partly of canvas and partly of wood, and has but one street. The signs are hardly in keeping with the structures to which they are attached. Over a shanty is painted in large letters, 'Pacific Hotel,' and over a tent, 'Club House.' One of the wooden dwellings attracts notice on account of the neatly arranged muslin curtains within the window. Unlike the others, it has no signboard to indicate its purpose, but a glance through the open door satisfies the curiosity of the passerby. He sees two or three smiling females ready to extend welcomes to whoever will enter in. This is characteristic of all these rude settlements in the wild Western country. In a canvas town, the abode of women with few scruples to overcome and no characters to lose is as distinguishable, and as much a thing of course, as the gambling hell and the drinking saloon. Of drinking saloons there are many at Promontory; but there is only one gambling hell as far as I could learn. This one is quite enough for the place. In its way the hell is unique. The object of its keepers is to entice the passengers halting here to try their luck. With

this view agents are sent to the neighbouring
stations, where they take their places in the cars,
and enter into conversation with the occupants.
Of course, as soon as the train stops at Promontory
these agents lead the way to the gaming table.
Nor have they far to go. It is in the open air,
within a few yards of the line. The game played
is three card Monte. It is as simple as thimblerig.
Three cards are laid out in line with their faces
downwards. Let it be supposed that these are a
Jack, a King, and a Queen, the denomination of
the cards making no difference—the dealer will
then challenge any one to point out one of them,
say the Jack. A stake of a twenty dollar gold
piece depends on the event. In front of the card-
dealer is a pile of these gold pieces. He addresses
the on-lookers as follows:—' Gentlemen, you have
your eyes against my hand. You see how I place
the cards,' moving the three backwards and forwards, and then laying them in a row. ' Now I
will bet any one of you that he does not point out
the Jack; if he does so at the first chance he wins
his money, if he fails he loses it.' One of the by-
standers inquires if he will bet without touching the
cards, to which the reply is, ' Certainly, sir; I will
bet anything, from 20 to 100 dollars, that you do
not point out the Jack.' The speaker steps for-

ward eagerly and excitedly, places a 20 dollar gold piece on the table, and points to a card, which, when reversed, is seen to be the right one. He gets his 20 dollars, which he clutches, and then makes off rapidly, as if surprised and delighted at his good fortune, carrying off, also, the winning card in the excitement of the moment. The card-dealer calls upon him to return the ' ticket,' adding, ' By golly, Sir, you have beaten me this time, but you are as welcome to the money as if you had worked hard for it.' This is repeated several times, the keeper of the table invariably losing. Indeed the game seems absurdly easy, as there is always a small black speck on the back of the winning card, and every onlooker thinks it a certainty to point out this card. At last, after the dealer had lost repeatedly, a man came out of the tent behind the table saying, ' Come now, partner, you had better stop; this won't do.' To which he replies, ' By golly I will play till I lose every cent I have in the world. I must win nine times out of ten, and I am ready to bet any gentleman 100 dollars that he does not point out the right card this time.' The truth is the men who had staked and won were what we call confederates, and what are here called ' cappers.' They certainly played their parts exceedingly well, and would have imposed on any other set of spectators than one composed of old Californians, who are too knowing birds to be caught by the chaff of cardsharpers. They are well acquainted with the trick of the game. I saw a poor German baker, destitute of experience and endowed with but little sense, dispossessed in a few minutes of all that he had in his pockets. The trick consists in being able to deceive the spectator by shifting the small black speck on the back of the cards in such a way as to make him point to the wrong one. When the betting is real the 'Bank' never loses. I have been told that the winnings on some days are as high as 1,700 dollars. It is the passengers who alone become dupes, and the emigrant trains yield the most plentiful harvest. A 'capper' with whom I conversed supplied me with what he deemed a defence of the 'institution.' This 'capper' strongly urged me to try my luck. I thanked him for his recommendation and expressed my deep regret at my inability to contribute an adequate amount to the gains of the Bank. I told him that I should not forget his advice, if at any future time I might be possessed of more money than I could easily squander, and that, rather than get rid of it all by throwing it out of the window, I should reserve a portion wherewith to visit Promontory station and lose the remainder at three card Monte. Thereupon he changed his tone, and said that the keepers of the table had been harshly treated by the press, had been called robbers and other hard names, whereas they were honest, straightforward men who laboured hard in order to earn their living. He added that the play was perfectly fair to those who took part in it. This was perfectly true if fairness consisted in uniform winning on the one side, and uniform losing on the other. He told me, moreover, that many emigrants had come to Promontory, had lost all they had, and had been kindly treated by these calumniated hell keepers. Their charity, he said with an accent of candour and an air of kindliness which would have done credit to the most practised adept in professional philanthropy, was conspicuously displayed towards those whom they had beggared, for they gave them a sum sufficient to pay their journey to their destination, or to keep them during the journey. I modify while translating his language, which was rather highly seasoned with vigorous and sonorous expletives. Although the small population of this place is composed for the most part of roughs and gamblers, with the admixture of a female element quite as obnoxious, yet the peace is tolerably well kept on account of the awe felt for the railway officials. It is tacitly understood that open lawlessness or any serious disturbance would end in the clean sweep of the whole nest of scoundrels. If those who had the power were at once to begin the cleansing process, they would do a service to all travellers over this railway.

'Pullman's palace cars' do not form part of the ordinary trains on the Central Pacific Railway. That company has what it calls 'silver palace cars,' of which the name is the best part. They are very inferior when compared with those of the Pullman Company. Besides, the system of management is far less perfect. In Pullman's cars there is a conductor whose duty it is to see that the passengers are properly cared for, and under him are coloured servants, one being attached to each car. The Central Pacific Company's cars are in charge of a coloured man, who also acts as attendant. This double part is generally done badly. The opinion prevailed throughout the train that at least one of these coloured gentlemen would suffer rough usage some day at the hands of ex-asperated passengers. His insolence and inatten-tion were unbearable. He was certainly the wrong man for the place. The conductors of Pullman's cars are patterns of good officials. They are hand-somely paid. They hold office on the condition that no complaint is preferred against them, instant dismissal being the consequence of any well-founded charge. It is this, among other things, which has rendered Pullman's Car Company a splendid commercial success.

If the cars of the Californian Company are inferior to those of its rival, the Californians are entitled to a large share of the praise due to those who constructed this railway. A few words may fitly be expended in stating what they did. Several years ago, when Sacramento was a much smaller place than it now is, some of its most intelligent residents convinced themselves of the feasibility of carrying a line of rail across the lofty and snow-capped Sierra Nevadas. At their own expense they had a survey made. A route was fixed upon, plans were drawn up, and the details of the project elaborated. Throughout the state of California the scheme became so popular, that to be a 'railroad man' was one of the best claims wherewith to secure the votes of electors. A state charter was formally obtained, and the promoters went to Washington to urge the measure upon Congress. This was in 1862, when the nation was alive to the necessity of facilitating intercourse with the Pacific States, in order that the perils to which the Union was then exposed might not be rendered more formidable in character or more extended in range. The desire of California to have the railway constructed was thus in unison with the heartfelt aspirations of the Eastern States. Accordingly, the assent of Congress was given to the proposed scheme, and the pecuniary aid of the Government pledged to carry it into effect. However, forty miles had to be completed before any money could be claimed from the Government, and these forty miles ran up the steep slopes of mountains so lofty as apparently to defy the science of the most skilful and sanguine engineer. Yet the formidable obstacles were vanquished one after another, and the prophets who predicted failure, and the cynics who styled the scheme a swindle, were put to open shame. The Californians allege that, while their section of the line presented the largest number of engineering problems to solve, it is far the better of the two. They might add that had they not had the advantage of the cheap and efficient labour of Chinamen it would still have been a grand project, or else but slowly advancing towards completion.

Meantime the train has been careering over the Central Pacific Railway, and along the shore of the Great Salt Lake, thus affording to the passengers a splendid view of that magnificent sheet of water, as well as of the bold mountain peaks which encompass it. The prospect is one to be enjoyed and remembered. But it is the only glimpse of scenery, worthy of special note, on which the eye rests with pleasure. We are still within the Territory of Utah. Promontory Point, where the junction was formally made between the railways of which the starting points were Sacramento and Omaha, is in that Territory. The Mormons constructed more than an hundred miles of the railway, and Brigham Young is said to have enriched himself by the way in which he manipulated the contracts. Yet, on the memorable day when the line was finally completed and officially opened, the very existence of the citizens of Utah was unrecognised, if not forgotten. The Governor of Arizona was present and brought with him a silver spike as the contribution of the dwellers in his remote Territory. The State of Nevada also sent a silver spike, fashioned by the hands of one hundred citizens. Some munificent citizens of San Francisco contributed two golden spikes, as an offering on behalf of the State of California, while the last 'tie' or sleeper was a beautiful piece of Californian laurel. The ceremony of driving the last spike was marked by an incident to which a parallel will be sought in vain among the many extraordinary feats of modern times. The hammer with which the

blows were given was connected to a wire in direct
communication with the principal telegraph offices
throughout the Union.   Thus the instant that the
work was consummated the result was simultaneously saluted on the shores of two great Oceans
and throughout the wide expanse of a vast continent by the roar of cannon and the ringing of
bells.*

Several miles westward of Promontory station,
the line traverses what, properly speaking, is the
Great American Desert.   This is supposed to be
the bed of ·an inland sea.   In barrenness it rivals
the Desert of Sahara; in desolation and dreariness
it cannot be surpassed.   A coating of alkali dust
gives to it the appearance of a snow-covered plain.
But snow is far less intolerable than the alkali.
Where it abounds nothing of service to man or
beast can live.   Shoe-leather is burned by it as by
quicklime.   The minute particles which float in the
air irritate the throat and lungs as keenly as the

---

* Lest any curious traveller should waste his time in seeking for
the precious spikes and the valuable sleeper, I may state that they
were removed almost as soon as laid, and that pieces of ordinary
wood and iron were substituted for them. But these, however, did not
long remain intact. The hoarders of relics hacked the sleeper into
splinters in the course of a few minutes, and attacked the last rail
with a vigour which had the effect of rendering it worthless.   The
sleeper had to be renewed three times and the rail once in the
course of a week. Even then, credulous visitors were still busied
in cutting mementoes of the ' last tie.'

steel dust which cuts short the lives of Sheffield needle-grinders. Long before Elko is reached, a station 200 miles distant from Promontory, the passengers in the train fervently pray to be delivered from this corrosive and ubiquitous alkali dust.

Soon after the opening of the railway, a party, of which ex-Senator Ben Wade was one, made this journey. Complaints were rife about the discomforts experienced on this section of the line. Wishing to make the best of what could not be remedied, the Mark Tapley of the party remarked that with plenty of water to lay the dust and congenial companions, the Great American desert would be, not only endurable, but delightful. Whereupon the ex-Senator observed:—' With plenty of water and good society, Hell would not be a bad place to live in.'

XV.

THE HUMBOLDT RIVER AND PLAINS.

AFTER passing through the Great American Desert the sight of a running river and luxuriant vegetation is most enjoyable. The stream which freshens and fertilises this region is the Humboldt, having its source in the mountains of that name, and flowing westwards for about two hundred and fifty miles. Along the banks of the river Humboldt is a thick fringe composed of willow trees and a variety of shrubs. It is characteristic of this part of the country that as soon as the land is irrigated almost any plant or vegetable can be grown upon it. The climate is genial. If it were not for the lack of rain millions of acres might be at once brought under cultivation. Hence the extreme value of the tract adjacent to a stream of water large enough to supply all that is required for the purposes of irrigation. When the emigrants formerly traversed this route, they timed their halting places so as to be within easy reach of a river. In many places there are numerous pools of water; but for the most part these are so strongly impregnated with alkali as to be even more undrinkable than sea water. The alkali water burns the tongue, inflames the throat, irritates the stomach. Those who essay it will agree with the American writer who says:— ' Taste it at the first opportunity, and you will wish that the first opportunity had come last, or that it never had arrived.' An animal will die of thirst sooner than drink a drop of it. Yet men have been known to struggle against an impending death from thirst and exhaustion by painfully swallowing small portions of this bitter water. Happily these trials are no longer among the dangers which beset the traveller across the Great American Desert and the Humboldt Plains. The railway has changed all that. Where there is no drinking water on the spot, it is brought by train. In several places tanks have been erected for containing a supply of water sufficient to meet all ordinary wants.

In the midst of the Humboldt Plains is the town of Elko, at which the train makes a long stoppage. This is one of the mushroom towns which abound to the west of the Rocky Mountains. It contains three thousand inhabitants. What Sacramento and San Francisco were twenty years ago, Elko is said to be at the present moment. It is laid out in streets, and these streets are lined with shops and dwellings. As names, Commercial-street, Main-street, Railroad-street sound well, while First, Second, Third, Fourth, and Fifth Streets convey the notion of an American city of size and import-ance. But it is one thing to read of those streets, and another and very different thing to walk in them. They are as much entitled to the appellation of streets as are the spaces between the booths of a country fair. Nor are the shops, houses, and public offices at all more imposing than the booths erected in a night for the business of a day. The thorough-fares are neither paved nor macadamised. They are as primitive in character as the pathways be-tween the tents on Wimbledon Common when the Volunteers are encamped there. The foot pas-senger walks among alkali, and as he moves along he raises a cloud of dust which whitens and damages his clothes, and excoriates his nostrils. Over the fronts of shops constructed of wood, canvas, or a combination of both, are signs intimating that everything the pedestrian wants is to be had within. If he enters one of these pretentious 'stores' he will find that with money, and plenty of it, he has at his command whatever he can desire, from a box of pills to a bottle of champagne, and from a cigar to a pot of blacking. On the outside of some huts is a board with the inscription that a lawyer or a doctor may be consulted within. One of these huts has these words painted above the door in large black letters:—'Office of the *Elko Independent.*' A newspaper office in such a locality specially attracts the attention of anyone to whom newspaper-offices are places of personal interest. I regret that the time at my disposal was insufficient to visit this home of journalism in what was little better than a wilderness. I was fortunate enough, however, to succeed in procuring a copy of the *Elko Independent.* It is published twice a week; is printed on good paper; its leading articles are quite as well written as those which grace the columns of an English provincial newspaper, while its advertisements are fraught with instruction of a new and curious kind. That the price of a copy should have been one shilling surprised me less than the fact that the journal was published at all, and was supported by the small population of this primitive town.

One of the advertisements was very noteworthy. It was worded as follows:—'Ung Gen, Chinese Doctor, Silver-street, between Fourth and Fifth, Elko, will attend professionally to all who may require his services. Having been engaged in a steady practice for several years, he is prepared to cure all diseases that may come to his notice.' This was not, as sceptical readers may suppose, an advertising trick. Chinese doctors are not shams here, but living realities, and, in their own way, useful members of society. In some parts of the Union mock Indians impose on the credulous, and deceive the unwary. At Saratoga, for example, the Indian camp is inhabited by persons bearing strong physical resemblances to Irishmen of pure blood and obstreperous patriotism. Around Niagara Falls the Indians have a very theatrical appearance. Their names and dresses alone recal the wild aborigines of America. But the Chinese in these parts of the American continent are genuine natives of the Flowery Land. They have been the chief constructors of the Pacific Railway. They are the most docile and trustworthy of servants. Along the line I saw squads of them at work. At this place they are so common as to attract no notice. Many of them were making their way through the crowd on the platform of the station. Four or five women and a few children were the momentary objects of interest, for Chinawomen are but seldom seen in public. Not less curious than the advertisement of the Chinese doctor, whose ' steady practice for several years' had prepared him ' to cure all diseases,' was that of a firm of druggists. This firm intimated not only that it was ready to supply all drugs and to prepare all prescriptions, but also

that it had on hand 'a large stock of paints, oils,
window-glass, castor oil; also a large assortment of
fishing lines and hooks of all kinds.' Another announcement may be repeated for the benefit of
future visitors to Elko. In it the keeper of the
'White Pine Saloon' informs his patrons that—
'The most delicate fancy drinks are compounded by
skilful mixologists in a style that captivates the
public and makes them happy.' Turning from the
advertising to the leader columns of the *Elko Independent*, I find that the Democratic party is
honoured with its support, and that the Chinese
are the objects of its aversion. A proposition for
excluding Chinese labour, without openly persecuting Chinamen, deserves mention on account of
the malicious ingenuity which inspired it. The
writer points out that it is characteristic of the
Chinese to desire that their remains should be interred among the graves of their ancestors, and that
to be buried in a foreign land is repugnant alike to
their religious sentiments and patriotic feelings.
Taking advantage of this, it is proposed to make it
a penal offence 'to disturb the remains of the dead
after burial, and to attempt to carry away from our
shores the mortal remains of one of that people, and
the good work of excluding them is accomplished.'
From conversations with fellow-travellers I learned

that the aversion to the Chinamen is very general on the Pacific slope of the continent. The Chinese I saw along the line appeared to be hard-working and good-tempered beings, ready to interchange words with whoever would converse with them in the broken English which they understand, and delighted when a passenger who had lived in China gave utterance to a word or phrase in their native tongue. One or two Chinamen entered the train here. Among them was a merchant who had amassed a fortune, who spoke English fluently, and who conversed intelligently on most subjects. He was not allowed a seat in the best cars, but was condemned to occupy a place in the emigrants' cars. All his money could not conquer the prejudice against his tribe. Though the negroes have been emancipated, yet the spirit of caste still works mischief in America. Indeed, as an American writer has forcibly remarked: 'The spirit of "Native Americanism" is but a thinly disguised aristocracy of birth.' Perhaps no two persons in the motley group on the platform at Elko station were more helpless and misplaced than a Frenchman and his wife. They were evidently very poor, were miserably clad and dirty, and downcast in spirit. They hardly knew a word of English, and those about them were ignorant of French. Their desire was to get to the silver mines in as cheap a way as possible, being under the delusion that if they once reached the mines their fortunes were as good as made. This was the second French couple I met in this far away region. The other wretched pair had taken up their abode in Salt Lake City, with a view to deal in furs. Both had been from ten to fifteen years in America, and the husband alone could make himself imperfectly understood. His wife spoke French only. They uttered warm expressions of satisfaction when they found one with whom they could converse in their own language. Unfortunately the pleasure was not reciprocal, seeing that this unhappy couple took advantage of the opportunity to pour forth a long and by no means interesting account of their sufferings and their disappointments. The couple at Elko thought less about telling their story than about finding a team of mules wherewith to start for the silver yielding region. They were clearly directed whither to go, but when last I saw them as the train moved off, they were walking in the wrong direction in a state of hopeless bewilderment.

What gives importance to this place is the fact that the road to the White Pine mining district branches off at Elko. This district is about 125 miles south of Elko, and is almost due east of

10

Virginia City, where the excitement with regard to silver mining in Nevada first broke out, and attracted general notice. The reputation of White Pine had been achieved in a very short time. In February, 1869, the population of the district was reckoned at four hundred people; five months later it had increased to twenty thousand. The dominant topic in every conversation is the silver mines of this State. Let me pause in the description of my journey to furnish a brief account of the silver mines of Nevada.

XVI.

THE STATE OF NEVADA AND ITS SILVER TREASURES.

PRIOR TO 1861, what is now known as the State of Nevada formed part of the Territory of Utah. The Mormons were in the minority and the Gentiles were dissatisfied with their own condition. Having resolved upon separating themselves from the Mormons, the Gentiles met together, passed resolutions, and formed a territorial organization. Congress approving of their conduct, gave validity to the arrangements they had made. The President appointed a Governor over the new Territory. The numbers of the citizens rapidly increased: their ambition prompted them to desire admission into the Union and, on Congress giving the necessary consent, the semi-independence and the valuable privileges accorded to a State became, in 1864, the portion of Nevada.

As early as 1859 discoveries of silver in Nevada had attracted the notice of adventurous miners in all parts of the West. Ten years had then elapsed since the gold excitement in California startled and fascinated the world. The Californian quartz mines

were as rich as ever, but the individual miner found
great difficulty in getting a return for his labour equal
to that which he could easily command before the
watercourses had been rifled of nuggets and all the
gold dust had been sifted from the sand and gravel.
To these disappointed and desponding miners the
news that silver was even more abundant in Nevada
than gold had ever been in California was received
with great joy, and an immediate rush was made to
the new Potosi.   The yield of the great Comstock
lode was such as to verify to the letter the most
highflown statements, and to gratify the most sanguine hopes.   Virginia City, in Western Nevada,
was built within easy reach of this lode and the
whole district was honey-combed with mines.   The
estimated value of the gold and silver obtained in
this district during ten years is twenty millions
sterling.   Sixteen millions of dollars are believed
to be the gross annual yield.   The sum is enormous,
yet the proportion of actual gain is very small.
The net profit is understood to be not greater than
half a million of dollars.   Worse than the insignificance of the return is the prospect that, unless a
desperate experiment prove successful, these mines
will have to be abandoned altogether.   To avert
this calamity a tunnel is now being driven into
Mount Davidson with a view to intersect the great

Comstock lode at the depth of 2,000 feet. The distance to be driven is four miles. Mr. Sutro is the projector of the tunnel, and it has been named after him. Opinions are divided as to the merits of the enterprise. Its very magnitude is regarded by some as an insuperable bar to its success, while more daring and confident spirits predict the brilliant triumph of the gigantic undertaking. It is not necessary to be a practical miner, an experienced engineer, or a volunteer prophet to state that the Sutro tunnel will either beggar its promoters, or else be the means of converting each of them into a Crœsus.

To the east of Virginia City another district rich in silver deposits attracted miners in 1862. This is called the Reese River district. The mines in it do not yield large quantities of ore, but the ore found in them is of a superior class. Austin City is the chief town of this locality. But the spot which at present surpasses all others, which has been more than a nine days wonder, and the theatre of an excitement which tends to increase rather than abate, which has been the haven of miners disgusted with the reality elsewhere, and is one of the most notable among the many rich repositories of silver treasure in the State of Nevada, bears the name of White Pine.

This district which lies due east of Virginia City was first ' prospected ' by some adventurous miners who left Austin City in the spring of 1865 with the design of carefully exploring untrodden wilds in the hope of making their fortunes. With such men the old saw, that the sea contains as good fish as have been taken out of it, is at once an article of faith and a stimulus to action. While thoroughly coinciding in the spirit of the saying they have materially altered its wording. Instead of sea, they read stream or flat or mountain slope, and for fish, they substitute the words golden dust or auriferous quartz, chloride of silver or argentiferous stone. A pickaxe is their ' open sesamé.' Wherever their keen and skilled vision detects traces of mineral, there the rending blow is struck and the stone detached to be tested by a rude chemistry, or subjected to the rapid and decisive scrutiny of eyes quick to discern and admire the true ore and trained to reject the dross. During many months of hard toil continued with indomitable vigour, and of trying privation borne with unflinching spirit, did they prosecute their search. Spring melted into summer and summer faded into autumn before the prize was won. They then satisfied themselves that what is now known as Treasure Hill contained incalculable stores of precious minerals. On the

10th of October they assembled together, made speeches and passed resolutions whereof the gist is contained in the mining records of the locality. The entry runs as follows : ' A company of miners met on the above day for the purpose of forming a district. Motion made and carried that this district be known as White Pine District—bounded on the north by the Red Hills, and running thence south to a point whence the mountains run into a foothill, thence east twelve miles, thence north, and thence west to the place of beginning.' The district thus mapped out had no attraction of scenery or site to recommend it. The trees which grow in the valleys or on the mountain sides are few in number and small in size. Desolation and sterility dominate the landscape. Nor is the absence of beauty compensated for by balmy winds and genial skies. All the year round the air is chilly, while, during the long months of winter, storms rage with incredible fury. The blast sweeps along charged with snow, and dust, and gravel. Those who suffer this ordeal are justified in believing that the demons of the storm have chosen as their appropriate home the bleak and barren mountains of Nevada. A name originally given to a thick white mass of cold vapour which sometimes veils the mountain tops and sometimes fills the valleys is employed to characterize these terrible storms. Tell a miner acquainted with White Pine that you have had to face the Po-go-nip and he will at once know that all your powers of endurance have been put to the test. The strength of the fascination produced by the silver deposits at White Pine is measured by the fact that the miners persevere in extracting the valued metal despite the terrors and the trials of the Po-go-nip.

Hamilton City, Shermantown, and Treasure City, are the principal centres of business in the district of White Pine. Many other names of 'cities' might be mentioned, but the 'cities' themselves are names and nothing more. They are glibly uttered by speculators: they figure in books and maps; but the greenhorn will search for them in vain. A new-comer desiring to learn some particulars about a city, questioned a miner who, on the strength of a month's residence in the neighbourhood, had a claim to the title of one of the oldest inhabitants, and received the reply that the city 'was about as large as New York, but was not built up yet.' Those which have been 'built up' are mere aggregates of miserable shanties and primitive tents. To construct a wooden dwelling is nearly as expensive here as it is to erect a marble palace elsewhere. Treasure City, perched up near the summit of Treasure Hill at an elevation of nine thousand feet above the level of the sea, is in close proximity to one of the richest of the White Pine mines. This is the Eberhardt, which is to White Pine what the famous Gould and Curry is to Virginia City. Not till the spring of 1868 was it vigorously worked and since then the returns have been prodigious. Its value has been rated at millions: at one time a purchaser acquired it for twenty-five dollars. A trustworthy writer has given the following sketch of the appearance of the mine underground:—'At the door a pack train of Mexican mules are being loaded with the precious ore for the mill two miles to the south-west, and two thousand feet lower down. In the shed men are busy at a great pile of brown, blue, red, green and black rock, breaking it to pieces and sorting it, the richest being thrown aside for the crucible, and the rest going into the sacks to be packed away to the mill. There is a princely fortune in this pile of ore, which to the uninitiated eye is but a heap of broken rock fit only for building walls or macadamizing public streets. Over one of the hoisting shafts there is a large wooden bucket with a rope and rude windlass such as you might see on the prospecting shaft of the poorest miner. It has served for hoisting all this wealth to the surface. In this bucket we descended into the mine. A long, narrow chamber, with dull, dark walls, and a few men at work with pick and gad, were all that the first glance revealed, and there was a momentary feeling of disappointment. A closer inspection showed that the walls, the ceiling, the floor, were silver; even the very dust on the floor was silver. This lump will yield five dollars a pound, this six, this seven, this eight, and this, which will flatten like lead under the hammer, is worth within a fraction of ten dollars a pound. They tell us that there is a million dollars worth of silver piled up before our eyes in this gloomy cavern, and such is indeed the fact.'* Keystone, Aurora, and Virginia, are the names of other productive mines. It is dangerous, however, to speak eulogistically of any mine, for before the ink is dry in which the words are written the mine's reputation may have been blasted beyond redemption. To-day its richness is the theme of every tongue and the envy of all who have no share in it, while to-morrow hardly a soul will deign to notice the concern which, in the slang of the locality, is ' played out' or ' busted.' Not only are the blanks more numerous than the prizes in the great lottery of silver mining, but the prizes often become converted into blanks. The miner makes what he calls

* Mr. A. S. Evans, in *Overland Monthly* for March, 1869, p. 279.

' a strike; ' he has found the hidden treasure ; his fortune, he now thinks, is made. Suddenly he discovers that the ore is ' refractory ' and will not pay to work, or the lode which sparkled with metal first becomes ' disordered' and then disappears. Moderate success will not suffice to enable him to live easily and accumulate wealth. He may work for others and receive 1*l.* daily ; but this barely enables him to subsist. In the early days of mining here, the prices of the commonest articles were exorbitant, while the sums charged for others were prohibitory. Rich men could alone afford to be ill, and all who fell ill were not rich. A doctor's fee would have ransomed a captive out of the hands of bloodthirsty Greek brigands. Laudanum sold at 5*s.* a drop. A single pill cost 2*l.* For extracting a tooth 10*l.* were charged. Even the trivial luxury of a cup of tea could not be enjoyed for less than 1*l.*, while the man who wished to eat an egg had to pay 15*s.* for the treat. Competition has now lowered prices, but there are several things which still command comparatively high sums. There is no water in Treasure City; every drop consumed there has to be brought in barrels up the steep mountain side, and a gallon costs as much as a gallon of wine on the Rhine or the Rhone. There is little wood in this district: a bundle of sticks costs one pound sterling. When these things are duly considered, it will not seem strange that the profits of those who work what are reputed to be the richest mines should be neither great nor lasting.

Although thousands will waste their substance and their strength in developing the silver mines of Nevada, yet the returns from these mines will probably suffice to double or quadruple the silver bullion of the world. That State has already produced as much silver as all the mines of Peru. What has been done within the brief space of a few years is but a trifle compared with what may hereafter be accomplished. There are numerous mountain slopes and Canyons yet untested in which many an Eberhardt mine may be discovered, or another Comstock lode laid bare. Nor of adventurers willing to risk all on the venture is there any lack. Perhaps the capitalist who is not addicted to speculations which differ in name only from staking money on the chance of a dice-box, on the roll of a ball, or on the colour of a card drawn at random from a pack, will act wisely if he watch rather than aid in the developement of the Nevada mines. Those who are on the spot may effect a profitable investment : those who are at a distance must trust to the representations of others; must rely upon the reports of assayers; must believe that the specimens

shown to them really represent the character of
the mines which they are asked to purchase. The
following story, despite its exaggeration, is fraught
with a useful moral. When new discoveries were
being made daily, the first duty was to get the
specimens assayed. If the result were encouraging
the claim would at once command a high price.
One of these assays was too satisfactory. According to the assayer's report the proportion of silver
in the stone was rather more per ton than if the
whole had been solid silver, while it was added that
gold to the value of 39 dollars was also contained
in it. 'Considering that the specimen assayed was
a fragment of a grindstone, the effort of the assayer
was terrific.'

XVII.

ACROSS THE SIERRA NEVADAS.

For 200 miles to the west of Elko the scenery continued to be monotonous, consisting of wide barren
plains bordered by mountain slopes. The Humboldt
river, with its banks fringed with shrubs and plants,
and the land for some distance on either side affording grazing ground for herds of cattle, alone gave
a slight variety to the scene. Now and then a
prairie wolf slunk aside as the passing train startled
it from its lair. More than one rude monument
was pointed out to me as indicating the spot where
a foul murder had been perpetrated or a bloody
combat had been waged. It was in this locality
that the Indians made a savage onslaught on those
engaged in constructing the line, murdering, scalp-
ing, and plundering several white men. Some
Indians were among the passengers by this train.
I was told that they are carried gratis. In return
they sometimes help to heap wood on the tender
at the appointed stopping-places. They were Sho-
shones, and were said to be very peaccable. With

their vermilion-stained cheeks, their lank black hair, their low foreheads, prominent noses, and sensual mouths, and an expression akin to the expression of a brute rather than that of a human being, they were as unprepossessing looking mortals as ever were seen in reality, while the very reverse of the Indians depicted in works of fiction. Indeed, the contrast was equivalent to a revolution between the doings of Eagle Eye, Little Hawk, South West Wind, and other warriors, now that they heaved billets of wood on the tender and when they scoured these plains with a view to achieve some deed of daring, and with a dislike deemed insuperable to perform anything that was simply useful. None of them had any scruples about asking and accepting alms. The squaws, who were far more hideous than the men, and the children, who were both ugly and naked, pestered the passengers for money or eatables. It was the rare exception for them to have anything to sell.

An American train resembles a steamer in this, that all the passengers are thrown together in a way which is impossible when they are cooped up in compartments as on an English railway. Every carriage communicates in such a way that it is possible at any moment to enjoy a welcome change by walking from end to end of the train. In my car there were several Californians on their way home after a visit to their native places in the Eastern States. One of them had several bottles of choice old Bourbon whisky with him, and he was persistent in asking his acquaintances to 'take a drink.' The whisky bottle was produced as early as six in the morning, and was passed from hand to hand at short intervals till the hour came for going to bed. The number of drinks must not be taken as a criterion of the extent of drunkenness. A sip of liquor constitutes a drink. It is the form rather than the effect which seems to give pleasure. The Westerners and Californians hold that, not to drink at all is the mark of a milksop, while to drink too much demonstrates a fool. One passenger could hold his own with most men of his years in drinking, smoking, shooting, and driving a bargain. He told some stories, which I should hardly have credited had they not been confirmed by independent and impartial testimony. He was thirty years old, and had seen more of life in all its aspects than many bold adventurers of double his age. More than one fortune he had made and squandered. He was now bound for California, with 150 dollars in his pocket, determined to enrich himself again. Everything by turns he had essayed; among others, the business of an auctioneer in Salt Lake City.

During four years he had driven a roaring trade among the Mormons by selling to them at high prices the second-hand and old-fashioned silks and satins disdained by the fashionable world elsewhere. Although a Gentile, he yet had succeeded in gaining the good graces and pocketing the spare cash of the Mormons. Judicious bribery and judicious reticence had commended him to the leaders among the Saints. Yet, while keeping his mouth shut, he did not shut his eyes also. Many examples of Mormon cruelty and tyranny had been witnessed by him, and these he detailed in a way which chilled the listener's blood. Another American, who had come from a two months' residence at Salt Lake City, was brimful of stories similar in kind. To their tales I attributed the greater credit, because they tallied in the main with what I had learned from personal observation of the practical working of Mormonism in the valley of the Great Salt Lake. It is noteworthy that no American who has visited Utah is a defender of the system in operation there. They all regard the Mormons as unworthy and dangerous citizens. The opinion seems universal that Congress must speedily legislate for Mormonism, not as a peculiar system of religion, but as a permanent conspiracy against equality and the impartial administration of justice.

Towards morning there was a commotion among the passengers. A sudden shock roused all from their slumbers. Many were greatly frightened, but no one was seriously hurt. A severe shaking was the only result of what proved to be a collision with a herd of cattle. The engine and tender had been thrown off the rails. Two oxen were crushed to death. Fortunately, the ground on either side was level; had the accident taken place farther on, where the embankment was very steep, the consequences might have been disastrous. As it was, a detention of eight hours between Wadsworth and Clarks' Station and the loss of breakfast were the only sufferings to be borne. Before many minutes had elapsed energetic steps were taken to replace the engine on the rails. The necessary appliances were at hand, and were put to their respective uses. This was not the only proof of the completeness of the arrangements for such a contingency. A telegraph clerk was in the train, and he had an instrument for tapping the wires. In the course of a few minutes the requisite connections were made, and messages were telegraphed to the stations East and West. An hour did not pass away before two locomotives were on the spot. What was still more important, the passage of trains over the line was stopped. As the line is a single one, the timely warning thus given by telegraph doubtless helped to avert the danger of other collisions. Some passengers were indisposed to forego their breakfasts without an effort to provide a substitute. There was plenty of beef alongside the line, and the sage-brush could be used for fuel. What more natural then, they argued, than to light a fire and cook a steak? The sage-brush was soon in a blaze, but the meat could not be procured with equal rapidity. Cutting through an ox hide and carving out a steak with a pen-knife was a task which baffled the passenger who made the attempt. While the ineffectual endeavour was being made, the fire threatened to produce serious consequences. The flames rushed along in the direction of the telegraph posts and the cars. A German gentleman of greater pluck than prudence had ignited the sage-brush, and he became ludicrously alarmed at the results of his act. He rushed about in frantic consternation, making energetic attempts to stamp out the flames. His vigour in undoing the mischief he had caused, led to the scorching and permanent injury of his boots and trousers.

Eight hours after the collision had occurred, the engine was replaced on the rails and the train was put in motion again. Not long afterwards the base of the Sierra Nevada range was reached, and the

wearying sight of plains covered with alkali and
sage-brush was exchanged for picturesque views of
mountain slopes, adorned with branching pine trees,
and diversified with foaming torrents. This was a
gratifying relief, as well as a fascinating prospect.
An anecdote is told of a lumber-man, who journeyed from his native State of Maine to seek his
fortune in the State of California. He was extremely taciturn and depressed in spirits during the
journey across the plains. When these mountains
came in sight, and his eyes rested upon the familiar
pine trees, he gazed earnestly for a moment, then,
rising to his feet, exclaimed, ' Thank God, I smell
pitch once more; ' and then, sinking back into his
seat, he wept for joy.

Reno is the last halting place of importance
during the Westward journey through the State of
Nevada. It is within a few miles of Virginia City,
the headquarters of the miners who work the
numerous silver and gold mines in this district.
Here, as at other similar places, a large number of
passengers left the train and a new set entered it.
The amount of the local passenger traffic was far in
excess of my expectations. Indeed, the proportion
of through passengers is very small when compared
with the number journeying from one intermediate
station to another. Near Boca, which is 127 miles

distant from Sacramento, the line crosses the boundary that separates the State of Nevada from the State of California. The Californians rejoiced when the train entered their State, and spoke with pleasure about soon basking in the sunshine which has made the Pacific slope a modern Garden of Eden. The ascent now becomes very steep, and two engines are employed to drag the train. At short intervals there are strong wooden sheds of about a thousand feet long, erected to guard the line against destruction from what we call avalanches, and what here are called 'snow slides.' Indeed, these sheds are very much like tunnels. They have been constructed at a vast expense, and in a solid manner. It has yet to be seen how far they will subserve their purpose. They have the drawback of interrupting the view of some of the most romantic scenery on the line. The glimpses one gets are just sufficient to tantalise and not prolonged enough to satisfy. The view of Donner Lake is the most charming of them all. This lake is picturesquely situated in a gorge of the Sierras. It was once the theatre of a terrible tragedy. An emigrant party, travelling to California in 1846, was overtaken by the snow within eight miles of Donner Lake. The party, which was composed of men, women, and children, numbered eighty in all.

They were blocked in by snow drifts and were compelled to encamp and wait for the return of spring. Long before the winter was over and gone, their stock of provisions was exhausted, the cattle had all been killed and eaten and even the hides had been devoured by the half famished party. Then came the bitter struggle between absolute starvation and a resort to cannibalism. The desire to live triumphed over every other consideration and the bodies of the dead became the sustenance of the survivors. While this horrible tragedy was being enacted, an event happened which has given rise to much speculation among the believers in supernatural occurrences. A hunter named Blount living in California beheld in a dream the situation and condition of the suffering party. The impression made on him was so intense that he mentioned the circumstance to other hunters who were well acquainted with the region around Donner Lake. They told him that his description tallied with the reality. This intelligence had the effect of making him resolve upon doing what he could to rescue the snow-bound emigrants. Being joined by others he went to their rescue and had the satisfaction of saving nearly thirty out of the eighty. The survivors were frostbitten and crippled; but their physical condition was less deplorable than their mental state. They had lived upon human flesh till they acquired a liking for it. One of them was detected smeared with blood and furtively roasting a woman's arm, after the supply of other food was ample. Such a story furnishes confirmation of the saying that truth outstrips fiction. It is more puzzling and revolting than any which the modern writer of sensational novels has yet produced for the gratification of depraved tastes.

Summit Station, though the highest point on this line, is not so high as Sherman Station on the Union Pacific. It is 7,042 feet above the level of the sea. This represents not the altitude of the Sierra Nevada range, but only the elevation of this mountain pass. Above the station the peaks of the mountains tower cloudwards. The scene is one of unprecedented grandeur. Owing to the delay caused by the accident I have described, the speed of the train had been increased. The engine-driver had been running extra risks in order, as the Americans phrase it, to 'make time,' so as to arrive 'on time.' The descent was thus made with exceptional rapidity. From Summit Station to Sacramento the distance is 105 miles. Between these places the descent from a height nearly half as great as that of Mont Blanc to fifty-six feet above the sea level has to be made. The velocity with which the train rushed down this incline, and the suddenness with which it wheeled round the curves, produced a sensation which cannot be reproduced in words. The line is carried along the edge of declivities stretching downwards for two or three thousand feet, and in some parts on a narrow ledge which had been excavated from the mountain side by men swung from the upper parts in baskets. The speed under these circumstances seemed terrific. The axle-boxes smoked with the friction, and the odour of burning wood pervaded the cars. The wheels were nearly red hot. In the darkness of the night they resembled discs of flame. Glad though all were to reach Sacramento, not a few were specially thankful to have reached it with whole limbs and unbruised bodies.

The charm of the last few hours is indescribable. It owed its effect to the striking contrast between the experience of the past and the pleasure of the moment. To nothing can it so aptly be compared as to that impressive passage in the inspired vision of the great Italian poet which tells how, after having painfully traversed the circles of Hell, he at last entered the ' dolorous realm ' ribbed in everlasting ice, then issuing forth through an outlet, he returned to the ' bright world,' beheld the beauteous

sights of Heaven, and saw the stars again.* But a
few hours ago we were passing through a region in
which desolation reigned supreme ; a region of sage-
brush and alkali dust, of bitter water and unkindly
skies. Still more recently the icy winds of the
snow-crowned Sierras had chilled us to the bone.
The transition was sudden and the transformation
magical. The sun descended in a flood of glory
towards the Pacific Ocean, while the train was
spinning down the ringing grooves of the mountains.
The canopy of azure overhead, unflecked by a cloud
and spangled with myriads of brilliant stars, surpassed in loveliness the brightest and most serene
sky which ever enchanted the dweller on the
luxuriant shores of the blue Mediterranean. No
Italian air was ever more balmy, nor evening breeze
through vineyard or olive grove more grateful to
the senses than the soft wind which, tempered by
the coolness of the distant ocean and odorous with
the rich perfumes of the neighbouring plains, now
fanned our cheeks and gave a fresh zest to life.
The journey is not yet over. San Francisco is still
upwards of a hundred miles to the west. But the
Rocky Mountains, the American Desert, and the

---

* 'Tanto ch' io vidi delle cose belle,
  Che porta il Ciel, per un pertugio tondo:
E quindi uscimmo a riveder le stelle.'

Inferno, canto xxxiv. lines 137-9.

11

Sierra Nevadas are far behind us and a new country is before our eyes. That the Golden State is one of extraordinary richness is well known to every traveller. To some, however, as to me, it may have been a matter for rejoicing to discover that California is also a land teeming with unexpected natural beauties and rare natural delights.

XVIII.

THE CAPITAL OF THE GOLDEN STATE.

THE passengers by the train in which I journeyed across the continent of America 'missed connections' at Sacramento. This is the American way of stating that the train which arrived did not correspond with that which departed. The accident which I have described was the cause of this. Had the train been punctual the passengers need not have rested for the night at Sacramento, as they might have continued their journey without pause till San Francisco was reached. However, they had no choice. For better or worse a night had to be passed at Sacramento, the capital of the State of California, and 125 miles distant from the chief and most notable city on the Pacific Coast. For my own part I had intended to stop here on the way Westward, in order to see something of the most remarkable among the cities of California.

My first personal experience of a Californian hotel was partly a severe trial and partly a new pleasure. The trial consisted in the demands made upon me by hospitable acquaintances; the pleasure in practically learning how persistent and expansive was Californian good-fellowship. I accompanied my travelling acquaintances to the hotel for which they vouched. One of them had been a member of the Legislature of California, and was consequently well acquainted with Sacramento, the seat of 'the legislature of a thousand drinks.' A few minutes after my companions and myself had inscribed our names in the hotel-register it was proposed that we should 'take a drink.' This proposition was received with general approval. As a stranger, I could neither object with good reason nor retire with courtesy. The 'drink' was duly enjoyed by the several members of the party. Hardly was the libation at an end than the friend of one of those present made his appearance. After a hearty greeting to his friend, the ceremony of introducing those who were strangers to him was performed with the accustomed solemnities. Then followed the invitation, 'Let us take a drink.' Again were healths pledged and glasses emptied at the hotel bar. The gratification was slightly diminished this time, seeing that the night was advancing, and the hour for supper was nigh. But remonstrance was useless, and would have been regarded as unsocial.

Under these circumstances cheerful submission is more commendable and wise than flat refusal and unmannerly opposition.   But a third and greater trial was at hand.   Fresh introductions were made, and new invitations to take a drink were proffered. With as good a grace as I could command, I submitted to an ordeal which was now becoming serious and unpleasant.   Happily, the end to the trying and novel welcome had arrived.   Each one was now permitted to go his own way and make his own arrangements.

In no respect was my experience exceptional. The custom of the country is to drink as often as possible.   The bar-keepers ingeniously speculate on this predilection of their fellow-citizens.   It is common to find a ' free lunch ' and a free supper provided in the more important Californian barrooms.   Any one may walk in and take luncheon or supper gratis.   He has several courses from which to choose, or he may take a portion of each. Soup, fish, made-dishes, joints, and vegetables, are on the bill of fare of a ' free lunch.'   At the free supper the variety is equally great.   In both cases the viands are good in quality, are well cooked, and are served by attentive waiters.   Although no charge is made, yet it is understood that every one who partakes of either meal must take a drink afterwards. He need not take more than one, nor pay more for this than a quarter of a dollar—that is, one shilling. This is the price charged for all drinks, from a glass of lemonade to a glass of champagne. The most common drink is 'whisky straight,' in other words, raw whisky. Each person helps himself from a bottle presented to him. Not merely is the quantity taken very trifling, seldom exceeding the contents of a liqueur glass, but a small tumblerful of iced water is always handed by the bar-keeper along with the bottle and glass, and is generally sent after the whisky by the drinker. It is the small portion taken and this subsequent draught of water which enables the operation to be repeated very frequently without inebriety being produced. Probably the climate has something to do with the result. This is the general belief. Whatever be the explanation, I entertain no doubt as to the fact that in California there is less drunkenness in proportion to the amount of drinking than in any other State in the Union, or in any place of corresponding size and population in the world.

As a city, Sacramento is less remarkable for what it is than for what it has survived. The conduct of the inhabitants of Salt Lake City is often cited as illustrative of an energy almost miraculous, of a faith almost unparalleled. But the trials of the Saints, though grievous, and their triumphs, though meritorious and laudable, have neither surpassed, nor do they merit more eulogy than those of the inhabitants of Sacramento. More than once fires and floods have destroyed their city and impoverished them. Yet the citizens never lost heart along with their fortunes. They re-built their ruined dwellings; the devastated streets they re-made. On each occasion their city became more beautiful in appearance and more commodious in fact. At present the entire city is in process of transformation. All previous efforts having proved futile to protect the locality from inundation when the rains flooded the surrounding plains and the snow melted in the distant mountains, a new and more venturesome course was resolved upon, and has since been pursued. The expenditure of capital upon embankments was suspended, and the elevation of the city to a height ten feet above its original level was begun. The immediate result is neither picturesque in appearance, nor agreeable in reality. Some of the streets have been entirely raised to the projected level. Others are in course of being elevated to a corresponding height. For these reasons a walk along the pavement, if prolonged for some distance, means the ascent and descent of sudden slopes. I have used the word pavement, but this is a misnomer here, there being nothing which precisely tallies with the word as used by us. In this case the American term 'side-walk' is at once applicable and correct. That part of the street which would be covered with paving-stones in an English city or town is often composed of wooden planking in the towns and cities of America. In the Far West, where wood is often cheaper than stone, wood naturally gets the preference. When the rain does not fall, and where snow is unknown, this wooden pavement is unobjectionable. In Sacramento it is employed under the most favourable conditions. A projecting roof springing from the sides of the houses overshadows and shelters the pavement. Thus a sort of arcade is formed, an arcade quite as effective, and far less gloomy, than the arcades which are peculiar to Turin and Bayonne.

Although I have said so much about wooden pavement, I am yet far from wishing it to be supposed that Sacramento is chiefly a city filled with unsubstantial and temporary wooden structures. Some of the houses and shops are built of wood, but the majority of the shops and dwellings are constructed of brick, or stone, or iron. Many of the more recent erections are both ornamental and solid in appearance and character. The number of buildings now being erected affords unmistakeable evidence that Sacramento is a prosperous and rising city. To it, more than to almost any other Californian city, the opening of the Pacific Railway has imparted a new and a vigorous life. It was here that the first advocates of this railway dwelt, and planned, and toiled. Their energy materially helped to arouse their countrymen to energetic efforts in furtherance of the grand and ambitious project. At the period of my visit a banquet was held to celebrate the successful completion of the scheme. The speakers on that occasion had no hesitation in appropriating to themselves, their fellow-citizens, their city, and their State, the major share of the credit for what had been accomplished. A few short extracts from the speeches delivered on this occasion may not only prove interesting, but will serve the purpose of showing the style of Californian oratory, and displaying the tone which the citizens of Sacramento adopt when their own affairs and those of other persons are under discussion. In response to the toast, ' California, a young giant refreshed with new wine,' Lieutenant-Governor Holden said, ' Suffice it for me to say that our skies vie in beauty with those of far-famed Italy; our valleys surpass in richness the famous Valley of the Nile; our plains in productiveness the sunny plains of France; our Sierra Nevadas, for beauty and grandeur of scenery, surpass those of the mountains of Switzerland. Who would not be a Californian? Why, sir, we have the bravest men, the handsomest women, and the fattest babies of any place under the canopy of heaven.' A passage in another speech I copy in order to show that the bravest men may blunder when indulging in the luxury of quotation after dinner. The toast proposed was the health of Admiral Farragut. The speaker, a Mr. Curtis, told his audience that the admiral was well qualified for practically inculcating the lesson first imparted to England by the gallant Perry, who, on the North-Western Lakes, ' met the enemy and taught them another motto than the one they had so long cherished that :

> 'Britannia needs no bulwarks
> To frown along the steep;
> Her love is on the mountain wave,
> Her march is o'er the deep.' *

This original and novel version of an old song was accepted by the company as correct, and was not

* It may be useful to give, as a contrast to the version of Mr. Curtis, the original by Thomas Campbell:—

> 'Britannia needs no bulwarks,
> No towers along the steep ;
> Her march is o'er the mountain-waves,
> Her home is on the deep.'

rejected by the newspapers as inaccurate. Indeed, the *State Capital Reporter*, in which I read these speeches, headed the report with an introduction wherein the ability which its reporters had displayed in furnishing a trustworthy version of the several speeches was singled out for special commendation. The last extract I shall give relates to a topic in which the speaker was more at home: —' Mr. Chairman,—It is not necessary that anyone should speak for Sacramento. I am no speaker, but Sacramento requires no speaker. There was a time, in the long ago of her history, when every son of Sacramento was required to work, and act, and speak for her. But, thank God, that day has gone by; the wheel of time rolled on with a velocity that amazed and entranced, while it cheered and gladdened. The devastation of fire and flood swept over her, but she arose, Phœnix-like, from her ashes, and the heart of every Sacramentan wells up with joy and gladness at the brilliant prospect of her future. The beautiful City of the Plains, nestling in her grandeur in the bosom of the valley, coquetting with the mountains and smiling on the sea, robed in Republican simplicity, modest and unpretending, constantly growing in wealth and importance, cultivating a pure and enlightened Christian civilization, has attained a proud position

among the cities of the Union. With her elements
of greatness and grandeur, her gallant sons, her
working men, her cosy cottages, her stately mansions, her happy homes, her lovely daughters, her
comely matrons, her churches and public schools,
her looms and anvils, her mechanics and artizans,
all speak in eloquent and thrilling tones of her
present importance and future greatness. Her
swift coursers of internal trade, whizzing through
valley and canyon, over hill-top and mountain,
rousing dreamy nature, and awakening glad echoes
all over the land; all—all attest her enterprise,
and proclaim her the Queen of the Golden State.'
This luxuriant rhetoric is temptingly open to criticism; but to criticise is not my business at present.
Yet I may note in passing that the ridicule which
it was thought had sufficed to finally extinguish
the Phœnix, has simply had the effect of compelling
that miraculous bird to migrate to the Pacific Slope,
there to prove serviceable to orators who use me-
taphor to conceal their lack of wit. Certainly,
nothing that I have yet said, or may hereafter say,
in praise of Sacramento will be thought worthy of
attention alongside of this glowing picture. While
it was still vividly imprinted on my mind, it was a
shock to read on a placard in the streets—' We
should all vote against Negro and Chinese suffrage.'

These words do not represent the utterances of a knot of foolish and shortsighted politicians; if that were the case it would be unfair to cite them. Unhappily, they express the opinions of the majority in this State; they form the watchword of the political party which has won the victory at the polls. In this city the Chinese constitute a considerable proportion of the inhabitants. They are the most hard working among the labourers who earn their daily bread by their daily toil. They are to be seen in every street bearing heavy burdens suspended from the two ends of a pole, which rests on one of their shoulders. They act as waiters; they are the most conscientious of shoe-blacks. Sign-boards over small shops announce that within Hung Lee or Sam Wah does washing and ironing, and repairs clothes with neatness. Through the open doors or windows these Chinamen may be seen scrubbing, starching, and ironing linen with a care and industry which not even a Parisian *blanchisseuse* could surpass. To all appearance their services are indispensable. That they should be obnoxious to those who cannot labour as cheaply is not surprising. The Irishman detests the competition of cheap negro labour; the negro is jealous of the Chinaman; if the energy of monkeys could be utilized, all of them would probably unite in denouncing the unfairness of employing labour which required no direct monetary compensation. But the validity of the reason for persons of higher position regarding Chinamen with intense aversion is not so easily discovered. As members of the community, the Chinese are acknowledged to be remarkably sober, singularly industrious, exceptionally quiet in demeanour, strict observers of the law. They do what they are commanded; they refrain from what is forbidden. It is indisputable that their labour is a great boon to the entire community. It is not so clear that the Democratic party will succeed in their one-eyed policy of keeping the Chinese in perpetual subjection, and treating them as social and political Pariahs.

Although no longer as busy a city as it was when the gold fever was at its height, Sacramento is still, and must continue to be, a place of great commercial importance. The Pacific Railway has been a great boon to it. As the western terminus of the Central Pacific it enjoys special advantages. The manufactories and machine shops of the company are situated here. Several hundred men are employed in constructing cars, in putting together and repairing locomotives. Other industries are successfully carried on. Three flour mills, capable of supplying 1,200 barrels of flour daily, are at work within the city's bounds. A woollen mill is being erected, and a company has been constituted for manufacturing sugar from beet-root. Among other strange notices, I remarked a sign-board with the inscription, ' Coal and Ice Depôt.' Excepting for cooking purposes coal is not in great demand, while the consumption of ice is very large. As the climate is mild a supply of ice cannot be procured in the vicinity at any season of the year; consequently, the ice used must be brought from the mountain lakes, many miles away. Of churches and of both public and private schools, there are as many as the most exacting could desire. Notwithstanding the partiality of the Californians for drinks, they profess to be as proud of the character of a church-going people, and wish to be thought quite as desirous that their children should be educated as are the natives of New England itself. The press of Sacramento is a recognised power throughout the State whereof it is the capital. One newspaper, the *Sacramento Daily Union,* is extremely well conducted. It aspires to be independent of party, making the interests of the community at large and of the country as a whole the objects of its especial care. I understand that its circulation extends far beyond the limits of the city, and that its opinions exercise great weight throughout California. There are, of course, the usual party organs and, like purely party organs in America, they are both rabid and indiscriminate upholders of their respective sides. As the seat of the State Legislature, this city has an element of importance in addition to those I have named. A new State House has just been completed. This is built on the conventional pattern of American Capitols. It has been decorated in a style of great splendour.

After all that I have said about this city, it may be a surprise to read that the number of its inhabitants does not exceed between twenty-five and thirty thousand. It is the more noteworthy, then, that it should merit so much attention. A glance at the spacious streets stretching away on all sides for long distances leads the beholder to suppose that, as the area of the city is large, the number of its citizens must be large also. The majority of the houses have gardens attached to them. Rows of stately trees line many of the streets. The vegetation is on a scale of tropical richness. The weeds appear to be shrubs, and the shrubs resemble small trees. Other pests besides weeds abound here in rank profusion. The mosquito curtains which closely surround the beds are significant tokens of the prevalence of a form of insect life with which most persons would gladly dispense.

When it is considered that not many years ago Sacramento was the haunt of the most reckless and depraved of the earth; the temporary home of men who came to dig for gold, and who lavished the gold of which they became possessed in riotous living and in the vilest profligacy, the marvel is to find how thorough has been the change, how complete the purification. The streets of Sacramento are as quiet at night as the streets of Boston. A Maine Liquor Law is unknown, drinking customs are in the ascendant, yet drunkenness is not the vice of the majority. Whereas formerly every man carried a revolver, and used it on the smallest provocation, or even out of mere wantonness of brutality, it is now the exception to go armed, and the rare exception to hear of dastardly murders having been committed either in passion or cold blood. At night the streets are ablaze with gas and guarded by vigilant policemen. The peace is strictly preserved, and the lawless stand in terror of the judges. One relic of the olden times still survives. Gaming, the miner's favourite pastime, flourishes in defiance of the law, or, perhaps, with the connivance of the authorities. It is true that the gaming hells are not places of resort into which the stranger is allured by publicity, or which the passer by, if uninitiated, can detect without difficulty. A thin veil of mystery surrounds them. But the secret is one which everybody can fathom at the cost of a drink. All the bar-keepers can point out where the hells are situated, and can generally tell, moreover, which of them is honestly conducted, and which is a den of sharpers. Nor is the entrance into any one of them attended with much trouble. The Cerberus at the door is easily propitiated. The game played is ' Faro,' a game which was the delight of English gamesters a century ago. In the United States the operation of staking one's money in a gaming hell is called ' Fighting the Tiger.' I witnessed the ceremony for the first time at Sacramento. Though the name of the game played is different, yet the result is identical with that which follows when money is staked at Baden-Baden or Homburg. As I was informed that the same spectacle of ' Fighting the Tiger' might be witnessed on a grander scale at San Francisco, I shall defer my account of the exhibition till after visiting the chief and the most renowned among Californian cities.

XIX.

SACRAMENTO CITY TO THE GOLDEN GATE.

THE western terminus of the Central Pacific Railway is at Sacramento. This city occupies the place at one end of the line which Chicago does at the other. Just as several routes lead from New York to Chicago, so are there more routes than one between Sacramento and San Francisco. For the third time is the traveller embarrassed by variety. He may select one out of two railways, or he may elect to take the steamer. His ticket gives him the option of a land or water journey. The difference in time is trifling. As nothing worth speaking of was gained by continuing my journey by rail, I decided upon completing it by water. Besides, I could return by train, and thus see more of the country than if, on both occasions, I had traversed the same route.

The California Steam Navigation Company's steamer leaves Sacramento at two in the afternoon, arriving at San Francisco at ten o'clock the same night. Like the majority of American steamboats, those of this company are large, commodious, and luxurious. None of our English river or coasting steamers are on a par with them. The upper saloon resembles a large hall in an English country house, furnished in the style and with the taste of a splendid drawing-room. It constitutes a fine promenade for those who like to walk under cover. In the soft couches the studious may recline book in hand, while those who are fond of meditating with closed eyes may do so in the numerous easy chairs. The dining saloon is in the lower part of the vessel. This is a lofty, airy, and well-lit apartment. During the day the light streams in through large windows; after nightfall many gas jets make it as brilliant as if the sun shone. A meal eaten in this saloon can be enjoyed all the more on account of the absence of the foul smells and stifling atmosphere which render the saloon of an English river steamer an earthly purgatory. It is hardly possible to infer from appearances that those who sit at table are not seated in the dining-room of a first-class American hotel. On the deck there is ample space for the comfortable accommodation of those who, when at sea or on the river, delight in walking or sitting in the open air. The return journey is made at night, and then the comforts of a well-appointed

state-room may be had for a small extra payment.
With the French the phrase ' English comfort ' has
taken its place in the vocabulary of those who desire
to express or typify what are deemed perfect arrangements for procuring and partaking of what
constitutes the acme of bodily enjoyment. An acquaintance with the railway carriages and the
steamers of America provokes a doubt whether in
the construction of either the exacting and comfort-
loving Englishman has not been rivalled by those
who are on the high-road to becoming his superiors.
I do not maintain that the steamer Yo-Semite, by
which these remarks have been suggested, is on the
whole a model craft. The boats on the River
Hudson, and those which ply between New York
and Newport, are far more noteworthy as examples
of floating palaces.   Even the less famous steamers
which make the passage between Boston and Port-
land are quite as complete and comfortable places of
temporary abode as the steamers on the River
Sacramento. What specially impressed me was to
find a similar degree of excellence in this department of travel obtainable within sight of the Atlantic and within a few miles of the Pacific, as well
as on the majestic rivers which form liquid and
silent highways between the inland States and the
two Oceans which wash the shores of the Continent.

At night the brilliant lights on these steamers give to them the aspect of fire-ships. At all times they are hardly less dangerous than floating powder magazines. This is their bane, as comfort is their characteristic. Costly decoration is frequently indulged in at a disregard for safety. The saloon is far more perfect than the engine-room. The machinery is better adapted for show than use, the boilers being very inferior to the berths. One of the passengers on the Yo-Semite told me that a year or two ago an explosion had taken place whilst he was on board, that many passengers were killed, and several maimed for life. This intelligence damped the spirits of some who heard it. Others argued that the fact of such an accident having occurred once was favourable to a safe voyage. My own feeling was one of indifference. After travelling for thousands of miles over roads reputed to be dangerous, the chances of an accident taking place cause but little concern, the accidents themselves being looked upon as parts of the programme.

At Sacramento, where the river of that name is joined by the American river, the united streams form a broad but shallow sheet of water. Not far from this point the memorable discoveries of gold were made in 1848. It is not true, as has been supposed, that this was the first time the existence of gold in California had been demonstrated. Many years prior to these discoveries the Indians were in the habit of bringing small parcels of gold dust from the interior to the coast, and selling them to the masters of the vessels which then came for cargoes of hides. Mr. Dana, the well-known author of ' Two Years before the Mast,' who visited the Pacific coast in 1836, relates that among the cargo which the *Alert* carried to Boston was a small quantity of gold dust. He adds that rumours of gold discoveries were then current. These, however, attracted little or no attention. It is no longer possible to procure gold with as little labour and trouble as at the period of its discovery. The gold digger's occupation is not gone, but transformed. Instead of washing the precious metal out of the sand and mud of the streams, he has now to make elaborate arrangements for excavating from the depths of the river bed or from the sides of the mountains the earth throughout which the glittering and valuable dust is interspersed. What is called hydraulic mining has had the greatest success in this part of the State, just as in other parts quartz-crushing has become the rule and the source of wealth. This hydraulic mining consists in diverting a powerful stream of water against the deposits of earth on the mountain slopes, and separating the metal from the semi-fluid mass which descends into suitable tanks. The earth or mud, or mixture of both, after having been carefully sifted, is thrown into the stream which runs into the river. The result of this is to add large deposits to the river's bed, and to cause the swollen stream to flood the surrounding country. This is the principal reason why the recent inundations have given the citizens of Sacramento and the inhabitants of the Sacramento Valley so much annoyance. The bed of the stream has become disproportionately high for its banks. Towards the winter, when the dry season is many months old, and the season when the rain falls has not arrived, the shallowness of the river occasions much inconvenience. The breadth of the river at Sacramento is equal to that of the Thames at Greenwich. But the numerous shoals seriously impede navigation. The water is of a dark brown colour. For several miles below Sacramento the scenery is very monotonous and unattractive. The view from the Scheldt below Antwerp bears a great resemblance to what may be witnessed here, with this difference—that no conspicuous object, like the fine spire of Antwerp Cathedral, attracts the attention and gives variety to the prospect. The banks appear to have been undermined by the swift and strong current. They are covered down to the

water's edge with a rank and unpicturesque vegetation. The land, though devoid of natural beauties,
is yet of the richest and most valuable character.
If little more than semi-liquid mud, it is a soil in
which anything will grow, provided the recurring
inundations are checked. At present, cultivation
is hardly possible here. Rising and falling with
the varying height of the river, the fields cannot be
tilled with ease, nor the harvest reaped with certainty. A house built upon it is reared on as
imperfect a foundation as a house built upon treacherous and unstable sand. To other drawbacks,
that of unhealthiness must be added. Conspicuous
among the natural products of this virgin soil are
huge reeds, many of which attain to the height of
ten feet. These are similar to the bulrushes of
Scripture among which the infant Moses was concealed. Here they are called ' Tules.' The ground
whereon they flourish is known by the name of the
' Tule Lands.' Millions of acres of this land could
be turned to profitable account if efficient embankments were erected. The pure vegetable mould
which constitutes the soil, coupled with the facilities for inexpensive irrigation, present every requisite for the growth of rice. The reclamation of
these Tule Lands is one of the problems which the
agriculturists and capitalists of California are long-

12

ing and labouring to solve. Experiments have been made by them, but without success, owing, it is said, to the imperfect nature of the works executed. If the Dutch had control over this land they would soon win it from the river, while if the Chinese were allowed to cultivate it they would soon convert it into remunerative rice-fields. What some Californians do is to discuss the course to be adopted, and to set fire to the ' Tules' once a year. The spectacle of these fires is magnificent. I was fortunate enough to witness the sight. The thick, sluggish volume of smoke rose grandly into the air, and was wafted slowly away by the gentle breeze. A purplish red tint gave to the canopy of smoke a strange and beautiful aspect. I have seen a prairie on fire in the State of Iowa, but the sight was infinitely less imposing than the blazing ' Tules' on the banks of the Sacramento River. After nightfall the effect produced resembled that which those can picture who have seen the furnaces of the Black Country or of Belgium belching forth flames in the darkness of a starless and moonless night, and illuminating the surrounding country with a lurid glare, only that in this case the flames were rolling and raging in an unbroken mass, extending over what appeared to be a limitless tract of country. The bon-fire was the largest and grandest

I ever witnessed. I should have preferred, however, to have seen the 'Tule lands' yellow with
harvest to seeing them the theatre of a gigantic
conflagration.

While the steamer Yo-Semite was descending
the Sacramento River, I learned some interesting
particulars, from passengers with whom I conversed,
relating to the agricultural capabilities and customs
of California. My informants were practical
farmers, and, like farmers in other quarters of
the globe, grumbled bitterly at their lot. But
their grievances were not the grievances of uncertain weather and untractable soil which vex the
hearts and try the tempers of English farmers. As
regards the weather, they had no reason to complain. They could make their arrangements with
perfect confidence that no outward change in temperature nor any untimely shower of rain would
blight their prospects by ruining their crops.
During certain months of the year they know that
rain will fall; during the remainder of the year
they can count upon uniformly fair weather. Indeed, the Californian farmer is sure of reaping, in
due season, the crop whereof he sows the seed.
He is under no apprehension that if he omits to
house his grain for a day the consequences may be
fatal to his hopes. On the contrary, he may post-

pone his harvest-home from day to day, and from week to week, with comparative impunity. His sheaves will not rot on the fields, owing to the moisture with which, after too long exposure in our fickle climate, they are certain to be saturated. Of sheaves, indeed, he knows nothing. The ears of corn are clipped from the stalks by a machine, and gathered into heaps until the time for thrashing them arrives. The straw is wasted altogether, being got rid of as an incumbrance, instead of being treated as a source of profit. It is set on fire. As the ash produced by its combustion partially and imperfectly subserves the purpose of manure, the process is a wasteful as well as barbarous one. The excuse for it is, that labour being scarce a loss must be incurred at some stage or other of the agricultural processes. If there were more hands to do the work much less waste would be occasioned. This, then, is one of the grievances of the Californian farmer. He is ready to pay farm labourers as much as a skilled mechanic is paid at home. What a Dorsetshire peasant gets for a week's labour he would readily receive in California for the labour of a single day. Moreover, he would be well fed and comfortably lodged, treated not as a servant but an equal, and expected to prove himself something nobler than a drudge touching his hat in abject submission to the squire, and listening meekly to the parson. To all who are willing to engage in field-work, the Western prairies of America and the vast plains of California offer inducements such as can hardly be over-estimated or exaggerated. But those who are ignorant of farming, and who cannot or who will not toil with their hands, had better stay at home. It is true that they may starve in England, but it is quite as probable that such persons will starve in the United States. Next to procuring plenty of labour—not cheap labour, be it remarked, for he is both willing and able to pay good wages—the Californian farmer desires to purchase cheap implements of husbandry. This is but another way of stating that he is a Free-trader to the backbone. He finds that Liverpool is the best market for his grain, and he argues that no obstacle should be interposed to hinder his getting in return cheap machinery and tools from England. These statements are not put into the mouths of imaginary farmers, but are the statements actually made to me by men with whom I conversed. More than one avowed that his conversion to Free Trade was a thing of yesterday, and had its basis in self-interest. Until California became a large grain-producing country, the injury wrought by a high protective tariff did not directly affect its inhabitants. They are otherwise-minded now, because they feel that they are the victims of a policy which enriches a section of the American people at the cost of the agricultural population of the country. The Californian farmers are at one with the farmers of Illinois and other States in desiring the proclamation of Free Trade as the policy of the nation. Moreover, what these men desire will probably be brought to pass, because they bid fair to become the majority at the polls.

Eighty miles below the city of Sacramento the Joaquin joins the Sacramento River, and the united streams flow into the Bay of Suisun. This bay is connected with the Bay of San Pablo by the Straits of Carquinez. On the right of the outlet from the Bay of Suisun is the town of Benicia, celebrated in Europe as the dwelling-place of the ' boy ' of that name, and notable here as the former capital of California. It is no longer a thriving and advancing place. The wharf seems falling into decay. The number of inhabitants is rated at 600, yet it still continues to enjoy a reputation of an enviable kind. Its schools are well-conducted and are largely patronised. The only law school of which California boasts is among the noted seminaries of learning that adorn Benicia. On the opposite side of the bay may be discerned Mount Diablo, a solitary eminence amid the surrounding plains. In its vicinity are extensive coal pits. The coal raised here is of excellent quality; but it has one great drawback. The volume of dense black smoke emitted from the ignited coal is much larger than is agreeable or desirable. A steamer or a locomotive, in the furnaces of which this coal is burned, is distinguishable at a considerable distance by the blackness and quantity of smoke issuing from its funnel or chimney. About 1,000 tons monthly are raised from the pits, and the surrounding towns and cities are beginning to use this coal in preference to that which is imported, and which is necessarily more expensive. The depth of water at Benicia is great enough to permit of ocean steamers sailing up to the wharf. Even the gigantic steamers of the Pacific Steam Navigation Company can be brought here for repairs, the company's foundry and machine-shop being situated at this place. The passengers who, at this season, descend the river in steamers, are rejoiced when Benicia is reached, because they no longer have reason to dread detention owing to the vessel running aground on the Hog's Back, or any of the other shoals which render the navigation of the river precarious and unsatisfactory. The Yo-Semite took the ground more than once; fortunately, however, the engines were powerful enough to move her into deeper water again.

After passing through the Straits of Carquinez, which are eight miles in length, the Bay of San Pablo is entered. This bay is fifteen miles broad and twenty long, and opens at its lower extremity into the great bay on which San Francisco is situated. The sun set while the steamer was ploughing her way through those noble sheets of water. The sky was of a brilliant blue, and not a cloud dimmed or concealed its brightness. As the sun rapidly sank behind the range of mountains which lines the coast of the Pacific the horizon was flushed with a soft rosy light, which the eye, accustomed to the varied splendours of the masses of golden and purple clouds that constitute the glory of a sunset in a Northern clime, views with an admiration mingled with wonder. The rapidity of the change from bright sunlight to pale starlight was still a novelty to me. Of twilight, that charming isthmus between the glare of the day and the gloom and mystery of night, there was hardly a trace. Scarcely had the last glimpse of the lord of light been caught than the deep blue heavens were glittering with stars. It is probable that the strangeness of the lovely spectacle made it more fascinating to me than to other passengers on board the steamer. To them it was literally an every-day occurrence. Each returning evening resembles this one, and they were not excited by a sight which was stale and commonplace to them. Moreover, they had an excuse for preferring the shelter of the cabin to a seat on the open deck. The breeze from the Pacific blows at nightfall with a coolness almost too great for those who have been oppressed by the heat of the day. Besides, a slight swell made the Yo-Semite rock with more violence than was perfectly agreeable to the majority of the passengers. She was now traversing the waters of San Francisco's unrivalled bay, and the waves rolling in through the Golden Gate demonstrated to the incredulous that the Pacific has breakers which are a match for the billows that rear their crests on the most stormy seas. About fifteen miles intervene between the wharf at San Francisco and the outlet from the Bay of San Pablo. At a considerable distance from the landing-place a fine view of the city is obtained. Seen as I saw it for the first time the appearance of San Francisco is enchanting. Built on a hill slope, up which many streets run to the top, and illumined as these streets were with innumerable gas lamps, the effect was that of a huge dome ablaze with lamps arranged in lines and circles. Those who have stood in Princes-street at night, and gazed upon the Old Town and Castle of Edinburgh, can form a very correct notion of the fairy-like spectacle. Expecting to find San Francisco a city of wonders, I was not disappointed when it seemed to my eyes a city of magic, such a city as Aladdin might have ordered the genii to create in order to astonish and dazzle the spectator. I was warned by those whom personal experience of the city had taught to distinguish glitter from substance, not to expect that the reality of the morrow would fulfil the promise of the evening. Some of the parts which now appeared the most fascinating were said to be the least attractive when viewed by day. Still, the panorama was deprived of none of its glories by these whispers of well-meant warning. Those who wish to have a favourable impression when they first behold San Francisco are strongly advised to view it from the deck of a steamer when the full-orbed stars twinkling overhead are almost rivalled by the myriads of gas-lights illuminating the land.

If this spectacle be poetry the landing is prose. The din and bustle soon recall the errant mind from aerial flights of fancy to the harsh realities of terrestrial life. A Babel of tongues rises from the crowded landing-stage as soon as the steamer has been moored. Hardly has the passenger set foot

on shore than he becomes the prey of men intent
upon earning a gratuity by doing, or professing to
render, him a service. The importunities of the
touters, porters, and cabmen are not only quite as
tormenting as those of their brethren at Calais or
Boulogne, but this bidding for employment is also
in marked contrast to what prevails in other American cities. The stranger who disembarks at New
York has to ask the hangers-on at the wharf to
carry his luggage, and he might have long to wait
before they voluntarily pressed their services upon
him. It cannot be doubted that the stories which
once were true about the independence of the
dwellers in San Francisco have ceased to be applicable and characteristic. At one time a new arrival
is said to have offered a shabbily-dressed man a
dollar to carry his bag a short distance for him.
He received the reply, ' I will give an ounce of gold
to see you carry it yourself.' The new-comer
thereupon acted as his own porter, returned and
claimed the ounce of gold, which he received, and
was in addition treated to a bottle of champagne,
for which his entertainer had to pay the value of
another ounce. At present the tables are turned,
and the supply of labour is in excess of the demand.
I had not long to wait before I discovered that if
certain kinds of labour were abundant, the prices

paid for labour generally were exorbitant. All payments in California are made in coin, and they are nearly as high as the corresponding payments made elsewhere in depreciated 'greenbacks.' A drive through the streets disenchanted me as to the fairy-like character of the city. Indeed, the streets, private houses, shops, warehouses, and hotels presented no remarkable and exceptional appearance. The journey had been made too rapidly to make the aspect of a large and populous city a thing to be beheld again with special satisfaction. Among the marvels wrought by the Pacific Railway is the comparative annihilation of ideas as to distance in the minds of those who travel by it across the continent of America. Some time elapses, after arriving at San Francisco, before the fact is fully realized that New York is three thousand and Chicago two thousand miles distant. The traveller who has come thus far thinks it but a trifle to continue his journey in the track of the setting sun, even though aware that he would have to sail for ten or twenty days before finding a halting-place at Honolulu, or Yokohama, or Hong Kong.

XX.

THE QUEEN CITY OF THE PACIFIC COAST.

THE Golden Gate was one of the many important discoveries made by Sir Francis Drake. He spoke eulogistically of the bay into which that opening in this rockbound coast furnished an entrance, and in token of his gratification with the surrounding country he named it New Albion. The Spaniards, however, were the first settlers in California. Till the year 1847, what is now known as San Francisco was called *Yerba Buena.* In like manner, Sacramento bore the name of *Nueva Helvetia.* Even these names are being forgotten, just as all traces of Spanish settlement are gradually dying out. When Mr. Dana came here in 1835, but a single wooden shanty occupied the site of the present city of San Francisco. As long ago as that year, and when the value of this place had not been ascertained, Mr. Dana made the following entry in the diary, which, under the title of ' Two Years before the Mast,' was given to the world in 1840:—' If

California ever becomes a prosperous country, this bay will be the centre of its prosperity. The abundance of wood and water; the extreme fertility of its shores; the excellence of its climate, which is as near to being perfect as any in the world, and its facilities for navigation, affording the best anchoring grounds in the whole western coast of America—all fit it for a place of great importance.' This prediction deserves to be ranked with the most successful specimens of fulfilled prophecy. Ten years later the population had increased from one man to an hundred and fifty souls. According to the most recent estimate the inhabitants of San Francisco now number 170,000. This rapidity of growth is wonderful; yet it is not unexampled in the United States. Other things than the increase of the population and the enlargement of the city have made the growth of San Francisco an event without a parallel, either in America or in any other quarter of the habitable globe Its name had become synonymous for all that was most shameless in profligacy, for all that was basest in depravity, for all that was wanton and brutal in ruffianism. In the open day men were murdered with impunity. At night the property of the citizens was at the mercy of the lawless. The scum of Polynesia, desperadoes from Australia, bullies and blackguards from the wild State of Missouri, Spanish cut-throats from the cities of the Pacific Coast, dissolute women and reckless adventurers from the slums of Europe, congregated in San Francisco, and there plied their several avocations and followed their devious courses in defiance of the prohibitions of a law which had lost its terrors for them, and in disregard of any other check save the revolver or the bowie knife. At that time, San Francisco was one-half a brothel, and one-half a gaming hell. There came a crisis in the annals of the city when the action of the law was forcibly impeded, in order that the reign of law might be restored. As the old Romans submitted to a Dictator, so did the citizens of San Francisco temporarily and voluntarily submit to a dictatorship, under the name of a Vigilance Committee. This body discharged the fourfold functions of police, judge, jury, and executioner. A short shrift and a lofty gallows was the fate of the criminal whom they took in the act of committing robbery or murder. The remedy was strong and dangerous. But the symptoms were so threatening as to inspire fear lest what men call civilization should cease to exist, and no peril incurred in applying the remedy was comparable to the risk of allowing the disease to spread and become intensified.

Never, perhaps, in the history of the world did the result more completely justify the means employed than in the case of San Francisco. The Vigilance Committee discharged its duties with unrelenting severity so long as professional thieves and systematic murderers were at large triumphing in their crimes. As soon, however, as order was restored, the Vigilance Committee decreed its own dissolution, and the dispensers of summary justice became conspicuous for their obedience to the administrators of the law. From being a by-word for its lawlessness and licentiousness, the city of San Francisco has become, in little more than ten years, as moral as Philadelphia, and far more orderly than New York.

With the knowledge of what San Francisco had been, and unacquainted by personal observation with what it had become, my first walk along its streets on the morning after my arrival was one of peculiar interest. I went along Montgomery-street, which is the Regent-street and Lombard-street, or Broadway and Wall-street, of this city. It is lined with handsome shops. The pavement is crowded with pedestrians, the majority of whom have the anxious look and the hurried gait of business men, while the minority are ordinary sight-seers, or persons who walk therein in order to be seen. Bankers' offices are very numerous. Their windows are filled with the paper-money of all nations, from the plain white notes of the Bank of England to the elaborately figured 'greenbacks' of the United States. These 'greenbacks' are not current in California. The State stretched its legal rights to the extreme point of refusing to accept as currency what Congress had proclaimed legal tenders. Nothing passes current here save gold and silver coin. Even the nickel and copper cents of the Eastern States are unknown. They are looked upon as curiosities. Men wear them on their watch chains just as some Englishmen wear 'spade' guineas. On my arrival at the hotel, a Californian who had brought some of these coins from the East was besieged with inquiries for them. Many persons had never seen one, and to them they were as great novelties as African cowries would be to us. Small sums are reckoned in 'bits,' which are imaginary coins having the nominal value of twelve and a half cents. Indeed, the absence of single cents causes something worse than confusion. A newspaper costs ten cents. Suppose that a quarter dollar, equal to twenty-five cents, is presented in payment for the newspaper, the seller will probably return a dime, which is equal to ten cents. Thus fifteen cents have been paid

instead of ten.   His excuse will be that he has not
any half dimes, these coins being extremely scarce.
In California this is taken as a thing of course by
the natives and the residents.   The visitors, however, are apt to regard it as an imposition.   The
gold coin generally current is the twenty-dollar
piece.   It is about the size of half a crown, is
worth nearly five pounds sterling, and is a very
beautiful coin.   The inhabitants, who are accustomed to high prices, part with these coins far
more readily than we part with sovereigns.   In
addition to paper money and specie, the windows
of the offices of the bullion dealers usually contain
a display of specimens of gold or silver ores.   These
are said in the labels affixed to them to be very
rich in the precious metals.   But statements of
this sort seldom impose on old and experienced
Californians.   About the richness of lodes they
are as sceptical as cynics are about the existence of
unalloyed and genuine patriotism.   Just as, with
many, 'patriot' has become a synonyme for impostor or place-hunter, so has a lode of great
reputed value come to be regarded by the mass
of Californians as worth little more than a large
property in the moon.   The difficulty consists in
ascertaining with certainty whether or not the
specimens have been really found in a particular

spot, whether they fairly represent the lode, and whether, if they have been dug out of the ground in question, they had not been discovered by those who, like the diggers in the 'Antiquary,' had concealed the specimens for the purpose of duping the credulous. To prepare a mine in such a way that it may appear to be extremely rich in valuable mineral is called 'salting' it. At this art many persons in California, Nevada, and Montana are practised adepts, and the desire of the majority is to escape falling into the trap ingeniously and carefully baited for them. When these things were explained to me, I ceased to wonder at the reluctance of the capitalists here to secure for themselves shares in the gold and silver mines, which were offered for sale on the most advantageous terms.

At its northern end Montgomery-street extends to the top of a steep hill. The latter portion is so precipitous that carriages cannot ascend it. A flight of steps enables the foot passenger to mount with comparative comfort. From the top a commanding view is had of the bay, the opposite coast, and the business quarter of the city. I was surprised to see the greater part of the lower town enveloped in a dense cloud of smoke. A large number of tall chimneys were emitting volumes of smoke such as in London would entail heavy fines on their proprietors. The reason was that Mount Diablo coal is burned in the furnaces, and this coal, as I have already said, has the drawback of giving forth much black smoke during combustion. The darkness and dinginess of the city surprised me less, knowing, as I did, that the coal was in fault, than did the sight of so many manufactories. I had supposed San Francisco to be a second Liverpool: I was not prepared to find that it was also a second Birmingham.

On inquiry I learned that the inhabitants of this city take pride in the fact that the manufactories of California are sufficient to meet nearly all the requirements of her citizens. There are several woollen mills here. The magnitude of the work done in these mills may be inferred when I state that in one the amount paid in wages is 6,000*l.* monthly, and that upwards of one million and a half pounds of the raw material are annually converted into woollen fabrics. Indeed, the blankets and flannels of California deserve a reputation even more extended than that which they enjoy. In fineness of texture they resemble the delicate hand-wrought fabrics for which Shetland is famous, rather than the corresponding articles produced by machinery in English mills. As railway wrappers and overcoats this blanket material is much in vogue here, and certainly there is nothing I have seen which can be said to surpass it. In these woollen mills the operatives are chiefly Chinese. In some, employment is given to hundreds of women; but the rule is to employ Chinamen in the proportion of two-thirds to that of one-third white men. The boots and shoes which the Californians wear are not merely home-made, but the leather is a home product also. One large establishment, ' The Pacific Tannery and Boot and Shoe Factory,' combines the double business of preparing the leather and working it up for wear. This is a marvellous change since the day when the raw hides were shipped in order to be carried to New England, returning after many days in the form of boots and shoes; and what adds to the wonder is, that little more than thirty years have elapsed since the period when the only commerce of California was the export of these raw hides. The cotton mills are less flourishing than the woollen ones. The supply of home-grown cotton is but small. A large quantity is imported from the Atlantic States, and it is employed in producing the coarser varieties of cotton goods. In other departments of industry an activity not less notable is persistently manifested. There are saw manufactories which rival those of Sheffield; locomotive and steam-engine works which compare favourably with those of Philadelphia and Newcastle; rolling mills, which are admitted to be most complete in their arrangements. The iron safes, manufactured by one firm have a high reputation, and are said to defy alike the ingenuity and force of the burglar. If I mentioned all the mechanical industries which flourish here, I should fill a long list with names and descriptions. Suffice it, then, to say that the most important are well represented, and that all are flourishing

In addition to the manufactories just named, and in which San Francisco is the competitor with many cities in America and England, there are branches of industry in which California has entered the lists with France and Germany, with Italy and Asia. One of these is silk culture. It has been proved that 'silk raising' is possible throughout the entire State, from the mountains on the east to the sea shore on the west, and from Arizona Territory on the south to the State of Oregon on the north. The climate is said to be so favourable to the process as to lighten the labours of those who have to superintend it, and that one person in California can do the work of six in Europe. If the statements made are trustworthy, and if the end should not belie the promise of the beginning, there is good ground for the prediction that the State of California will yet become the largest silk-producing region in the world. Silk-weaving has already been attempted, and machinery for carrying on operations on a large scale is in course of construction. The success of the silk culture has been placed beyond doubt. But the cultivation of the tea plant and the production of tea are still in the experimental stage. I found no fears entertained as to the result. Hitherto all has gone well. The Japanese, who have come hither to cultivate the tea plant, have succeeded as far as they have gone, the plants having thriven as rapidly as could have been desired, and giving promise of yielding a satisfactory tea crop when they come to maturity two years hence. The culture of the vine, like the production of silk, has passed out of the domain of experiment, and acquired rank among the most remunerative and successful of Californian industries. Looking eastward across the bay, extensive vineyards and orchards may be discerned. On inquiry, it is ascertained that year after year the area of land devoted to the growth of vines is extending in various parts of the State. Most pleasing of all is the fact that the land thus devoted to the grape has not been withdrawn from the corn plant. It resembles those patches of soil which, on the banks of the Rhine, cannot be used for any other purpose than to grow vines, and which as vineyards are valuable beyond measure. Before being set apart for vine-growing purposes the land here is valued at 25 cents the acre; after the vines have come to maturity its value rises to more dollars than the cents for which it was purchased. A notion of the extent of the wine trade may be formed from this, that the estimate for 1868 was seven millions of gallons of wine as the product of the vintage. In 1869 the yield was expected to be larger still, though 1869 is not considered a good year.

The Jesuit missionaries first planted vines in California, and the wine made from these grapes is by no means the worst among the wines produced now. Nevertheless, in 1861 the State authorities resolved upon importing cuttings from the vines in the most celebrated wine-producing districts of Europe, and hundreds of different varieties were imported. Of these 250 are now in fruit-bearing condition, and all of them have retained their European characteristics, with this exception, that here the grapes ripen more thoroughly, and are richer in saccharine matter than the grapes of Europe. Among the Californian wines are some resembling sherry, madeira, claret, hock, burgundy, port, and champagne. The sparkling wine is distinguishable from the best among French champagnes only in being newer and less perfectly matured. None have those drawbacks which render Cape wines unpopular. I do not wish it to be supposed that all the wine made in California is palatable and pleasant. The first bottle I tasted in a San Francisco hotel was disagreeable and disappointing. I have been told, however, that two systems prevail here, and that the results of each differ widely and materially. The one consists in making wine from the grapes grown in the vineyard possessed by an individual or a company, the other in purchasing all wine of a certain quality and standard from the growers, and then preparing it for the market. The latter is the practice of the most notable firms in the wine-growing districts of France and Germany. The large establishment in Jackson-street, San Francisco, of which Mr. Landsberger is the head, is conducted on the European model. For the production of what he honestly calls sparkling California wine, Mr. Landsberger has already made himself a name. It is but two years and a-half since he first began to supply this wine, and he now produces 12,000 bottles monthly. For other wines, such as port and white and red Sonoma, the monthly demand is equal to five hundred dozen. The sparkling wine is his greatest triumph. Were it not so

new, it might be ranked with some of the best
European vintages. Chinamen are employed in the
several stages of manufacture. They are not quick
workers, but they are painstaking and trustworthy.
Whatever they do is done thoroughly. One advantage this establishment has over those on the
Rhine, the Moselle, and in the Champagne district, consists in dark underground cellars being
dispensed with, the several processes being carried
on and the rows of bottles stacked in large and light
and airy apartments. A change in the barometer is
not dreaded. No precautions have to be taken to
keep the temperature from suddenly rising too high
or as suddenly falling very low. This adds to the
ease with which the operations can be carried on,
while it conduces to the perfect maturing of the
wine. A few years hence the wines which have
been made and kept here will rival if not far surpass
the wines imported from Europe. They have the
attraction of cheapness as well as that of genuineness
and excellence in quality. They cost one-half less
than imported wines. Strange to say, notwithstanding all these recommendations the chief market for
Californian wines is not the State of California.
They are readily purchased in Chicago and New
York, while in San Francisco they are not half so
popular as the more expensive, but not better wines

which have been brought from Europe, and which are sold at a high price. At present wheat is the only native article of produce which is exported to England on a large scale. The trade is still in its infancy. Not till very recently did the farmers of California learn that Liverpool was the best market for their grain. On account of its extreme dryness and its general superiority over the grain of other countries, the wheat grown in California sells at a higher price than the wheat which is grown elsewhere. This discovery has stimulated production. In 1860 the wheat crop was 5,928,470 bushels. It was more than double this amount in 1865. In 1866 it amounted to 14,080,752 bushels. It may now be rated at twenty millions of bushels, with the probability of indefinite and continuous increase. Thanks to Free Trade the poor of London are not only blessed with a cheap loaf, but they are certain to have the farmers of icy Russia competing with the farmers of sunny California in order to supply them with wheat.

A walk through the markets of this city suffices to convince the visitor that in this State the necessaries of life are furnished in unexampled profusion, and on a most extensive scale. Fish and game are plentiful and cheap. All the common fruits and vegetables are to be had for a trifle, while fruits which are luxuries elsewhere are here within the reach of the multitude. Nor is this abundance the most noteworthy circumstance. The change from summer to winter is discerned with difficulty in the market-place. As far as the supply of vegetables and of most fruits is concerned there is neither seed-time nor harvest. In this favoured city potatoes are always new, and strawberries always in season. The size of many products of the garden and orchard is gigantic. The huge turnips, cabbages, pears, and apples which at home form the subjects of paragraphs during the dull season, are here substantial and purchasable realities. Now and then an unusually large natural product is sent to the newspaper offices of San Francisco for the inspection of the proprietors. I was in the office of the *Alta California* when some stalks of Indian corn which had been grown at San Diego, a locality which wiseacres had pronounced unsuited for the growth of the plant, were examined and measured. The tallest were $17\frac{1}{2}$ feet; the others were 15. Fancy a field covered with stalks like these! Yet it would not be more extraordinary than the groves of trees at Mariposa or Calevaras, of which the trunks are 30 feet in diameter and 300 feet in height. Indeed, everything is on a large scale here. The Bay is 50 miles long; the steamships which ply between this port and China or Japan are of 4,000 tons burden; some farms cover an area of 30,000 acres. A farmer, when speaking to me about his affairs, incidentally mentioned that he was then holding 120 tons weight of wheat in the hope that prices would rise at Liverpool. He mentioned this not as a boast, but merely as a piece of information. Indeed, the contrast between the Californians and the New Englanders is very marked. The latter are remarkable for ingenuity in detail. They beat the world in producing machines which enable one man or woman to do the work of many hands. The Californians have invented no machine for peeling apples or shelling peas, but they have carried a railway over the Sierras, have filled up a portion of their great Bay, in order to add new wharves and streets to San Francisco, and have levelled hills, in order to make the streets of that city more convenient and the dwellings more commodious.

The public buildings are not objects of great note, yet several of the banks and merchants' offices are noble erections. Four of the hotels are equal in size and arrangement to the largest and best appointed hotels in New York. The churches are the most striking and imposing edifices in the city. The Jews of San Francisco have erected one of the finest synagogues in the United States. There are two Roman Catholic Cathedrals. All the best knows sects of Protestants have their own places of worship, the churches of the Episcopalians being the most attractive, and the Episcopalians themselves forming the most numerous sect. They occupy the place in California which the Unitarians occupy in New England. I confess to have been surprised to find the press of San Francisco not merely flourishing, but meriting a eulogy which cannot justly be conferred on the press of New York as a whole. The articles in the *Alta California*, for example, are animated by a praiseworthy spirit of impartiality, and are singularly free from blemishes due to the prejudice which hinders the comprehension of anything outside the writer's narrow sphere of personal experience and limited observation. Having complex problems to solve with relation to China and Japan, and finding that these problems are treated by the journalists of the Eastern States in a flippant and foolish style, the journalists of San Francisco are not prone to regard the opinions of the New York papers on subjects of general concern as worthy of implicit confidence and unalloyed respect. Unfortunately, the journals of New York are supposed in Europe to represent the American press, and the least reputable of these journals is generally, though erroneously, considered to be the leader of that press. In addition to the *Alta California*, there is the *Bulletin*, also a first-class paper, while the *Morning Call* is a journal filled with chit-chat and gossip, retailed with a view to piquancy and effect, and without marked consideration for the rules of etiquette and the canons of good taste. Among weekly journals, the *Golden City* and *Sunday Mercury* are what Americans would call 'real live papers.' A monthly magazine entitled the *Overland Monthly* has recently been established. Already, it is acknowledged to be one of the best among American periodicals. Several English periodicals of repute are infinitely inferior to it. With considerable difficulty could many magazines be named which are both better written and more worthy of being read through from the first page to the last. Its articles on the affairs of China, Japan, and of the Pacific slope, are filled with details which are invaluable. Having become acquainted with the press of this city, I am disposed to concur with the compiler of a guide-book, who, after naming the several journals, and indicating their character, thus concludes his remarks:—'If among these papers you can find nothing to suit you, nothing new, why, then, we advise you to read the Bible, and profit by its teachings.'

When the citizens of San Francisco are anxious

to exchange the air of the city for that of the open country, they can easily gratify their longing. If they sail across the bay to Alameda or Oakland, they are in a beautiful country and surrounded by new scenes. Santa Clara and San Matteo, on the south, can be reached by rail, and there sights which recall the magic gardens of the Arabian Nights may be beheld and enjoyed. A shorter and more popular excursion is to the Cliff House, which is five miles distant from the city, and built on the shore of the Pacific Ocean. In front of the house may be seen the sea lions, a species of seal, gambolling on the rocks, over which the heavy ocean swell rolls and foams. In the house itself a pleasant meal may be enjoyed. Indeed, the Cliff House is to San Francisco what the Trafalgar at Greenwich is to London, and what Taft's at Point Shirley is to Boston.

XXI.

THE 'TIGERS' AND CHINESE IN SAN FRANCISCO.

ONE afternoon, after having been treated to drinks at the bar of the Cosmopolitan Hall by Californian friends, I had some interesting talk with a gentleman to whom I had been introduced, and with whom, as with several others, I had formed a drinking acquaintance. He was a man of middle age, of quiet demeanour and pleasant manners. He resembled a gentleman who had retired from business after having made his fortune as a banker or a solicitor. Like the rest of his countrymen he conversed with fluency on the most various topics, from the prospects of gold-mining to the nature of the Alabama claims. He resembled his countrymen also in being as 'cocksure about everything' as Lord Melbourne asserted that Macaulay was. I had previously been fortunate enough to make the acquaintance of distinguished lawyers, and of one who was about to leave the bar for the career of diplomacy, having been appointed United States

Minister at an Eastern court. Between these
gentlemen, one of whom now occupies the highest
judicial office in the gift of the citizens of San
Francisco, the Minister to whom I have referred,
others who were considered notable men by their
fellow-countrymen, and the gentleman of agreeable
talk and smooth demeanour, no external difference
was perceptible. Shortly before parting he told me
that he was engaged in the pasteboard business,
and that I might possibly like to visit his establishment. As I had come here in order to see everything of a novel and interesting kind, I expressed
my readiness to pay a visit to his pasteboard manu-
factory. Perceiving that I had misapprehended
him, my acquaintance entered into an explanation,
in the course of which he asked me if I had ever
heard of Faro, and if I knew the meaning of
'Fighting the Tiger.' Soon afterwards I learned
that I was conversing with the keeper of one of the
most notable among the gaming hells of San Francisco. He was a prosperous man and a respected
citizen. He courteously invited me to visit his
establishment, which, he said, I should find open all
the night. He added that he would rather I did
not play, as he should regret were I to lose money
after having come at his invitation. These kindly
sentiments I reciprocated, assuring him that he

would not grieve more bitterly and sincerely than I should were I to lose my money while madly engaged in 'Fighting the Tiger.' The following description of what I saw will give a fair notion of these banks as a whole, without reference to any particular one.

Admittance into a Faro Bank is not always a matter of course. At Sacramento, indeed, the one which I visited was accessible to any who ascended the stairs leading to it. All of them appear to be on the first floor, both in Sacramento and San Francisco. The visitor rings a bell, and before the door is opened he is generally reconnoitred through a small aperture or grating. As soon as the guardian is satisfied, either from appearances, or from personal knowledge, or from the inspection of a card in the proprietor's handwriting, that no objection exists, the door is opened, the visitor takes a few steps forward, and is brought face to face with the 'Tiger.' He sees what he is told is a Faro table. This table is small, and will not accommodate more than six or eight persons. The dealer occupies one side, and sits with his back to the wall. Facing him, one of the players holds a marking-board, on which the cards, whereof the chances are exhausted, are scored for the information alike of the players and the lookers-on. A double row of cards, with the faces uppermost, is fastened to the table. On these cards the stakes are placed. The cards in play are dealt from a small box which holds them, so that but one at a time can be separated from the pack. Two cards are dealt in succession—the one being put alongside the box, the other a little way from it. The card which falls either near to, or away from the box determines the result of the stakes in the row of cards nearest to or farthest from the dealer. Indeed, the game is but a complicated Blind Hookey. It is, perhaps, even better adapted for ensuring the loss of money on the part of the players than Roulette or Rouge-et-Noir. I was told that the difficulty of cheating is greater at Faro than at other games of chance, and this consideration has tended to render it popular. The Californians may be great gamesters, but they naturally prefer a game played with some regard for fairness, or one which they style a ' square ' game. In some of the rooms I visited the coloured photo-lithograph of a Bengal tiger's head was affixed to the wall above the dealer, and facing the players. The blood-shot eyes, the rows of sharp fangs visible through the half-parted jaws, the general aspect of infinite ferocity which marks the tiger about to pounce upon his prey, were all effectively rendered in this picture. It was at once a symbol and a warning, yet the hidden meaning excited no thought, and the implied menace no dread.

As a rule, money was not staked. The dealer or banker sells ivory counters to the several players. These counters are of different colours and sizes, so as to represent different values. I suppose the reason for using counters to be the evasion of the law against playing for money. In all the hells the costume of the keepers and dealers, or rather the absence of it, was the same, shirt sleeves being their full dress. Those who superintended the game also sat without their coats. The shirts of all were spotless. The superintendents, dealers, and game-sters all smoked cigars. Nor were their manners more formal than their apparel. All the company seemed to be on terms of intimacy; each one not only addressed the other by his Christian name, but as Tom, Dick, or Harry. What conversation there was consisted of trivial remarks of a personal kind. Between the dealers and the players there appeared to exist a perfect understanding that the work in hand was pure matter of business. A player some-times uttered an ejaculation to the effect that his luck was bad, and received from the dealer a few pithy words of commiseration. The losers, who ap-peared to be in a large majority, took their mishaps most philosophically, while the rare winners did not exult in their good fortune. Indeed, ' Fighting the Tiger' in San Francisco seems to be a pastime which, if neither harmless nor praiseworthy, cannot fairly be denounced as fraught with immediate evil consequences. Were I to venture on an explanation of this, I should attribute it to the fact that those who play at Faro have acquired their money very easily and rapidly, and know that if they would but take the like pains they might again enrich themselves by speculation, or by drawing a prize in that lottery which here goes by the name of gold and silver mining. To such persons, and under these conditions, gaming is almost a matter of course. It is simply another form of the every-day life which men of business consider natural and legitimate. It cannot be said that there are extraneous provocations to spur on the jaded gamesters. In some of the hells a supper is provided, but this is merely what their frequenters can get gratis at nearly every bar-room. A drink may be had for the asking; but this, again, is not a special incentive, but a part of the ordinary social arrangements. Californians do not seem happy unless they are either taking drinks or treating their friends and acquaintances to them. That they should find drinks provided for them in the gaming hells is merely what they consider themselves entitled to expect. I believe that the law forbids gaming, and I have been informed that the amount of gaming indulged in now is but a fraction of what was openly permitted a few years ago. What goes on at present is supposed to be continued in defiance of the law. Perhaps the authorities wink at what they cannot entirely repress, and make no sign so long as public scandal is eschewed. One of the keepers of a Faro Bank told me that the police had sometimes put the law in force against him, but that the only serious result was a payment by him of 1,000 dollars as a fine. This diminished his profits, but neither this penalty nor any other punishment entailed the closing of his establishment and his own ruin. Lest it be supposed that the prevalence of gaming proves the utter demoralisation of the Californians, I must add that Faro Banks are to be found elsewhere throughout the Union, and that in no city are they more flourishing than in New York. I have described them as they exist in San Francisco and Sacramento, because they are among the sights of these places. 'Fighting the Tiger' is an occupation which is usually conducted without any bloodshed, with but little loss of temper, and with no more marked result than that of furnishing a practical illustration to the old saw that fools and their money are soon parted.

While assured that I might enter a gaming hell without dread of pickpockets, sharpers, or bullies, I was told by the same persons that to explore the Chinese quarter was a very different and far more dangerous undertaking. Sir Charles Dilke relates in his 'Greater Britain,' that when he went through this quarter he was accompanied by two detectives, who, if they aided his researches, also acted as a drag on his movements. Holding the opinion that when the gratification of curiosity, not the prosecution of business, is the object, guides are incumbrances, I resolved upon seeing as much as I could without presenting my introduction to the police authorities, and availing myself of the aid which they would doubtless have rendered with readiness and courtesy. An experienced Californian of my acquaintance, whose company I requested, spoke in strong terms of the folly of running the risk proposed, and refused to join me. I thought then that he exaggerated the danger, in the same way that dwellers among the Alps and the Pyrenees are wont to exaggerate the peril of crossing a glacier or scaling a mountain, and now I feel convinced that I was right.

In every street Chinamen are to be seen engaged

in some occupation of a menial kind. They may be met with ascending the stairs of the hotels with baskets filled with clean linen; in some hotels they officiate as servants. According to a return made to the State Legislature, the number of Chinese on the Pacific slope is 89,500. What proportion of them inhabits San Francisco is a matter of uncertainty. Some persons estimate it at thirty thousand. But, though San Francisco is not a very populous city, yet, as it covers a vast area, thirty thousand Chinamen might be quartered in one of its long streets or spacious squares without attracting general notice, or without being often seen by the pedestrian walking along the principal thoroughfares. Let any one, however, turn accidentally or intentionally to the left after traversing Montgomery-street almost to its northern extremity, and he is suddenly transported into a new region. A few steps behind him are the shops, dwellings, manners, apparel and language of England and America, while before his eyes are the people, the shops, the houses of the natives of that curious and over-populated land, which is metaphorically styled Flowery or Celestial, and in simple speech is called China, or Cathay. My first visit to the Chinese quarter was made by daylight. I entered it without design, having no exact know-

ledge of the locality in which the Chinese had made
their homes in this city. The effect was as startling
as the transformation scene in a pantomime, with
this difference, that the personages are neither
fairies nor sprites, neither princes nor princesses in
difficulties, beings of unearthly mould gifted with
supernatural powers. Nor did the Chinamen
whom I saw resemble clown, pantaloon, or colum-
bine in dress or demeanour. They were clothed in
plainly-cut blue tunics, had straw or cloth cover-
ings on their heads, and shoes on their feet resembling slippers down at the heels. The shops were
adorned with pendent flags bearing inscriptions in
Chinese. An entire street was filled with these
strangely decorated and as strangely arranged
shops. In some of them merchants of the highest
respectability do business, and accumulate wealth.
The articles they sell are the best of their kind,
and as these merchants are satisfied with small
profits, the low prices attract purchasers. Other
industries than those of dealers in tea, silks, lac-
quered ware, and porcelain are carried on in a
humbler style by men of less ambition and capital.
In cellars which are certainly dark, and probably
unhealthy, silent Chinamen may be seen washing
or ironing clothes, manufacturing cigars, or shaving
the heads of their countrymen. Here and there a

shoemaker is actively engaged in making the semi-
slippers which the Chinamen wear, or else repairing
old ones with extraordinary neatness and patient
care. Now and then a butcher's shop, filled with
joints of new shape, attracts attention, while cook-
shops, filled with prepared viands, which, if savoury,
are very uninviting, are also very plentiful. At
the corner of a street I remarked a lofty stone
building, which proved to be a Chinese hotel. As
no objection was made to my entering it and
inspecting the arrangements, I had an opportunity
of seeing the Chinaman at home. Within the door
on the right a porter or clerk sits with a book
before him corresponding to the visitor's book of
other hotels. When I saw him he was engaged in
making out the accounts of the several occupants,
and producing bills which were long in a material
sense, inasmuch as they were written lengthwise
on narrow strips of paper. Opposite to where he
sat was what appeared to be a kitchen combined
with a butcher's and poulterer's shop. Plucked
fowls with long yellow necks were suspended in
rows by their heads, pieces of meat were affixed to
hooks, while beneath were vegetables of various
kinds. I was told that the visitors purchase their
own provisions, and either cook them or employ
some one to do so. The Chinese have the reputa-

tion of excelling as cooks; they are called the
French of the East. They take a great deal of
pains in preparing the several dishes, and they excel
in sauces. To those unaccustomed to their ways
one thing they do excites surprise. Whether they
season a dish or sprinkle a shirt preparatory to
ironing it, they adopt the same method of proce-
dure. This consists in filling their mouths with
water, and squirting the required quantity over the
garment. In cooking, they do not, as I supposed
they did, simply spit into the dishes they prepare,
but they season them by mixing the condiments in
their mouths, and then ejecting as much of the
seasoning as they think necessary. Those who
employ Chinese cooks will relish their meals all the
more heartily if they never enter the kitchen when
they are at work. The accommodation in this hotel
is not luxurious, nor is the furniture sumptuous.
A few wooden benches serve as seats, and wooden
shelves are couches by day and beds at night.
Every inch of room is turned to account. The
common saying about being packed as closely as
herrings in a barrel expresses, with but slight exaggeration, the manner in which the Chinamen are
packed in this hotel. It appears large enough to
contain about two hundred persons; as many as
twelve hundred are said to occupy it during the

busy season. That some do not die of the effects
of the overcrowding is a marvel. But it is even
more credible that the mortality should not be
enormous from this cause alone than that anyone
should be able to inhale the indescribably horrible
smells for an hour, and live.

Not far from this hotel I passed an alley wherein
crackers were exploding, and small bonfires burning. The inhabitants appeared to be making
holiday. The women were gaily dressed, and had
wreaths of artificial flowers on their heads. I
fancied that a wedding was being celebrated. A
Chinaman, however, told me that the day was
Sunday, and that the crackers were being let off,
the fires lit, and the dresses worn, in honour of the
day. At more than one doorstep a ceremony was
performed which bore a resemblance to the heathen
sacrifices of antiquity, whereof descriptions have
been handed down to us. A tray was brought, on
which were three cups filled with liquid, a small
quantity of rice, several pieces of coloured paper,
plaited into patterns like the summer ornaments of
a stove, and a few slender sticks like the spills
used for lighting lamps or cigars. These sticks, I
was told, were sacred to 'Jossy.' They were first
ignited and placed upright at the corner of the
tray, then the coloured papers were set on fire, and,

while they blazed, each of the cups was emptied over them in succession. Lastly, the rice was scattered abroad to different parts of the compass. Although the intelligent Chinaman to whom I spoke told me that the day was Sunday, yet I have reason to suppose that he used this word for lack of a more suitable one wherewith to give an explanation of the occurrences. I learned afterwards that the ceremony was one in which the Chinese indulge whenever they think it necessary to lay the devil. Of the infernal powers they stand in great terror, and propitiate them with offerings like those described. But if this be the case, it is still possible that the desire to enjoy a holiday and make high festival combine to render the operation of laying the devil one for which they are not sorry to have an excuse. Some of the more practical and frugal Chinamen signify their disapproval of this tendency by saying that there is ' too muchee debbil in Californy.'

The Joss House which I visited is in the building set apart as the Chinese Hospital. The room in which the idol is enthroned in state, with lights burning before it, is a dingy apartment. When I entered no priest nor any attendant was present. An iconoclast might have done his worst with impunity. On passing through the rooms set

apart for the sick I was surprised to see most of
the patients at work.   The Chinese do not accept
illness as an excuse for idleness.   So long as a
patient can move his hands and his feet he is made
either to carry water, chop wood, or perform some
other task.   It was pitiful to see the haggard in-
mates struggling over their occupations.   Many
were in the last stage of consumption, and several
were cripples.   If the disgusting stories current
about the medicines used are well founded, the
death of all the patients who take them is what
might be expected.   For a time Chinese doctors
were the fashion.   But an analysis of the medicines
they prescribed and supplied has rendered them far
less popular.   The ingredients were found to be
chosen rather on account of their rarity and nasti-
ness than for any other apparent reason.   These
doctors are not afflicted with modesty as to the
nature of their powers.   At the entrance to an
alley I saw a sign-board projecting from the side of
the house, and intimating that ' Dr. Hung Ly
cures all diseases upstairs.'   In the newspapers
those doctors advertise regularly.   Thus may be
seen among other announcements one to the effect
that Dr. Jay Hon Chung, graduate of the highest
medical college of China, has opened an office in
Washington-street :—' The most obstinate and pain-

ful chronic diseases treated with entire success, and cures guaranteed. Dr. Jay Hon Chung will make no charge for medical advice to those who are too poor to pay for the same.' These doctors have rapidly and thoroughly imitated the style of advertising quacks in England and America. Perhaps it is in order to compete with them successfully that the quacks who trade on human credulity in California are, if possible, even more audacious in their statements than their brethren elsewhere. A gentleman of majestic stature, whose head was adorned with long flowing locks, who styled himself 'The King of Pain,' was harvesting dollars when I arrived at San Francisco. He professed not only to cure all diseases, but also to inform the patient of his malady without asking any questions. Like others of his tribe, he had a specific for the cure of every malady with which human beings are afflicted. In disposing of this he displays an amount of ingenuity which casts into the shade the advertising tricks in which English quacks are adepts. Driving through the city in a handsome carriage, he halts now and then, and makes a short speech. While he is retailing some of the miraculous cures which he has effected, a passer-by having the appearance of a sailor, or a mechanic, stops and exclaims, 'What's that you say about Boston?'

The quack replies, 'Sir, I have just told these gentlemen how Mr. John A. Jones, a prominent citizen of Boston, was cured by a single bottle of this specific after all the other doctors had given him up.' 'Well, sir, that's so. I come from Boston, and I know that Mr. Jones was cured by a bottle of your medicine.' This independent testimony induces several among the audience to give the 'King of Pain's' specific a trial. He then drives off, when he can no longer exchange his bottles for the dollars of dupes, and the farce is played over again in another quarter of the city, the confederate, of course, changing his attire and his story. It is clear that the Chinese quack doctors will have a hard struggle to keep themselves abreast with their American competitors.

At night, when I strolled through the Chinese quarter again, the spectacle was more curious. The pavement was crowded with Chinamen talking incessantly and in loud tones. Entire alleys were filled with small houses, at the open windows of which painted female faces were clustered, and whence invitations, couched in broken yet very broad English, were sent to every male passer-by. The theatre is easily found by those who listen for the sounds of gongs and cymbals. A quarter of a dollar is charged for admission. As a rule the

14

Chinese are disinclined to admit foreigners into their theatre. The doorkeeper has to be propitiated before he will admit that a seat is to be had. Inside, the house is arranged after the manner of lecture rooms. Rows of seats slope upwards from the pit to the opposite wall, and above this is a gallery. The orchestra is at the back of the stage, and is composed of three or four performers, who keep up an incessant clashing of cymbals and beating of gongs. The noise is overpowering. When all the performers have momentarily left the stage, the unmelodious and ear-rending sounds are diminished in volume; but, when the performers come forward and begin to speak, the gongs are beaten and the cymbals clashed with increased vigour. It seemed as if the object of the members of the orchestra was to drown the voices of the players. In order to defeat this design the players yelled at the top of their voices. Never before did I hear musical instruments made to give forth louder and more discordant noises, and human throats utter words in equally shrill tones. As to the merits or demerits of the piece I can say nothing. The first act had been performed several months ago, and the last would not be reached till several months hence. Regarded simply as a pantomime, it was a curious and clever performance. Some of the scenes required no explanation in words. The love passages were, so to speak, emphasized in a manner which rendered the meaning intended to be conveyed almost too clear. The difficulty consisted in detecting the line which separated acting from reality. Feats of agility and trials of strength were common. The single combats were horribly real; spear-thrusts being delivered with wonderful energy, and sword-cuts made with such rapidity, that they could only be eluded by the exercise of a practised eye, and by extraordinary dexterity of fence. When the actors chased each other along the stage, impediments were surmounted in the style of the circus. Over chairs and tables they vaulted, turning summersaults in the air before alighting on the ground. They fell heavily, no spring-board or mattress being placed to aid them in jumping and to break the force of the fall. How they escaped with their ribs whole and their legs unbroken is incomprehensible. The costumes and make-up of the actors were very good. They always entered by the right door, and made their exits by the left, each entrance being a sort of triumphal procession. It was but seldom that the audience testified their satisfaction with the performance. The attention was rivetted on the stage, not a sight being missed or a sound lost. Nearly everyone had a Manilla cigar or a cigarette in his mouth, and all smoked with a deliberation which demonstrated a desire to enjoy to the full the pleasure of the moment.

The Chinese have their own gaming hells. The stakes are small, but the players never cease till they have lost everything. Lotteries are also plentiful. A thousand chances can be bought for a dollar. The tickets fill a small volume and are beautifully ornamented by hand. The highest prize is a thousand dollars. Near the Chinese quarter, and in the streets leading from it, are streets wherein more danger is to be feared than among the Chinese themselves. Nearly every house is tenanted by women who, scantily dressed in gaudy apparel, stand on the door steps or at the open windows, proclaiming their profession by look and gesture. Underground dancing saloons are numerous, and in them are to be seen what are here significantly styled 'pretty waiter girls.' These saloons are but traps baited and set for the unwary. They are the relics of San Francisco in bygone days, when its very existence was a scandal. The Vigilance Committee did invaluable service in clearing it of the thieves and murderers who were then a terror to the peaceable and well-disposed citizens. There is still plenty of work for the police to perform in the interest of decency and good manners.

What impressed me most in the Chinese quarter was not any particular phase of life and novel kind of house, church, shop, hotel, or theatre, but the general aspect of the place, and its inhabitants regarded as a whole. In China itself the like number of people dwelling, doing business, and enjoying themselves in the same way, would not produce a similar impression. The force of contrast operates with irresistible effect. At one moment I am in Kearney-street or Montgomery-street, surrounded by tokens of Western civilization, and a few minutes afterwards I stand in what is a small section of an actual Chinese city. It is impossible for the most cursory observer to witness these things and to fail being struck with the fact that their continued existence involves the solution of a great problem. Of this the citizens of San Francisco are perfectly conscious. What they have done hitherto towards finding the desired solution does not entitle them to unstinted praise. At present, Chinese labour is as much a necessary of their existence as the clothes they wear. In private houses, John—all Chinamen being called John—is a far better servant than Biddy. He takes lower wages; he is temperate, honest, and respectful; he does his work with extreme care, whether it consists in washing dishes or nursing babies, scrubbing floors or waiting at table. Manufactories would have to be closed, vineyards suffered to run wild, and many railways would continue to be projects, were there no Chinamen to watch the spindles, tend the vines, cut the sleepers, build bridges, and lay the rails. Chinamen, however, are chargeable with the unpardonable fault of being Chinamen. The shape of their eyes, the hue of their skins, the cut of their clothes, nay even their virtues, such as prudence, patience, abstemiousness, attachment to the land of their birth, a desire that their bones should be laid amidst the bones of their ancestors, are all regarded as disabilities unfitting them for being treated as rational human beings. It is considered dangerous to stand on the platform of a street-car, and passengers are prohibited from standing there. Yet Chinamen and Chinawomen are compelled by a regulation of the company to stand on this platform, and are forbidden to sit inside. This barbarous and disgraceful regulation exceeds in wickedness the prohibitions which in other days excluded the negro from the street and the railroad car. It is illiberal to refuse to take the Chinese as passengers, but to carry them at the same rates as other passengers and to make them occupy places which are supposed

to be dangerous can hardly be characterised in
language sufficiently strong.   Attempts have been
made to subject them to the bitterest injustice of
which men can be the victims.   In courts of law the
evidence of Chinamen has been proclaimed inad-
missible.   They might be wholly in the right, and
yet be adjudged as wrongdoers.   There was nothing
to prevent a non-Chinaman entering a house inhabited by a Chinese family, committing robbery,
rape, or murder in the presence of several wit-
nesses, and being held by the court to be innocent
of any offence against the law.   Happily this
monstrous violation of the rights of the individual,
which the statutes of California sanction, will not
be possible in the future.   I had the satisfaction of
learning that Ah Hund, who was defendant in an
action which came before a court of law during my
stay in San Francisco, and who, if not permitted to
testify, would have been robbed of his property,
was placed in the witness-box, in accordance with
the judge's ruling that the Fourteenth Constitutional Amendment, while extending equality to the
negro, likewise entitled the Chinaman to sue for
justice, and ensured that he would not sue in vain.
That the Supreme Court of the United States will
confirm this decision if appealed against, is regarded

as certain. In any case, however, the Fifteenth Constitutional Amendment will be an effectual bar to the repetition of iniquitous proceedings like those in question. How far the efforts made by the Democrats, who are now the majority here, to persecute and expel the Chinese will prove successful remains to be seen. The *Alta California,* which is an upholder of the Union rather than a mere organ of party, has made a bold and firm stand in favour of justice to the Chinaman. In one of many articles on the subject it remarks that if the Chinese were expelled, the value of landed property would at once decline 25 per cent.; that if they were excluded, the act would be a token of barbarism; and that not only unrestricted intercourse with China, but also kind treatment of the Chinese, is demanded by the spirit of the age. Furthermore, it is said that the old war cry of ' America for Americans ' is out of date, and there is no probability that ' America for Irishmen ' will be substituted. It is unquestionable that Chinese labour is a great boon to California. It is reasonable that if the Chinamen obey the law they should be protected by the law. Fortunately, the statesmen of America have recently succeeded in rendering it all but impossible to desecrate the grand principles of the Republic by persecuting men on account of accidents of parentage, and establishing a class of Pariahs in the great home of a people in whose eyes rank is but a trivial distinction, and who glory in maintaining that birth alone neither entails disgrace nor confers honour.

XXII.

CHARACTERISTICS OF CALIFORNIANS.

AMONG the earliest questions put by an American lady or gentleman to a traveller from England who lands at Boston, New York, or Baltimore this one is certain to be included :—'How do you like America?' If, however, the traveller should first tread the sacred soil of the Union when stepping ashore at San Francisco, he will as certainly be asked :— 'What do you think of California?' In the former case, the reply is expected that America is a great country; in the latter, that California is a paradise. The observer to whom the second inquiry has been addressed is soon led to think that the love of the Californians for their country has been absorbed in a singular and exceptional affection for their State. They sometimes appear to consider the old Bear flag as noble an ensign as the national Stars and Stripes. They talk as if 'the States' were mere adjuncts to California, satellites revolving round their sun. This sentiment is more excusable than the inflated provincial arrogance which puts the native streamlet on a par with the foreign river; which rates the native hills as the equals of distant mountains; which regards the native village as the centre and measure of the universe. The frog would never have striven to match the ox in size had the frog been less contemptible. Were California a small and insignificant State the exaggerated provincialism of its inhabitants would be simply ludicrous It is, however, the reverse of paltry and despicable. So extensive is its area that twenty such States as Massachusetts could be carved out of it. The population is small, yet it exceeds that of the old State of Connecticut. San Francisco alone contains more citizens than the entire State of Rhode Island. In the State of California there are 65,000,000 of acres which can be brought under tillage, and as yet not more than three per cent. of the whole has been cultivated. Within the ample bounds of this large and fertile State 20,000,000 of people can be accommodated with pleasant homes. The soil yields everything which human beings require to support and ameliorate existence. All the metals which men value most highly can be procured in abundance and disposed of at a profit. The rivers swarm with fish; the woods are filled with game; the fields are alive with the savoury birds which, in less

favoured localities, are the luxuries of the rich.
The climate is as glorious as that which must have
prevailed in those 'summer isles of Eden lying in
dark purple spheres of sea,' which the poet has
depicted as the regions of perfect terrestrial beauty
and happiness. That the dwellers in a State lavishly
endowed by nature and incontestably superior to
many other States in the Union, should be prone to
forget that they are the least part of what they see
and enjoy, is by no means unnatural, yet it fairly
lays them open to criticism.

Indeed, the Californians have so thoroughly iden-
tified themselves with their State as to be among
the greatest self-deceivers on the Continent of
America. They appear to live under the delusion
that the rich gold mines, the unrivalled grain,
the magnificent fruit, the delightful climate are all
creations of their own. Tell them that gold is
quite as abundant in Australia, that nature has
been as kind to dwellers on other portions of the
globe, and they will appear to think that an affront
is intended. Add that in some respects they are
not the equals of others who inhabit this Continent,
that the culture and polish of New England are
not among their adornments, that they pay a dis-
proportionate respect to material when compared
with intellectual achievements, and they will repel

the charges as malignant calumnies. In short, Californians in general will marvel at the temerity of the daring speaker or writer who ventures to assure them that, even if they live in a paradise, they are not wholly without spot or blemish.

It is hardly possible to reside for a day in California without hearing some reference made to the 'Pioneers.' To have come here in 1849 is held to be a mark of distinction like that accorded in Massachusetts to the Puritans who crossed the ocean in the *Mayflower* and like that awarded in England to the descendants of those who crossed the Channel with William the Norman. In Europe the spirit which originally led to the formation, and still sanctions the continuance, of orders of nobility is the same as that which prompts the pioneer-worship of Californians. The spelling of 'lord' may be greatly varied without altering the actual result. The Virginians had a form which, if clumsy in appearance, answered the purpose nearly as well as any other. The man who, in the Old World, would be dubbed a viscount or a baron was known in the Old Dominion as an F. F. V., that is, he belonged to one of the First Families in Virginia. It is probable that the two-fold effects of war and emancipation may prove fatal to the continuance of this petty form of aristocracy. Yet so long as the 'Pioneers' of California are regarded as exceptional men, the Great Republic will continue to have specimens on a small scale of the antiquated arrangements which its enlightened citizens regard as the bane of the Old World. These 'Pioneers' are aristocrats at heart if not in name; they are 'nobles' in their own estimation. If to have settled in California in 1849 be admitted to be so meritorious as to command admiration, the children of the 'Pioneers' will claim superiority over others on the ground that their fathers were the most distinguished citizens in the State and thus a hereditary hallucination will be propagated.

It was at Chicago that I first had the gratification of seeing several of these remarkable 'Pioneers.' A deputation arrived there with a view to fraternise with their Eastern brethren and exhibit themselves as examples of Californian greatness. They were welcomed with the warmth shown towards conquerors returning home after the performance of heroic exploits. Had the 'Pioneers' saved the Union single-handed their presence could hardly have aroused greater enthusiasm. It was also my good fortune to become personally acquainted with some of these extraordinary men. They described California in a way which led me to suppose that the country must be a modern Eden. If they had added that it was Eden after the fall they would have guarded themselves against exciting expectations which were doomed to be unfulfilled. By omitting to do this they led me astray. They assured me that the citizens of California were the superiors of all others on the Continent, were endowed with every excellence of character which adorns and exalts mankind. Their achievements, I was emphatically told, had been unparalleled in grandeur and unequalled in importance, while all that had been performed and all that was now rendered easy and possible had its source in the conduct and character of the ' Pioneers.' Such is the gist of the statements to which I listened with attention. If I do not accept them as wholly accurate, it is because I have failed to substantiate them by an examination of the facts. Moreover, granting the truth of the allegations, I am reluctantly obliged to challenge the propriety of the homage of which the ' Pioneers ' are the willing and gratified recipients. They went to California in order to get riches: they succeeded in their object; that their enrichment must be pleasing to them is quite in the nature of things. But to bow down before them because they have been successful is simply to revive the worship of the Golden Calf. When a man makes a fortune, he is not necessarily transformed into a demi-God.

Two qualities, I was told, distinguished the citizens of San Francisco. They were generous to a degree almost unique, and noted for hospitality beyond the rest of the world. Among my introductions were some to gentlemen who, by common consent, were ranked as representative men, citizens who occupied prominent positions as magnates and millionaires. Soon after my arrival I presented my introduction to one of these gentlemen. He was a banker, and I thought it natural that he should be rich; he was an ornament to San Francisco, and I deemed it a matter of course that he should be estimable. His reception of me surpassed any which I had received from the many affable Americans whose acquaintance I made in a similar manner. To call it cordial is but imperfectly to characterise it. Everything this gentleman could do to serve me he professed himself anxious to perform. His country-seat, his horses and his carriage were placed at my disposal with an alacrity which was startling. It resembled nothing so much as the sham politeness of the Spaniard who asks the stranger to consider himself the proprietor of all his possessions, and who never for a moment thinks that he will be taken at his word. I am sorry to have to record as the result of experience gained not only from this case, but from others, that among the legacies of the Spaniards to the Californians the peculiar Spanish views about hospitality have been included. It so happened that I had no occasion for availing myself of the banker's services, and was unable to put his kindness to the test. Shortly before my departure, I called to thank him for his courtesy and to express regret at my inability to profit by his liberal offers. Fancying, apparently, that I had come to ask him to give effect to his promises, he appeared strangely oblivious as to having seen me before; but, no sooner had I explained my errand, than his countenance cleared, the former cordiality of manner returned, and he emphatically expressed a hope, of which I perfectly understood the meaning, that he might have the pleasure of seeing me the next time I visited San Francisco.

If the Californians were less addicted to eulogising themselves, they might be praised more unreservedly by strangers. It is wise policy for the citizens of a new State to imitate the custom of the inhabitants of Tasmania and New South Wales and studiously refrain from provoking indiscreet and minute inquiries. That society in San Francisco and Sacramento should be composed of heterogeneous materials, and that the 'prominent citizens' should not always be conspicuous for their high breeding and their learning ought to excite no astonishment. The gold discoveries acted as a magnet which drew to the same spot a mixed crowd of adventurers. Some came to dig for gold; others to get gold in exchange for goods, for their personal charms, for their professional advice. In this keen struggle the most illiterate and unscrupulous had a great advantage over the scholar and the man of honour. The men who achieved the greatest success were in some respects changed for the worse. If vulgar and commonplace before, their rapidly acquired riches served to render these failings still more obvious. Their greatest gain consisted in the training which had made them self reliant to a degree which is unattainable except by those who have lived in a community where Judge Lynch administers the wild justice of revenge, and where a bullet from a revolver or a stab made by a bowie-knife is the only argument potent enough to command instant acquiescence. The dwellers in cities well guarded by policemen know nothing of what it is to inhabit a mining camp swarming with robbers and murderers. Those who have passed through the ordeal have gained an experience like that of the hunter who has lived for years by the produce of his rifle, and has executed the double task of shooting the game wherewith to sustain life and guarding himself against being shot by Indians who hate and pursue him as they do a wild beast. The hunter's career generally unfits him for living in the society of his fellows: he prefers a lonely but active life in the forest or on the mountain to a dreary and monotonous existence amid the solitude of a great city. This was not the case with respect to the gold-hunters. Having suddenly grown rich, they were eager to enjoy the luxuries which money can purchase. They imported into the city the manners and customs of the camp. To order drinks for ' the crowd ' was the habit of a hospitable Californian miner: to give drinks to their acquaintances is the habit of the prosperous Californian citizen. A gentleman who was pointed out to me enjoyed immense popularity in San Francisco. He was very rich. His greatest merit, as far as I could learn, consisted in this, that sometimes he expended 500 dollars a day in treating his friends to drinks. When, then, Californians vaunt about their hospitality they mean that they are the most liberal with their whisky of any people on earth.

It would be an error, however, to regard the Californians as spend-thrifts. While parting ostentatiously with their money, they are perpetually anxious to amass more wealth. The shrewdest Yankee cannot excel them in looking after the main chance. They seem to think that the whole duty of man consists in getting money. But to employ their accumulated wealth in a way which will benefit the less fortunate, cannot be numbered among the objects of their ambition. Many stories of unpardonable niggardliness are current. One of the best authenticated relates to 'The Mercantile Library' of San Francisco. Seventeen years ago the lovers of literature resolved upon founding a library here which should resemble the public libraries which do credit to the generous foresight of the inhabitants of the principal cities in the Eastern States. This collection of books and periodicals is large and valuable; the building wherein it is stored is a noble structure. Yet the existence of the association itself has been a never-ending struggle with poverty. The stranger who visits the library learns with amazement that the managers 'cannot point to one bequest or donation, save by some kind-hearted actor, musician or lecturer, the proceeds of whose generosity have been devoted to the purchase of new books.' The undertaking was originated and has been sustained by a few private citizens, 'most of them young and dependent on their daily employment for a livelihood.' It is added, by the unimpeachable authority from which the foregoing quotations have been made, that 'these facts, so creditable to the literary culture of San Francisco, are less so to the intelligent liberality of her millionaires.'* Until these millionaires shall have ceased to be living incarnations of purse-proud selfishness, it will be permissible, when describing them, to employ the stinging sarcasm of Burke, and say that the ledger is their Bible and Mammon their God.

Happily, there is another and a brighter side to be contemplated. Although the lowest form of materialism is the creed of the majority, and Dives alone commands general respect, yet in California there is a small and precious leaven of men who cultivate letters and art with pure affection, and who promise to become masters of their craft. I visited a gallery of paintings by Californian artists, and saw enough to warrant the belief that the landscapes of the Pacific slope will hereafter be worthily reproduced on canvas by artists who have lived among the scenes they portray. The desire and ability to do this have been unmistakeably manifested. Of material there is no lack. That California will hereafter be illustrated by its artists as well as enriched by manufacturers and merchants is one of

* *The Alta California*, 3rd October, 1869.

the most cheering among the possibilities of the future. In literature the harvest bids fair to be sooner ripe and more copious. The number of books of native growth is but small; yet the capacity for producing books bright with the charm of originality and impressed with the stamp of home production has been clearly demonstrated. Two years ago a magazine entitled the *Overland Monthly* was first issued by an enterprising publisher of San Francisco, and that magazine has already taken rank with the best periodicals which America produces. Were a competitive examination instituted, the *Overland Monthly* might even take high honours among the magazines which do credit to England. It is entitled to the rare distinction of being readable from cover to cover and yet to be able to maintain its place without being propped up by an instalment from a novel. The short tales in it are noteworthy alike for artistic treatment and freshness of subject. They are based on actual experience of life at the gold diggings; hence they have the attraction of displaying new varieties of existence and new types of character. It is probable that their authors were educated men who joined in the rush to California in the hope of succeeding better by wielding pick-axes than they had done by the exercise of their pens. Whether they were disappointed or not in their immediate design, it is certain that they gained much profitable experience which they are utilizing for literary purposes. These productions are not the only coinage of note from the intellectual mint of California. The critiques on current literature are quite refreshing in their genuineness, and very effective pieces of writing. The conventionalities of literary cliques do not seem to hamper and emasculate the writers. Having opinions of their own to express, they couch them in plain and straightforward language, and they appear to write with a thorough knowledge of the subjects which they discuss. Many literary oracles of greater age and pretensions, give forth feebler and more uncertain sounds and do less towards maintaining a high standard in literature, than the *Overland Monthly.* In support of these opinions and in justification of this praise I ought to cite examples. If I could do so within moderate limits, I should have no difficulty in substantiating my case. The discerning readers whose curiosity is piqued, or whose scepticism is aroused, can easily ascertain how far I have written at random, and whether I have strewn flowers of eulogy in error. If they turn to the *Overland Monthly* and judge for themselves they will have their reward, for they are certain to discover therein much of which the originality will afford them pleasure even should they be unable to admit the relative excellence and absolute superiority of the magazine as a whole.

The Pacific Railway has been regarded as an instrument designed to advance the prosperity of San Francisco and to multiply the attractions of California. As regards the people themselves that means of intercommunication will prove fraught with results quite as important. Their comparative isolation has led to the growth of a local pride hardly justified by facts and not deserving of admiration. The young men who left their homes in the Eastern States twenty years ago, and are now wealthy citizens of California, have remained practically ignorant of the changes which, during that long interval, have been wrought in the cities of their birth. They have not known that progress has moved with giant strides in New York, St. Louis, and Chicago as well as in San Francisco and Sacramento. They compare what they see around them with what they imagine to exist elsewhere and they glory in their achievements. Now that facilities for travel enable them to draw just comparisons, their self-importance may possibly receive a shock and the 'Pioneers' may soon be deposed from the high pedestal which they have occupied in the estimation of themselves and their neighbours. In reality there is no more merit in having been a ' Californian Pioneer ' than in drawing a prize in a lottery. The holders of prizes deserve congratulations, but no honour. Having made money these men may think that they have earned glory. The folly is not theirs so much as of the simpletons who accede to a ridiculous demand.

Nature, which has already done much for California, will doubtless do as much to render the race which is being moulded here a splendid branch of the human family. The physical conditions under which human beings exist in this favoured region are well adapted for imparting to them the qualities which lead to greatness in all departments of exertion. A century hence it is probable that the Californians will be a power in the Union and will make their influence felt throughout the world. As their intrinsic merit becomes more tangible their shortcomings will afford less ground for comment. When they have stronger reasons for boasting, they will leave to others the task of trumpeting forth their praises.

15

XXIII.

THE GOLDEN GATE TO THE AMERICAN ATHENS.

THE boldest figures of speech used by poets hardly outstrip the figurative names which have been conferred upon cities and places. It is difficult to fathom the reason for calling the harbour of Stamboul the Golden Horn and the entrance to the Bay of San Francisco the Golden Gate. There is nothing auriferous about either. With regard to the latter, however, there is an explanation which justifies the title. Along the Pacific coast a range of mountains rises to the height of five thousand feet. The bank of fog, which nearly always broods over this locality, seldom ascends above the summits of these mountains. The only break in the rockbound barrier forms the inlet to the quiet waters of San Francisco Bay. When the fog is dense and the sky obscured without, the sun shines brightly and the sky is clear within. The effect observed, upon the gap being reached, is that of a mellow golden haze. Hence the origin of the appellation. The sailors who came hither long before the discovery of the famous gold diggings or the advent of Californian ' Pioneers '

rejoiced when they could distinguish the glittering
yellow veil which indicated that the desired haven
had been reached, and they were nearly as enchanted at the sight as they would have been if the
rocks between which they sailed were in truth portals
of solid gold. If the earlier mariners who approached
this coast had, on landing, ascended the mountain
known by the name of Tamalpais, or Table Rock,
and beheld the detested fog rolling beneath their
feet and gazed on the beautiful prospect around
them, they might have entertained thoughts identical with those of the storm-tossed wanderers when
arriving at the land of the Lotos Eaters. Indeed,
the spot itself under circumstances such as these
could not be described more fittingly and beautifully than in the choice lines which are among the
most finished that Tennyson ever penned:—

'We have had enough of action, and of motion we,
  Roll'd to starboard, roll'd to larboard, when the surge was seething
      free,
  Where the wallowing monster spouted his foam-fountains in the sea.
  Let us swear an oath, and keep it with an equal mind,
  In the hollow Lotos-land to live and lie reclined
  On the hills like Gods together, careless of mankind.
  For they lie beside their nectar, and their bolts are hurl'd
  Far below them in the valleys, and the clouds are lightly curl'd
  Round their golden houses, girdled with the gleaming world.'

'Surely, surely, slumber is more sweet than toil, the shore
  Than labour in the deep mid-ocean, wind and wave and oar;
  Oh rest ye, brother mariners, we will not wander more.'

The Spaniards who first settled here were indeed little better than Lotos-Eaters. They lounged through existence. But their successors are men of more vigorous race and less tranquil temperaments. The Californians of whom Sir George Simpson wrote in 1846 that they were indolent and good-for-nothing, have been displaced by Californians whose fault is not want of energy and whose delight does not consist in folding the hands and dreaming like the sluggard. Had they done nothing else than construct the more difficult portion of the railway across the Continent, they would have vindicated their claim to be among the most enterprising and dauntless of mortals.

The completion of that railway has placed San Francisco almost midway between two Easts. If the traveller embarks in a steamer bound for China or Japan he will be carried towards that ancient and far East which is associated in our minds with all that is gorgeous in colouring, marvellous in story and romantic in adventure. Having journeyed 'Westward by Rail' the traveller is thus enabled to reach this East while following in the track of the setting sun. As I had attained the limit assigned to my present journey, nothing remained but to retrace my steps. While doing so and turning my back upon Asia I was able to proceed over what is to the Californians a 'new route to the East,' to an East far younger than the other yet more mature, not peopled with imaginary genii like the other, but the home of men who have yoked fiery dragons to their chariots and tamed the lightning to do their bidding. The Asiatic merely imagined a Sindbad and an Aladdin. In England and America hundreds of Sindbads and Aladdins exist who, without professing to work wonders, eclipse the achievements of the fabled heroes of romance.

By poetic licence the Atlantic and Pacific Oceans are said to be united by an iron highway; but, in reality, there are several breaks in the line and one of the greatest is here. It is possible to pass from the extreme East to the extreme West in a railway carriage, just as passengers might be transported from Charing-cross to the Northern Station in Paris or Brussels, provided the carriage were embarked on board a steamer and ferried across the Channel. Moreover, in this case it is possible for the water journey to be avoided altogether, for a railway runs between San Francisco and San José, and San José and Alameda. Yet, though this route is practicable, it is as roundabout and inconvenient as that from London to Portsmouth by way of Brighton. The rule is to cross the Bay in a steamboat, and to enter the train at Vallejo, Oakland, or Alameda. The crossing occupies nearly an hour. Starting at a quarter past seven o'clock in the morning, the view from the steamer's deck is far-reaching and splendid. A good notion of the extent of the Bay and of the quantity of the shipping is thus obtained. The city itself is seen to advantage. Its greatest drawback is also perceived with distinctness. Although the sky is clear overhead, yet the greater portion of the city is shrouded in smoke. The volumes of dense black smoke issuing from the chimney-stalks of innumerable furnaces, dim the brightness of the sky, and darken the streets and buildings. The effect produced by a London fog is hardly less unpleasant. If a choice had to be made between an occasional fog and perpetual smoke, the fog would certainly be regarded as the lesser evil. At the landing stage of Alameda, the train of the Western Pacific Railway is in readiness to transport the passengers to Sacramento. The line is here carried for a considerable distance on piles. Were the train to run off the rails, the carriages would fall into the water below. This is a contingency which will occur to any one who looks out of the carriage window, and speculates as to results. But another and a greater danger seems impending when the solid earth is traversed. The oscillation of the carriages is very great. They swing from side to side in a way resembling the rolling of a screw steamer. The inequalities of the surface cause shocks like those which shake a steamer when a head wind and sea rush and dash against her bows. Indeed, it is difficult to imagine that rails have been laid at all, or that, if laid, they have been bolted to the sleepers. A worse line I have never travelled over. It is nearly as rough and unpleasant as the common roads which, in the wilder parts of the Western country, seem to have been traced in the beds of watercourses and to have been unprepared for traffic by the exercise of engineering skill. The scenery along the line is not so attractive as to divert attention from the character of the line itself. The ground is undulating for the most part. As the winter rains had not yet fallen when I passed, the fields and trees and shrubs were of a monotonous dull brown, while the dust on the roads was about a foot deep. More than once I have spoken in terms of praise of the Californian climate, and I have, perhaps, omitted to make some necessary qualifications. Properly speaking there are three climates in California—the climate of the sea-coast, of the plains, and of the mountains. San Francisco has this advantage, owing to its situation, that when the sun shines most brightly a cool breeze blows in-shore through the Golden Gate. This wind has the great advantage of bracing the system, which otherwise might become debilitated by uniform warmth. The best proof that I can give of the actual superiority of the climate of San Francisco, after allowance has been made for draw-backs, consists in the fact that neither men nor women require to wear clothing specially adapted for summer or winter. The ladies wear dresses differing in texture and colour, in order to follow the fashions which are set elsewhere, but for all the purposes of clothing these dresses do not vary. At times, however, the transition from the extreme warmth of the day to the coolness of the night is sudden and trying to sensitive constitutions. To all appearance the children are healthy and robust. Their rosy cheeks are a great contrast to the trans-parent skins and pale complexions of New England children. If the child be a criterion of the man, the native-born Californians will hereafter be fine speci-mens of humanity.

Proceeding inland to the country intersected by the railways which run to Sacramento, the climate becomes far hotter. Yet, though less temperate it is not so tropical as to interfere with the easy and profitable cultivation of the soil. In the plains and valleys the year may be divided into spring and summer. Winter and autumn are mere names there. Rain falls in November, not rain like the torrents of water which fall in tropical climes, but gentle showers, like those which on a fine spring morning in England cool the air and moisten the parched ground. From December to April the Californian may plough and plant. At the end of June his crops are ripe; he may then cut the grain, and having done so, he may allow it to remain on the field till October. No barn is required to shelter the sheaves which are about to be thrashed; everything may be done in the open air within the time above-mentioned. Excepting during the season when it rains, all operations may be conducted in the open air, and animals need not be put under cover. The plains of California are a paradise for the farmer. In the mountains there are two seasons also, but these are winter and summer. Snow falls and ice forms on the slopes of the Sierra Nevadas. There are some localities in which the cold is perpetual and where the snow never melts. To the Californian the choice of climate and of scenery is as great within the compass of his own State as it is within the limits of Europe. Among the Sierras he has the glaciers and the mountain peaks, the gorges and the grand scenery of Switzerland; in the plains he finds the rich fields and the rivers

of mid-France; while along the sea coast all the
glories of the Mediterranean are reproduced on a
grander scale, and in larger numbers.

Six hours after leaving Alameda the train stops
at Sacramento, the terminus of the Western Pacific
Railway. The only intermediate station of importance is Stockton, a place of 10,000 inhabitants,
and the centre of the grain trade of the surrounding
region. It is also the spot whence supplies are
derived for the important gold-mining industry at
Mariposa. At Sacramento the passengers bound
eastwards take their seats in the train of the Central
Pacific. Immediately after leaving Sacramento the
ascent of the Sierras begins, and the difficulties
surmounted by those who made the railway are
fully realised. At the end of fifty miles the elevation of the line is 2,400 feet above the level of the
sea; when one hundred and five miles have been
traversed the height reached is 7,000 feet. This
great and sudden rise towards the clouds is accompanied by a great fall in the temperature of the air.
The transition is trying to the delicate chest, and
is borne with difficulty by the most robust. Indeed,
the journey eastward taxes the system more than
that towards the west. In the former case the land
of perpetual sunshine is exchanged for variable
weather and murky skies. It is not surprising that

those who have lived in California should be reluctant to leave it, and after having gone elsewhere
should long to return thither. In the train were
several passengers who had migrated to California
from the States to the east of the Rocky Mountains, in those days when gold discoveries attracted
thousands to the Pacific slope. These men are now
availing themselves of the railway to visit what
they call 'the States,' and to see their relations
once more. Nothing so strikingly illustrates the
comparative isolation in which the inhabitants of
California have lived, as the way in which they
speak of themselves, not as Americans, but as Californians. Even the passengers who had not been
'Pioneers,' who had gone to the Pacific coast a few
years ago in quest of health or fortune, were nearly
as enthusiastic as the older inhabitants. One who
held a high position in the medical staff of the
Western army throughout the war, and whose
health had been shattered by his labours, told me
that after a trial of two years he had resolved to
abandon his home in Wisconsin and practise his
profession in the exquisite climate of San José.
He was now on his way eastward, in order to complete the necessary arrangements. But there is
another side to the picture. I conversed with others
who had visited San Francisco in the hope of

finding lucrative employment there, and who were returning home disappointed and dissatisfied. The labour market is overstocked with young men fitted to do the work of clerks, and with professional men generally. Such persons are warned against seeking in San Francisco that which they cannot find in New York or London. There is room in California for thousands of emigrants, but these emigrants must be prepared to engage in manual labour, and especially in agricultural pursuits, if they would escape starvation. For the man who can rear vines or do farm work, and who has a small amount of capital at his disposal, there is no place in the world where he can make for himself a comfortable home and accumulate money more easily and certainly than the State of California. He can purchase excellent land for 5s. an acre, and can enjoy what a Sovereign, condemned to live in less favoured parts of the world, cannot command—a climate which keeps him in good health, lightens his toils and enables him to reap what he has sown. I have insisted on the advantages to be enjoyed in California as respects climate, because this is the chief consideration in the matter of bodily comfort, as well as the chief agent in making a nation. That the praises I have vented on the Californian climate are not exaggerated may be inferred from this circumstance. It was some time after settlers had flocked here from other parts of the American continent and from Europe before the honey bee was introduced. This useful little insect soon made itself at home, and filled hives with honey. After a year or two had elapsed the store of honeycomb was diminished to a minimum. The bees found that as flowers were in bloom all the year round there was no necessity for laying up a large supply of honey against a barren and blossomless winter season. Consequently, arrangements had to be made to deal with the bees as with hens, abstracting the honey in small portions in order that the formation of the honeycomb might go on uninterruptedly. Perhaps it may prove interesting to add what I have learned at second-hand, but from unprejudiced sources, that the highest eulogiums passed upon the soil, sky, and climate of California are literally applicable to Vancouver's Island also, and that if Americans are to be congratulated on having such a Garden of Eden as California among the States of the Union, the English people are quite as fortunate in numbering Vancouver's Island among the possessions of Great Britain. My informants were Americans, who did not conceal their desire to substitute in British Columbia the Stars and Stripes for the Union Jack.

It is hardly creditable that a possession so valuable should be almost disregarded. Those who are concerned in the organization of emigration from England might do their fellow-countrymen a service by investigating the advantages of settling in British Columbia.

These subjects formed the topics of conversation between myself and several passengers by the train. I have recorded them in preference to repeating for the second time particulars about the route itself. It was as unpleasant in some parts and as enjoyable in others as on the previous journey. The season being more advanced, the cold was more intense. Thus another discomfort was added to those which render the alkali plains the dread and torment of the traveller. While crossing these plains, and while still in the State of Nevada, several miners entered the train at one of the stations. They, too, were bound East, in order to see their friends. Some of them were wild in aspect, as well as rough in speech. From one of them I obtained some interesting particulars respecting the present state of the silver mining region. He carried a revolver and bowie-knife strapped round his waist, and a bottle of whisky in his pocket. When going to his sleeping berth on the night that he entered the car, an open display was made of the deadly weapons, and a distinct token was given of the whisky bottle having been called too frequently into requisition. Early on the following morning as I was standing on the platform of the car, and watching the sun rise, this 'gentleman' made his appearance, and, after a few preliminary remarks, asked me to 'smile.' I had learned by experience that this is the slang phrase for 'taking a drink.' I 'smiled' all the more readily because the morning was intensely cold, the pools of water being coated with ice. In the course of a few minutes this miner told me his name, his history, and his intentions. He became the more communicative when he discovered that I was personally acquainted with one of the 'prominent citizens' of Austin City, Nevada, a gentleman with whom he had been allied in some mining enterprises. He told me that he was known by the nickname of 'Slim Jim,' that he had crossed the plains when quite a youth, had 'made his pile' by lucky hits at mining, was now about twenty years of age, was bound for Chicago, in order to pay a visit to his parents, and that he purposed returning in the course of a few weeks in order to 'prospect' certain parts of the Territory of Utah which had not, in his opinion, received sufficient attention. Like all the miners with whom I formed a temporary acquaintance he had many specimens of ore in his pockets. He carried them for the avowed purpose of showing them as samples to those who might be disposed to buy a share in some of his mines. He insisted upon my accepting some of these specimens, which were certainly very rich in silver. There was nothing disinterested in this. I had been favoured in a similar way on many previous occasions of a like nature. In this part of the United States it is as common to advertise by distributing pieces of gold quartz or silver ore as it is in others to give away handbills of some nostrum for healing diseases.

At Promontory Station, the sharpers, whom I have already described,* were still actively plying their nefarious trade ; and at the other stations in the Territory of Utah, Mormon girls and boys were as assiduous as formerly in disposing of both fruit and hand-wrought gloves to the passengers. The scenery had lost none of its aridity or sublimity. The great Salt Lake still presented a spectacle of wonderful impressiveness, the Weber and Echo Canyons produced an impression of even greater majesty and wildness than when I passed through them earlier in the year. On reaching the Laramie Plains a change came over the scene, for the snow began to fall heavily, and the landscape was draped

* See p. 186.

in white. This gave a variety to the prospect, and rendered the hills more imposing in appearance. On the other hand, it retarded the progress of the train. The engine became unequal to its task, and two hours were consumed in passing over the distance of four miles. This detention led to a break in the arrangements. The line being a single one, the rule is for a train which is behind time to lose the right to the road, and the result is, that it must stop at the appointed sidings till the trains coming in the opposite direction have passed along. Thus it happened that when Omaha was reached, the corresponding train on one of the railways running east had left, and the passengers who had through tickets over that line had to pass the night at Omaha. Others who, like myself, were bound for Chicago by the North Western, were able to continue our journey, as the train had waited our arrival. In due time we arrived at the chief city of the Western States, and continued our eastern journey amidst a snow-storm. I now learned the advantage of having the cars comfortably heated by hot air stoves. In an English railway carriage this journey would have been disagreeable beyond measure, if not fraught with serious consequences to health. As it was, the Pullman car in which we

travelled was as comfortable as the best warmed
room in an English house.

The superiority of these cars is rendered the
more apparent when the traveller has to exchange
seats in them for those which run over the lines in
the States of New York and Massachusetts. At
Albany the carriages which go to Boston are separated from those which go on to New York.
Springfield and Worcester are the chief places of
note between Albany and Boston. The former is
the seat of the United States Arsenal. Near the
latter is Lake Quinsigamond whereon the annual
boat races are contested between the Universities of
Harvard and Yale. The scenery along the line is
varied and picturesque. The abundance of wood
and water seems a fine feature in the landscape to
those who have just crossed the treeless and arid
plains in the heart of the Continent. This contrast
is alike great and pleasing, but it is neither greater
nor more gratifying than that between the capital
of Massachusetts and the largest city on the Pacific
slope, between Boston with its classic memories, its
long-established order, its intellectual triumphs, and
San Francisco with its lawless episodes, its tardy
submission to the reign of law, and its feverish chase
after material riches.

XXIV.

BOSTON CITY AND HARVARD UNIVERSITY.

SEVERAL VISITORS to the Capital of Massachusetts have been struck with its resemblance to an
English city. Its inhabitants deem the likeness
creditable, and seem flattered when it is detected
and praised. The similarity, however, is purely
superficial, being confined to the irregular arrangement of the streets, the form and colour of the
houses. These things are but as rouge on the skin
of a beauty and of a wig on the head of a beau.
They are accidents and not essentials, external
marks which do not typify the hidden and ani-
mating essence. In those things which differentiate
one city from another Boston is unlike any other
city in either the Old World or the New. Bostonians
have better reason to rejoice in the points of dissimilarity than in those of resemblance. They have
substantiated a claim to the honourable title of
the Athenians of America; they are members of
the select and glorious company which, while not

despising wealth and material prosperity, yet counts
such things but as dust in the balance and contemptible dross unless the riches are gilded with
intellect and the success is ennobled by the pursuit
of a lofty ideal. They are in the van of that form
of civilization which is distinctively American and
of which the mission and the pride consist in demonstrating to a sceptical and sneering world that
the most uncompromising and perfect Republicanism
tends to elevate rather than to vulgarize, to beautify
rather than to tarnish, to quicken the pulse of
generous self-sacrifice rather than to repress all the
finer feelings of human nature, and enshrines in
men's minds, as the only idols to which homage can
fitly be paid, the highest form of social breeding
and the most finished patterns of mental culture.

Boston is notable among the cities of the Union
for its purely English origin and its genuine
American development. Those who first settled
here were English to the backbone, and they were
the flower of their generation. According to them
there was something more to be desired than the
favour of a Prince and the highest worldly honours.
They prized as a second heritage of their race the
right to exercise their opinions without reference to
what they considered were the corrupted tests of
degenerate men, and to regard the present world

as an arena in which the pure in heart were destined to strive for a heavenly crown. In thus thinking they were directly opposed to the predominant notions of their age. Their whole life was a revolt against the existing authorities and accepted canons of interpretation. It was to preserve themselves unspotted from the world that they crossed the Atlantic, and when they set foot on Plymouth Rock they brought with them the prolific germs of the ideas whereof the Constitution of the United States is the accurate and logical expression. From the beginning they manifested an irrefrangible resolve to do what they believed to be right and to dare everything when giving practical effect to their convictions. Unfortunately for the minority among them, the majority were too confident that they were the sole repositories of the truth. There is something ludicrous as well as sad in the interference exercised with regard to the concerns of the individual. This was, however, nothing more than the necessary product of their education, combined with the fruit of their theories. To stigmatise the Puritans of New England as petty despots is not to blame them with exceptional severity; but to make the charge and overlook or disregard the explanation is to become their accomplices. They could not shake off the influence of old traditions or emancipate themselves from the yoke of evil example in a day or a year They had lived in England, where the ways of the Tudor and Stuart autocrats had become examples which it was deemed right to copy, so long as the end in view was reconcilable with Scripture. Their fathers had taught them to obey decrees which prohibited certain persons from wearing apparel of specified colours and patterns, and eating food of a particular kind. They knew that even the High Court of Parliament had not respected the sanctity of the coffin, but had enjoined, under a heavy penalty, that the dead should be laid in their last home wrapped in a woollen shroud. When these men had the power, they abused it after the fashion of those whom they had been trained to respect. Under the pretext that certain acts were snares of the Devil and abominations to the Lord, they put in force a hateful system of interference with personal freedom. The Pilgrim Fathers were undoubtedly sincere, but they had the misfortune to be mistaken men. In due time their blunders were perceived and atoned for. The claims of the individual conscience were recognized as being subject to no other appeal than to the individual himself. The affairs of what was really a straight-laced theology, but was supposed to be religion, were eventually severed from the affairs of State.

Yet with this separation the ardour for promul-
gating and enforcing what was considered the truth
did not wax cold or die out. The Puritan spirit
survived the intolerant Puritan creed. The cause
for which the enlightened progeny of the original
settlers combated was happily in complete accord
with the precepts of world-honoured sages and the
conclusions of the greatest among philosophers.
In vindication of the immortal principles which
prescribe how absolute justice should be executed
between man and man, the citizens of Boston
were the chief instigators and the heroes of two
decisive and embittered conflicts, the first of which
established the independence of their country, the
second justified that independence by annihilating
slavery.

There is much in the early history of the settlers
in New England that seems to us utterly contemptible. The incessant wrangling about religious
dogmas and human duties, which constituted their
daily occupation during many years, appears to the
men of the nineteenth century quite as frivolous and
foolish as the controversies of the schoolmen. Yet
the talk was not all empty, nor were the discussions
all aimless. They necessarily implied and compelled
an acquaintance with subjects which education
could alone impart, and the controversies engen-

dered by the pulpit led to the foundation and main-
tenance of the school. The man who could not
read was a useless member of society. It was felt
that, in order to promote the objects which were
generally admitted to be laudable, the education of
the young was indispensable. Hence an impetus
was given to teaching which outlasted the special
reason whereon it was based. It became as much a
matter of course that the youth of Massachusetts
should cultivate their intellects as that they should
learn how to handle a gun or guide the plough.
The result is now beheld in the position which
mental attainments have enabled the citizens of
Boston to acquire despite the disproportion of
numbers and wealth. Their weight in the councils
of the Union is due to their indisputable superiority
in culture and learning.

Coming as I did from San Francisco, where
culture is the exception, to a city where it is the
rule, the transition was impressive and noteworthy.
On the Pacific coast I found that the men of wealth
cared for nothing but to heap up money, and would
not even aid in helping those who were labouring
to stock a library with the treasures of the mind.
Within sight of the Atlantic the reverse was the
fact. Merely to name the libraries in Boston would
fill much space, while to describe all that the

wisdom of the civic authorities and the munificence of individuals have done towards promoting the acquirement and increase of knowledge would require a volume. If then I would give any illustration of my statement, I must confine myself to a single case. Nor is it difficult to do this satisfactorily. Recent events have made the name of Harvard a familiar one to English ears. An account of what Harvard has been and now is may then be welcome to English readers, while serving as an example of the manner in which the citizens of Massachusetts have honoured and advanced the higher departments of learning.

Earl Bellamont, Governor of Massachusetts, said in his message to the General Court in 1699, ' It is a very great advantage you have above other provinces, that your youth are not put to travel for learning, but have the Muses at their doors.' This was intended as a high compliment to Harvard College, then the chief seminary of sound learning on the North American Continent. That college was neither young nor undistinguished at the time the Governor wrote. It was then sixty-three years old, and had been presided over by some of the most distinguished among the many able men who were engaged in founding on land reclaimed from the wilderness, and haunted by savages and wild beasts,

16

a new and a mighty England. Sixteen years after the Pilgrim Fathers disembarked at Plymouth Rock, the Legislature of the colony of Massachusetts Bay resolved to establish a college. A sum of money was set apart for the purpose. This resolution was as remarkable as it was wise and high-spirited. In one of the great speeches of the late Mr. Everett, the occasion was justly eulogised as the first ' on which a people ever taxed themselves to found a place of education.' The same renowned orator further said that Harvard College 'was an institution established by the people's means for the people's benefit,' and he was able to make the proud boast that at no period had Harvard ever been 'indebted to the Crown for a dollar or a book.' Yet Harvard owes a debt to England and Englishmen which she has never ceased to acknowledge with undissembled gratitude. The Rev. John Harvard, an English clergyman, who emigrated to America, took up his abode in the colony of Massachusetts, and died in 1638, bequeathed his library and the half of his fortune to the infant institution. The example was speedily followed, and money flowed in on all hands. Not long afterwards the name of the locality was changed from Newtown to Cambridge, in honour of the many Cambridge graduates, who, like Mr. Harvard, had thrown in their lot with the settlers. It has been estimated that in 1638 there was one Cambridge graduate to every 200 or 250 inhabitants of the New England villages. Hardly less memorable than this is the fact that the American offshoot from the grand old University which has done so much for the cause of English liberty, sent forth the earliest protest made in America against pusillanimous submission to the tyranny of the civil magistrate. Among the records in which the alumni of Harvard still take delight is one chronicling how, in 1743, Samuel Adams, when taking his degree, maintained the thesis, ' that it was lawful to resist the Chief Magistrate if the State cannot otherwise be preserved.'

It is not my design to write an elaborate historical sketch of the career of ' the University at Cambridge,' as Harvard College is designated in the constitution of the State of Massachusetts. Such an account would contain many statements not wholly creditable to those who, in bygone days, were in authority here. Like other seats of learning Harvard has had its share of jealousies fomented by rivalry and of dissensions having their root in theological differences. These, however, have neither checked the growth nor lessened the popularity of the University itself. Besides, they are events of days which have passed away, and possess little in-

terest for any one but the historian or the antiquary.
Nevertheless, before proceeding to speak of Harvard as she now is, a few extracts from official documents illustrative of what she was in olden times may prove useful and interesting. As in the statutes of our English universities, so in those of Harvard many of the provisions are admirable, while others appear harsh to modern readers, and ridiculous to modern students. For example, it is ordained in 'The Laws, Liberties, and Orders of Harvard College,' dated 1642-6, that the students 'shall be slow to speak, and eschew not only oaths, lies, and uncertain rumours, but likewise all idle, foolish, bitter, scoffing, frothy, wanton words, and offensive gestures;' that 'none shall pragmatically intrude or intermeddle in other men's affairs;' and that 'no scholar shall buy, sell, or exchange anything, to the value of sixpence, without the allowance of his parents, guardians, or tutors.' The last proviso seems to have been framed with a view to stifle that love for bargaining and bartering with which New Englanders have long been credited. The following is in still more direct opposition to the practical spirit which is universally regarded as the leading characteristic of Americans :—' The scholars shall never use their mother tongue, except that in public exercises of oratory, or such like,

they be called to make them in English.' In the orders issued by the overseers in 1650 there is the following prohibition against the use of tobacco:—
' No scholar shall take tobacco unless permitted by the president, with the consent of their parents or guardians, and on good reason first given by a physician, and then in a sober and private manner.' Quite as curious as these obsolete regulations are the successive changes which Harvard's motto has undergone. On the College Seal, made in 1642, the simple, yet significant word ' Veritas' was alone engraved. Subsequently, this was exchanged for the motto ' In Christo Gloriam,' and finally the present one was adopted, which is ' Christo et Ecclesiæ.' On the outside of one of the halls a facsimile in stone of the original seal is to be seen. The first four letters are inscribed on the inside of two open volumes; the last three are on the outside of a third volume. This has been ingeniously explained as indicating ' that no one human book contains the whole truth on any subject, and that in order to get at the real end of the matter we must be careful to look on both sides.' While nearly everything has undergone some change or a complete transformation throughout New England, the University at Cambridge is substantially the same now in spirit and fact as it was two centuries ago.

Old buildings remain to show to the present generation what manner of edifices their forefathers erected and occupied. In the proximity of halls over which centuries have passed are modern edifices in the style of a period which thinks quite as highly of ornament as of utility, or rather which strives to combine them both. Most striking among the latter is the library. This is a substantial stone building in the plain Gothic style. It contains nearly 200,000 volumes in every department of literature, the collection of scientific works being very large, and the collection of pamphlets being exceedingly valuable. Just as one Englishman gave a stimulus to the good work of founding Harvard College, so have other Englishmen contributed to increase the treasures of its library. The attention of the visitor from England is pointedly called to the munificent benefaction of Mr. Hollis, of Lincoln's Inn, an Englishman who, in the last century, enriched the library with his own splendid collection of books. His name, along with those of other distinguished donors and notable men, may be seen in conspicuous parts of the principal room. No hindrances are put in the way of non-students profiting by this fine library. With a liberality which cannot be too strongly commended or too widely imitated, the University authorities have treated their

library as the common property of thirsters after
knowledge, and have rendered access to it very easy
to all respectable persons. Speaking generally, it
may be said with truth that the system in operation
at Harvard is the same as that prevailing in our
Universities at home. One of the differences is the
method of teaching, which resembles that in vogue
at Edinburgh and other University cities of Scot-
land. The students are more youthful than English
undergraduates, and the professors teach more than
they lecture. Another essential difference is the
custom of regarding all the students who have
entered during the same year as belonging to one
class. The class does not cease to exist when the
University course is at an end. An honorary secre-
tary is elected, whose duty consists in compiling a
catalogue of the several members, with a short bio-
graphy of each. Once a year every one who thinks
fit to do so forwards such particulars as he may
deem interesting to his classmates. These records
are preserved, and when the class dies out the
whole of the documents are deposited among the
University archives. Being printed for private circulation only, the class lists are more minute in
their details than they might be were the information communicated to the public. Judging from
those which I have been permitted to inspect, I

may affirm with perfect confidence that the public does not always lose much which is really valuable by being kept in ignorance of what the members of each class think of themselves and of each other. If many of the facts communicated are worthy of record, others are so trivial as to merit oblivion. Amateur theatricals combine with boating to give the students scope for the display of their powers in other fields than those of science and the arts. How far proficiency on the stage contributes to a student's success in after life is a problem as difficult to solve as that which relates to the value of rowing as an element in University education. As the result of investigation, it may be asserted that the average number of reading men at Harvard is the same as that at the Universities of Europe. All the world over, a large proportion of young men has a decided taste for that kind of work which can with difficulty be distinguished from play.

A notice of Harvard would be as incomplete without a reference to the Porcellian Club as a notice of Oxford or Cambridge would be in which the Union Debating Society held no place. This and the Hasty Pudding Club, an association for performing amateur theatricals, are the two lions of Harvard. The Porcellian Club is hardly a place of resort for those who cultivate the intellect at the expense of the body. It is a very mundane and by no means unpleasant institution. The list of active members is small, owing in part to the largeness of the annual subscription. The great desire of every student is to become a member of it, or, in default, to learn what its members really do and enjoy. As the doings of the club are shrouded in secrecy, many curious stories are current on the subject. All that can be said by a stranger who has been privileged to step behind the scenes is that the mysteries are rites which can be practised without much labour, and yield a pleasure which is fraught with no unpleasant consequences. On the whole, the alumni of Harvard have good reason to glory in their ancient University. She has proved the fruitful mother of great men and of patriotic citizens. The roll of her teachers is studded with famous names. To the energy and enthusiasm of her teachers and graduates much of the vigour displayed in the heroic struggle for American independence, and much of the foresight and wisdom manifested by the framers of the American Constitution, are unquestionably due. Nor did the second great contest, when the issue between justice and tyranny was again fought out in the war which slaveholders began and in which slavery was extinguished, find the University at Cambridge an unconcerned spectator. There is something irresistibly touching in the stories, told without ostentation but with justifiable pride, of the students who went forth to serve as eager volunteers in the ranks of the great National army. Of these many fell on the battlefield, others perished in the camp, while few lived to return home unscarred and sound in limb.

In one respect, the Harvard College of to-day is far in advance of what it was two centuries since. For those who profess different creeds there is now a latitude and kindly toleration such as the early Puritan settlers neither practised nor understood. In other respects the transformation has been complete. The unbending and gloomy Calvinism of the first settlers has been repudiated by their descendants. While all religious sects are represented here, the religion of the majority is that liberal, tolerant, and rational creed which is professed by Unitarians.

If Harvard University owes much to the Englishman who bequeathed to her the larger portion of his substance—a gift she has amply acknowledged, to use the late Mr. Everett's words, by giving to ' an unknown stranger a deathless name '—she has also done much to conquer the admiration of all who speak and honour the English tongue. While the alumni of Harvard demonstrate their daring and prowess in friendly rivalry with their English brethren, it is meet that the latter should visit the oldest and most famous among the Universities of America, for by so doing they would find much to admire, something to learn, and many things in which to glory.

XXV.

NEW YORK TO EUSTON SQUARE.

THE PACIFIC RAILWAY was primarily designed
to link the Atlantic and Pacific shores of the United
States. That passengers and produce should be
carried with the greatest possible speed between the
principal cities of California and Oregon and those
of the Middle and Eastern States is what everyone
who had at heart the development of the internal
resources and the commerce of the country felt
naturally bound to further. The railway is a means
towards the accomplishment of the desired result.
But it has also been regarded as an instrument for
the promotion of a still grander object. It is supposed to be destined to revolutionize the commerce
of the world by affording increased facilities for
the reciprocal transference of goods and passengers
between China, Japan, Australia, and Europe. The
nearest way from Paris or London to Yokohama,
Shanghae, or Sidney is said to lie across the
Atlantic, the Continent of America and the Pacific

Ocean.   An important element in any calculation
relating to the subject is the certainty of the journey
being completed within a specified time.   This
matter is one still open to speculation.   There is
no question that, if existing arrangements were
carried out to the letter, the value of the new route
would be demonstrated.   For my own part I cannot
maintain that the traveller who puts his trust in
time-tables, whether these relate to steam-boats or
railway trains, exhibits a well-founded confidence.

When I journeyed from New York to San
Francisco the time occupied was nearly a day longer
than the allotted period.   The same thing occurred
on the return journey.   The traveller whose destination is not New York but London must take note of
another consideration.   He probably has a decided
preference for one out of the many lines of steamers
which make the passage across the Atlantic.   If
forced by circumstances to be economical, his chief
desire will be to travel at the cheapest rate, yet he
may not wish to forego comfort.   If he be one of
the favoured few who need take no thought about
money, he will probably yearn to secure his personal safety.   The outlay necessary to secure a
first-class passage ranges from thirteen guineas to
twenty-six pounds, according to the Company which
is patronized.   Although a steamer is said to sail

daily from New York, yet there is generally the interval of a week, and sometimes of a fortnight, between the days of sailing of the vessels belonging to a particular Company. When these facts are duly considered it becomes clear that to journey from San Francisco to London with entire satisfaction in the space of eighteen days is a feat much more easily performed on paper than in reality.

When New York is the place whence the traveller begins his Atlantic voyage, the opportunities for examining the steam-ships of the several shipping lines prior to engaging a berth are greater than those which can be enjoyed elsewhere. The vessels which sail from Bremen and Hamburg, Brest and London, Liverpool and Glasgow, all take up their moorings at one of the wharves on the North River. To those who are unbiassed by national prejudices, and uninfluenced by pecuniary considerations or personal prepossessions the variety of choice is almost too great. First comes the Cunard line with its high fares and high reputation. Second on the list is the Inman line which is struggling to rival the Cunard by making more rapid voyages, and which charges lower fares. The Guion and the National lines are of more recent date and rely for patronage rather upon lowness of charge than upon rapidity of passage. The steamers of these lines sail to

Liverpool, touching at Queenstown. Those of the Anchor line touch at Londonderry, on the way to Glasgow. The steamers of the Hamburg and New York line touch at Plymouth and Brest when voyaging between the cities of which the names form its designation, while those of the North German Lloyd touch at Southampton on the way between New York and Bremen. The London and New York line has a fortnightly service between the Thames and the Hudson, while the *Compagnie Transatlantique* conveys passengers between Brest and New York. In this list the name of an American steamship company does not appear, for the conclusive reason that no such company exists. The carrying trade as well as the passenger traffic across the Atlantic is in English, German, or French hands; even the mails of the United States being transported in foreign vessels. That this should be the case is due not to deficiency in enterprise, but to the ascendency of a system which is supposed to give protection to the native industry and to the shipping interests of the American people. At present the shipbuilders of the Clyde can supply iron steamships at lower prices than the shipbuilders of any other part of the world. Nearly all the companies named above have had their vessels built on the banks of the Clyde. Even the French shipowner has found it profitable to purchase British-built iron steamers. But the American shipowner cannot do this if he would. Consequently, he is at a disadvantage when compared with his foreign rivals. They are free to make contracts which redound to their profit, while he is so carefully protected against using his own discretion as to be helpless to perform that which he deems the best for himself. The political freedom enjoyed by the citizens of the United States has made their country the envy of less favoured nations and one of the wonders of the world. When the enlightened policy of free exchange shall be substituted for the mediæval policy of protection, not only will the condition of the American people be vastly improved, but the progress of their country will be even more rapid than it has been, while the admiration of those who watch and welcome its advance will be all the greater and all the more sincere.

A countryman and travelling companion, whose attachment to the flag and liking for the Cunard line were too strong to be overcome by the temptation of novelty even when presented in the form of German steamers famed for the comfort of their arrangements, having resolved to return home in the *Cuba*, I took my passage in that steamer also. It is noteworthy how those who frequently cross the

Atlantic acquire preferences for certain steam-ships.
They do this for the same reason that a traveller returns to the hotel at which he is specially welcome
because there he is personally known. An Atlantic
steam-boat is but a floating hotel, and acquaintance
with those who are permanently on board ensures
an amount of attention for which the new-comer
looks in vain. Some Americans who were among
my fellow passengers spoke strongly in favour of
the *Cuba*. They had sailed in her at different
seasons of the year and when on board felt less
apprehension for their safety than when in other
steamers or when in a railway train. She had not
a reputation for speed; but she was a good seaboat.
Starting an hour after the *Colerado*, a vessel belonging to the Guion line, we had an opportunity of
seeing which was the more rapid sailer. The
struggle was not a long one, nor was the race hotly
contested. In nautical phrase the *Cuba* walked
away from the *Colerado*.

The incidents of the voyage were too unimportant
to merit special notice. Most striking of them all was
an Atlantic gale lasting two days. The prodigious
mass of water which unceasingly rolls over the lofty
rocks at Niagara is supposed to convey one of the
best examples of irresistible power to be seen in
Nature. I cannot but think, however, that the

ocean heaving and foaming under the influence of a gale is a spectacle quite as imposing and majestic. The mighty sweep of the limitless waves appears fraught with ruin to everything in their path. As the infuriated wind shrieks and battles with the rising billows, the insignificance of man is the thought which takes possession of the mind only to be expelled however by the proud reflection that the powers of the air and the water are put at defiance by the vessel which triumphantly keeps her course and thus demonstrates the perfection of man's handi-work and extent of human resources.

The progress of invention has given to man the empire over the sea, but it has not yet enabled him uniformly to enjoy his triumph. To but a small minority is it given to take pleasure in a sea-voyage and to laugh at the very notion of being painfully affected by the motion of a vessel. Dr. Chapman has proclaimed that if his remedy of applying ice, enclosed in an India-rubber bag, to the spinal cord were universally adopted by those who are subject to sea-sickness, the malady would be almost unknown. But the sufferers commonly refuse to adopt any plan which does not accord with their own views. Each one has his private panacea. On board the *Cuba* I witnessed some experiments in this line which were at least novel. One passenger had implicit faith in port wine, freely administered. He bore bravely up for two days and then was seen no more. Another had perfect confidence in hot West Indian pickles mixed with potatoes. Of this compound he ate heartily and he alleged that it did him good. Appearances prompted another conclusion. A third said that there was nothing like marmalade and of this he took large quantities after every meal. More noteworthy than the remedies themselves was the childlike belief which those who employed them manifested in their efficacy. If sea-sickness could be cured by faith, then sea-sickness ought never to affect a large number of persons. The majority, however, generally learn by agonizing experience that Neptune is a deity neither to be offended with impunity nor propitiated with ease. Nowhere but at sea can the minority who are always well, practically appreciate the nature of the satisfaction which, according to Lucretius and Rochefoucauld, is the most perfect that human beings can enjoy, the satisfaction of being in rude health and entire comfort while others are living pictures of woe, and are bearing witness by their acts to the truth of Sir Thomas Overbury's saying that the sea is a 'moving misery.'

It is so common to praise the steamers of the Cunard Company, and these steamers are in many respects so admirable, that the duty of pointing out defects has been considered too invidious a one to be discharged willingly. In consequence of this the managers of that company may remain entirely ignorant of minor, but not unimportant, complaints made by passengers in their steam-boats. One of these is not applicable to the Cunarders alone, yet that is no excuse for the arrangements of these steamers being open to the strictures which I am about to make. When the passage-money is paid, the steward's fee is professedly included in the amount. This plan commends itself to most persons, as it saves trouble and obviates annoyance should the contract be rigidly carried out on both sides. In reality, however, the payment is a sham, or an imposition. If no steward's fee were included in the passage-money, a saving would be effected to the extent of at least one sovereign. The cabin steward, the saloon steward, and a personage calling himself boots, all make it clear that they expect fees. Payments made under these circumstances are simply black mail levied in modern guise. It is reasonable that if extra trouble be given, an extra payment should be made; but in no case should money be handed directly to the servants. The purser is the proper person through whose hands permissible gratuities should pass, or a box might be provided to contain the sums which

might be contributed voluntarily, the total being divided pro rata among all those entitled to share in
the distribution. There are other matters which the
company would do well to consider with a view to
rendering their steamers as comfortable as they are
safe. What these are I shall not specify; if the company desire to learn further particulars, let them send
an agent during one voyage, and report what the passengers say openly and without reticence. It would
be wise not to treat these things with contempt, for
competitors are pressing close on the heels of the
Cunard Company. In many points of detail the
steamers of the German lines are arranged with
far more consideration for the convenience and comfort of passengers, than are the finest among the
Cunarders.

On arriving at Euston-square after a journey
which, if not unbroken, was yet very rapidly made
from San Francisco to London, the mind naturally
dwells on the railway which has rendered such a
journey possible. Regarded as a whole the Pacific
Railway is a great triumph of engineering skill and
patriotic enterprise. It will contribute as much to
consolidate and perpetuate the Union as the most
splendid and thorough of Grant's victories, either
as soldier or statesman.

Even more satisfactory than the fact that the

Pacific Railway has virtually opened out a new country, as well as provided a new route to the East, is the stimulus it has given to continue and extend the work of which its originators were the daring and devoted pioneers. A second line through Kansas will soon be completed, thus opening up the country to the south of the present one. A third line is in contemplation which will open up the country to the north of it, bringing traffic from Lake Superior to the mouth of the Columbia River. In this rivalry the Canadians are about to take part. A line has been projected which will bring Halifax as near to Victoria as New York is to San Francisco. This line will traverse the Dominion of Canada from ocean to ocean and render millions of acres of the richest land in the known world accessible to the emigrant and adapted for the settler. As a route to the East, the Canadian Pacific Railway will shorten the distance between Liverpool and Hong Kong by 700 miles, compared with any other railway traversing the Continent of America. Thus, the three greatest enterprises of recent years —the Atlantic Cable, the Pacific Railway, the Suez Canal—are of inestimable value as examples as well as achievements. The success in each case has led to the prosecution of undertakings which would otherwise have long continued to be mere projects, exciting the derision of the foolish and the doubts of the prudent. It is a good omen for the future of humanity that England, France, and America, should have become vigorous rivals in works far more worthy to be praised than the competition which aims at covering the sea with iron-clad men-of-war, and the land with soldiers armed to the teeth, works of which the good is never interred with the bones of those who have aided in their achievement, but survives and operates to make the race of man happier by rendering the globe more habitable.

XXVI.

IMPRESSIONS AND OPINIONS OF AMERICA

'What do you think of America?' 'How did you like the Americans?' These two questions were frequently put to me, after returning home from the United States. Possibly, the readers of the foregoing pages may not object if the substance of the replies which I made, is appended to this volume by way of conclusion. The answers which I shall furnish must necessarily be short and superficial. All that I profess to do is to note one or two salient points and comment on some unmistakeable peculiarities. To do more would fill a volume. Adequately to do as much, within the narrow compass of a few pages, is a task of no small difficulty.

Great interest has always been felt throughout the United Kingdom about the condition and destiny of the vigorous off-shoot which has rapidly waxed great on the American continent. In order to gratify this natural and praiseworthy curiosity many English travellers have paid visits to the United States and placed on record their experiences and their prognostications. Unfortunately the anxiety to compose a saleable work has been more apparent than the determination to produce a fair and accurate one. Hence it is that English books of travel in America are for the most part either bundles of prejudices artistically arranged, or else deliberate caricatures skilfully drawn.

The circumstance that the Americans are living and active incarnations of modern Republicanism, is an element in the calculation which has had undue influence in moulding the conclusions of some English visitors to their land. Even among educated men in the United Kingdom there lurks the silly and baleful notion that all English-speaking Republicans are dangerous animals; semi-lunatics or utter knaves; human gorillas imperfectly tamed and wholly uncivilized. For the Republicans of antiquity and for Republics which have foundered in the seas of time are manifested true admiration and fervent sympathy. Nor is it impossible to find several persons of note who will admit that Frenchmen and Spaniards are justified in preferring a Republican form of government to a cruel and grinding despotism.

In the case of the Swiss an exception is always unreservedly made. The patriotism which inspired the fabulous deeds of William Tell, the proximity to a mountain so famous as Mont Blanc, or some

17

occult reason, has surrounded the Swiss with a halo of romance, and caused those who abominate the very name of a Republic to approve of such a Republic as that of Switzerland. The reasons commonly assigned for the approbation bestowed upon the form of government in existence among the Swiss are that Switzerland is a small country, is sparsely populated, is inhabited by a frugal and industrious people, and is very mountainous. These reasons are deemed conclusive, chiefly because they are supposed to justify the remark that, in a country of vast area and containing a population as large as that of the United Kingdom, the Republic established there is either a 'bubble' destined to burst, or the precursor of anarchy. I have been unable to discern a tittle of evidence confirmatory of these views. The tokens of failure do not lie on the surface. It is impossible for any one who is not the slave to foregone conclusions to travel through the United States and converse with persons of every rank in the social and intellectual scale without becoming convinced that the system of government prevailing there, a system which has its basis in the possession of brains and disregards altogether the accidents of birth, is a system at once popular and efficient, and that, if imperfect in minor details, it is as a whole a finely devised and carefully co-ordinated scheme for the government of the people by the people.

This opinion will be regarded in some quarters as rank heresy. It does not accord with the conclusions of many able writers. The statements of some recent travellers may be used to refute my conclusions. These travellers would be entitled to the greater weight as authorities if they had proved themselves capable of arguing logically and desirous of chronicling facts with impartiality. One of them passed an adverse judgment upon Republican institutions because he got a bad bed-room in the best New York hotel and because he detested the street and railway cars. Another writer has insidiously endeavoured to discredit the Great Republic by giving unfair prominence, in his description of what he strangely christened 'New America,' to some abnormal phases of pseudo-religious life, and by inducing his readers to infer that the most discreditable and profligate aberrations of sexual relationship constitute all that is characteristic of American society. Still more recently, a gentleman who journeyed over a large portion of the world in order to test mankind by a new standard, has drawn a ghastly picture of the Republic of the West. In the opinion of this writer, wherever pew-rents are charged, there everything is out of joint.

When he found pew-rents in combination with Republicanism he was obliged to ransack the language for terms of vituperation sufficiently strong wherewith to testify his abhorrence and disgust. Writers whom their friends deem merely eccentric and perfectly harmless may yet be able, if gifted with a command of invective and trained to wield the pen, to work more mischief than the wisest can ever repair.

While convinced as to the worthless or mischievous character of many books written about the United States, I am ready to admit that some American citizens act in a way which occasions misunderstanding and provokes retaliation. Their insolent assumption of superiority irritates and offends not a few. In addition to vaunting the perfection of the system of government founded by their predecessors, they foolishly sneer at and wantonly revile the systems in force elsewhere. While on the one hand, the prejudiced native of the Old World dislikes arrangements of which the inherent defect is their novelty; on the other, the uncultured citizen of the United States scoffs at the institutions of the United Kingdom simply on account of their antiquity. The one thinks that everything new must be bad; the other that everything old must be rotten. What I deplore is the disposition frequently manifested on both sides to be captious and critical rather than to study and comprehend, the readiness to decide on insufficient data, the dislike to make allowance for unavoidable imperfections. Each is apt to be offended if the expected flattery be withheld. Both naturally resent what is styled good advice, but which in reality is veiled malice. This kind of good advice is hardly less dangerous than the proverbial good intentions. If administered too freely, or inopportunely, it creates a hell of which the existence cannot be excused by saying that the supply of pavement is ample.

The English traveller in America has reason to take special note of the hotels. They materially differ from what he has seen either at home or on the Continent of Europe. For convenience of arrangement the first-class American hotel is unrivalled. Everything the visitor may require is within his reach. Shops of various kinds are generally in communication with the spacious entrance hall, while within that hall is an office whence telegrams may be sent off, and where railway tickets may be purchased. In one respect the English first-class hotel is preferable. It generally has, what the American has not, a reading-room containing, in addition to the daily newspapers, the weekly journals, monthly magazines, and quarterly reviews. The reading-room in an American hotel is meagrely supplied with newspapers, the frequenter being expected to buy his newspaper or periodical at the adjoining book-stall. Another drawback is that the American hotel is designed as much for the accommodation of the lounger as for the reception of the traveller. The idle public of the city makes free use of the entrance hall and reading-room, monopolizing the fireplace in winter and the seats near the window in summer. As a rule, bachelors, and married men travelling without their wives, get the worst rooms in all hotels; but in an American hotel they are treated with marked disrespect. The rooms set apart for them are in striking contrast to those which married couples are allowed to occupy without paying more for the superior accommodation. Making this fact the foundation of a theory, the ingenious speculator might advance a new explanation of the early marriages for which Americans are remarkable.

Travelling by rail has become very luxurious in several States, while, in others, it is a very fatiguing means of locomotion. The Western States are gradually teaching those of the East to carry passengers from place to place in perfect comfort. Nothing can be less agreeable than the ordinary

American railroad car: no carriage is more admirable than the car which has given to Mr. Pullman wealth and fame. Why an English railway company should not try the experiment of running some of these sleeping or drawing-room cars is a mystery to which I can find no clue. If it be said that the distances are too short, I answer that five hours in a railway carriage need not necessarily be hours of torture. The journey between London and Edinburgh, Glasgow, Aberdeen, and Inverness is surely long enough to warrant the employment of the improved carriage. Such a carriage is used when the Queen journeys from Windsor to Balmoral. Now, that provided for her use is neither more sumptuously decorated, nor more commodiously arranged than the best of Mr. Pullman's cars. To travel in them involves payment of an additional charge. This extra fare is cheerfully paid in America. Is it probable that Englishmen would refuse to buy luxury on the rail if they had the option? Besides, the system has been found to be not only popular but remunerative. The shareholders in 'Pullman's Car Company' receive dividends at the rate of 12 per cent. If one of these cars were shown at the Exhibition of Works of Utility to be held next year at South Kensington, the English public would blush to perceive that in this matter they have been surpassed, and would form an opinion most favourable to the spirit and enterprise of the active citizens of Chicago.

The observant and unprejudiced visitor who has spent a few days in the United States begins to doubt the correctness of what he has read about the manners and appearance of the people. After the experience of a few weeks his new notions become more precise and appear still more plausible. The result of a few months' travel and scrutiny is to transform his earlier views altogether and make him feel that, in trusting certain travellers, he has been the victim of misplaced confidence. As for the repulsive Yankee of the novelist he is nowhere to be met with in the flesh. He has apparently been evolved out of the novelist's consciousness. The typical American has not yet been sketched with the writer's pen or the artist's pencil. This is not surprising, for the task is one of which the difficulty is only second to that involved in portraying the typical European. The external marks and latent variations which separate and characterise Englishmen, Frenchmen, Germans, Spaniards, and Italians are scarcely more distinctive than those which separate the native of Maine from the native of South Carolina; the native of Ohio or Illinois from the native of Connecticut; the native of Massachusetts from the native of Texas, California, or Oregon. All of them are citizens of the United States, but each is an American with a difference. The type must include and express both the points of agreement and the points of dissimilarity, and I repeat that such a type has yet to be exhibited to the world by the word-painter or the draughtsman. If Mr. 'Punch' would make a note of this he might hereafter gratify his admirers not only with exquisitely drawn cartoons, but also with a typical American as true to nature as is his typical Frenchman or German.

It is as great a blunder to group Americans under one category as to confound the Highlander of Skye with the Cornish miner, the London cockney with the Dublin Irishman. No one acquainted with the French would regard the Frenchmen who perambulate Regent Street or Leicester Square as worthy representatives of the quick-witted, mercurial and polished Parisians, while able to trace a likeness between them and the swaggering and boastful Gascons. Now the discrimination to be exercised in such a case as this should also be displayed when opinions are passed upon Americans travelling in Europe. Some of them have no claim whatsoever to represent their country. Probably they have become enriched by speculation. The discovery of a petroleum spring or the possession of a fat army contract may have suddenly filled their pockets to overflowing. They have got wealth, but no manners; they have the desire to shine, but cannot do so at home. The best American society is as exclusive as that of London, Paris, or Vienna. Foreign adventurers may gain admittance into it; but the native upstart is carefully excluded. The latter has no choice but to seek in Europe that which he cannot obtain at home. In the twofold capacity of a rich man and an American citizen he is welcomed everywhere; his bad-breeding being laid to the charge of Republicanism; his wealth being attributed to the possession on his part of extraordinary abilities. At the fashionable watering places of Germany during the summer and at the fashionable resorts in the south of France and Italy during the winter these men, accompanied by their underbred wives and ill-bred children, are to be seen in all the glory of upstart millionaires. Highly paid couriers rob them and translate for them. They occupy the most expensive rooms in the hotels; eat the delicacies which are not in season; drink wines of the rarest vintage. They are the targets for criticism and scorn as they loll in splendid carriages alongside of their wives resplendent in dresses of the newest fashion and glistening with gems of great price. These men can sign their names and write intelligible letters. Newspapers they can read and enjoy. But of culture they are bereft, and of manners they have not even a varnish. To regard these blustering and unattractive members of the 'Petroleum' or 'Shoddy Aristocracy' as anything but Americans in name, is to err in a way of which the grossness cannot be adequately apprehended by anyone who has not visited the United States and formed the acquaintance of Americans in the land of their birth.

The notion prevails that the Americans are far too free and easy in manner to please the fastidious stranger. It is true that they often shake hands. This, however, is a custom which has no special significance. It resembles what the French designate 'hat-politeness.' An American cordially shakes hands with those whom he does not care to meet on terms of intimacy. Introductions are made with great formality; utterance is given to the pleasure which it gives the one to make the acquaintance of the other, while, should they see each other again, they may appear to be perfect strangers. In the Western States the old English custom of interspersing sentences with 'Sir,' a custom which, in high-bred Eastern circles, has almost died out, is still in force and the observance of it supposed to be the mark of good breeding.

English words are often used in America to signify something different from that which they convey to an English ear. A list of these words would show the inevitable change which is being wrought in the language. These alterations in meaning, accompanied by deliberate alterations in spelling, must sooner or later make the order which the Emperor Nicholas, when enraged against England, gave to substitute the teaching of American for English, one which it will be easy to obey. For my own part I am unable to side with those who profess to be shocked at the alleged deterioration of the English language in America; nor can I see the propriety of taking the people to task on account of their accent. A great deal too much has been made of this trivial detail. In itself it is a matter of no moment whatever. Moreover, neither side will convince the other, nor will denunciation of the American accent alter it one iota. The American climate has attuned the American voice. Nor is the accent uniform. It varies in different States. In New England the voice is sharp and shrill; in the South slow and liquid; in the West deep-toned and resonant. Indeed, the differences in this respect are as notable as those which exist between

the accent of a Londoner, of a native of Dublin, of
a native of Edinburgh. The like variation is ob-
servable in other countries also. The pronunciation
of a Parisian is in marked contrast to that of a
native of Alsace, Provence, or Auvergne. A
trained ear has little difficulty in noting the peculiarities of accent which distinguish the native of
Hanover from the native of Frankfort or Leipsic,
Berlin or Vienna. There is nothing new, though
there is something very contemptible in interna-
tional jealousies being cherished on account of the
way in which the identical language is spoken by
those who owe allegiance to different flags. Yet the
aversion which Frenchmen exhibit to the Swiss
and the Belgians is partly due to the supposition
that the French of Geneva and Brussels is a bastard
tongue.

There is, however, another side to the question
which has been wholly overlooked. Strangely enough
the purists who are displeased with the accent and
English of Americans have taken no thought of
the consequences which might ensue were it impossible to tell an Englishman from an American as
soon as either had uttered a few words. Sometimes
this difference is so slight as to escape detection,
and then Americans hear statements which are
more frank than flattering. When the war raged

certain northern gentlemen of great influence in the councils of the nation were travelling for their health in Europe and were thus brought into contact with those eccentric British tourists who excite the wonder of foreigners and are a disgrace to their country. The latter being ignorant of the nationality of those with whom they conversed in their mother tongue gave expression to sentiments which did not increase the admiration of the Americans for the part played by the United Kingdom. Misadventures of this kind have had results much more serious than might have been expected. So far from regretting that the language spoken in the United Kingdom should not be the exact counterpart of that spoken in the United States, I am certain that, the greater the divergence within reasonable limits, the better will it be for all parties.

From points about which travellers differ, it is a pleasure to turn to one about which there has been, and must be perfect unanimity. The beauty of the women is without the pale of controversy. It cannot be likened to the beauty for which English girls are deservedly and universally admired ; for which Italian maidens have been immortalized on canvas or in verse ; for which the sprightly damsels of France and the coquettish ladies of Spain have won applause and by means of which they have made conquests. If I were to select a particular locality in the United States, I might truthfully compare the type of beauty predominant there to that of a particular country in the Old World. But America is a world in itself. Within the bounds of the Republic of the West are all the climates which give diversity to Europe, from Rome to Copenhagen and from London to Madrid. Where climates vary, female faces vary also. In New England may be seen those delicately chiselled features and transparent complexions which in Europe are characteristic of the fascinating beauties of the North. In the Southern States the imperious and indolent Spanish women, with their amorous eyes and raven hair, have been reproduced at the distance of many thousand miles from Andalusia and Castile. Let the traveller cross the continent till the Pacific slope is reached, and there the soft and delicate beauty of Italy, combined with an intelligence wholly American and a physique wholly English, delights and surprises him. Nor are good looks the sole dower of American girls. They are more French than English in the acuteness with which they argue. They are passionately fond of the frivolities of existence, yet they follow with interest the course of the graver topics of the day. On political questions they are ready to take sides, and they discuss the issues involved in a controversy with zest and understanding. Their patriotism is not a profession, but a passion. The intensity of their devotion to their country imparted superhuman vigour to the struggle when North and South faced each other in battle array. The women of the South were the soul of the Confederacy. The women of the North saved the Union. If the women of America were more kindly disposed towards England, the relations between the two countries, at this moment, would be more cordial and more secure.

While misunderstandings are rife in Europe about the American people, mistakes quite as serious are commonly made with regard to the American press. The opinion of the entire country is supposed to be represented by the press of New York, or rather by a few New York newspapers. At one time there was an excuse for entertaining such an opinion, but that time has long since passed away. No one American newspaper is entitled to the rank of a national organ. Each expresses the views of well-defined sections; of particular interests; of individuals whose personal crotchets inspire respect or excite curiosty.

In this respect the press of New York differs

essentially from the press of London. The news-papers which guide and instruct Englishmen are in no sense of the word the organs of those who con duct them. One editor may give place to another without any variation in the courses of *The Times*, *The Daily News*, or *The Standard*. Under all circumstances and at all conjunctures *The Times* will strive to mirror the public opinion of the moment; *The Daily News* will uphold the doctrines of progress; *The Standard* will defend and repre-sent the principles of conservatism. On any given question the line which each is sure to take may be predicted beforehand with a confidence amounting to certainty. A sudden and unexpected conversion would be fatal to the newspaper's reputation. The positions of each may vary, while the relative dis-tance between each remains unaltered. To employ Macaulay's illustration;—the tail may appear to have taken the place of the head yet the space between the head and tail is the same to an hair's breadth.

Newspapers like the *New York Times*, *Tribune*, and *Herald* are managed on a plan totally dif-ferent. The conductor of each is known to the public. The opinions of the editor constitute the policy of the paper. When Mr. Raymond was alive, the side which the *New York Times* took during a presidential campaign, or on a question of national policy, was the side which Mr. Raymond was known to favour. Should Mr. Horace Greely crown his noble career by an honourable recantation of Protectionist heresies, *The Tribune* would at once become the ardent apostle of Free Trade. When Mr. Bennett has a friend to serve or a grudge to revenge, *The Herald* is a powerful instrument for giving effect to his wish in either case. What injures an American journal the most is not inconsistency, but ill-success in collecting news. Readers are indifferent to the tone or quality of the leading article so long as the latest intelligence is complete and trustworthy. The telegraphic despatches which, in our newspapers fill a column, often fill an entire page in an American newspaper. Owing to the personal nature and local influence of these journals many false impressions are made on those who, in Europe, look to any one for an index of national opinion. If the desire be entertained to trace the current and estimate the character of American thought by studying the press, the research must not be confined to a single New York journal, or terminate when all the journals of that city have been scrutinized, but must be extended to the leading journals of Boston and Philadelphia, of Richmond and Cincinnati, of Chicago and San Francisco, and even then it will be wise to hesitate before pronouncing a decision which may be vitiated by the error of mistaking a part for the whole.

Nothing gratified me more than the feeling of kindliness towards the Old Country which I found pervading the American people. The bitter and undying animosity about which much has been written exists on paper only, or in the distempered minds of irreconcilable Fenians. In this particular the press is not a faithful exponent of the public sentiment. A disposition to construe in the worst sense all the actions of the United Kingdom and to discredit her on every occasion and in every imaginable way, is certainly the characteristic of the press of New York. I believe this to be mere sound and fury wholly devoid of significance. It is the relic of a traditionary policy, rather than the token of a living and active hostility. To find a parallel to it, we have not far to seek. Long after the English people were on a footing of amity with the French, the tone of the press towards France was little more friendly and complimentary than in the days when it was the bad fashion to style Frenchmen our hereditary foes. The change in public opinion has now been responded to by the press of England, while that of France, reluctant to allow old jealousies to subside into oblivion, still harps on the imaginary plots and intrigues of perfidious Albion.

The Americans certainly entertain the belief that the United Kingdom has often been unjust towards their country and was wilfully unkind in the hour of her sore tribulation. Moreover, there is an indisposition on their parts to give a cool hearing to any explanations which may serve to render the grievance of America less clear and substantial. That the matter can have two sides is what few Americans readily admit: that the one party should be altogether in the wrong and the other altogether in the right seems to them a defensible position to assume. Notwithstanding a state of things alike painful and complicated, I consider that it is within the power of English and American statesmen to find the key of the puzzle and to agree to an arrangement which would both settle existing differences in an honourable and equitable way, and also ensure increased harmony in the future.*

That an amicable adjustment of grievances and a close alliance in opinion and policy should be effected between the United Kingdom and the United

* This is not the place to discuss in detail the problems which cluster round the Alabama claims. Besides, I have done so elsewhere. Any reader who cares to learn the nature of my conclusions has but to turn to the *Westminster Review* for January, 1870, and read an article entitled 'American Claims on England.'

States must be the ardent desire of any one who, like myself, being fondly attached to his own country and glorying in her renown, has had the advantage of traversing the greater portion of the magnificent continent of America, has enjoyed special opportunities for witnessing the working of the government, and has profited by conversations with all sections and classes of its energetic and high-spirited inhabitants.

THE END.

States must be the ardent desire of any one who, like myself, being fondly attached to his own country and glorying in her renown, has had the advantage of traversing the greater portion of the magnificent continent of America, has enjoyed special opportunities for witnessing the working of the government, and has profited by conversations with all sections and classes of its energetic and high-spirited inhabitants.

THE END.

THE ORIGIN OF SPECIES,

By CHARLES DARWIN.

A new American edition of "The Origin of Species," later than the latest English edition, has just been published, with the author's most recent corrections and additions.

In the whole history of the progress of knowledge there is no case so remarkable of a system of doctrines, at first generally condemned as false and absurd, coming into general acceptance in the scientific world in a single decade. From the following statements, the reader will infer the estimate that is now placed upon the man and his works by the highest authorities.

"Personally and practically exercised in zoology, in minute anatomy, in geology; a student of geographical distribution, not on maps and in museums only, but by long voyages and laborious collection; having largely advanced each of these branches of science, and having spent many years in gathering and sifting materials for his present work, the store of accurately-registered facts upon which the author of the 'Origin of Species' is able to draw at will is prodigious."—Prof. T. H. HUXLEY.

"Far abler men than myself may confess that they have not that untiring patience in accumulating, and that wonderful skill in using, large masses of facts of the most varied kind—that wide and accurate physiological knowledge—that acuteness in devising, that skill in carrying out experiments, and that admirable style of composition, at once clear, persuasive, and judicial, qualities which, in their harmonious combination, mark out Mr. Darwin as the man, perhaps of all men now living, best fitted for the great work he has undertaken and accomplished."—ALFRED RUSSELL WALLACE.

In Germany these views are rapidly extending. Prof. GIEKIE, a distinguished British geologist, attended the recent Congress of German Naturalists and Physicians, at Innspruck, in which some eight hundred *savants* were present, and thus writes:

"What specially struck me was the universal sway which the writings of Darwin now exercise over the German mind. You see it on every side, in private conversation, in printed papers, in all the many sections into which such a meeting as that at Innspruck divides. Darwin's name is often mentioned, and always with the profoundest veneration. But even where no allusion is specially made to him, nay, even more markedly, where such allusion is absent, we see how thoroughly his doctrines have permeated the scientific mind, even in those departments of knowledge which might seem at first sight to be farthest from natural history. 'You are still discussing in England,' said a German friend to me, 'whether or not the theory of Darwin can be true. We have got a long way beyond that here. His theory is now our common starting-point.' And, so far as my experience went, I found it to be so."

D. APPLETON & CO., Publishers.

THE ORIGIN OF CIVILIZATION;

OR, THE

PRIMITIVE CONDITION OF MAN.

By SIR JOHN LUBBOCK, Bart., M. P., F. R. S.

380 Pages. Illustrated.

This interesting work is the fruit of many years' research by an accomplished naturalist, and one well trained in modern scientific methods, into the mental, moral, and social condition of the lowest savage races. The want of a work of this kind had long been felt, and, as scientific methods are being more and more applied to questions of humanity, there has been increasing need of a careful and authentic work describing the conditions of those tribes of men who are lowest in the scale of development.

"This interesting work—for it is intensely so in its aim, scope, and the ability of its author—treats of what the scientists denominate *anthropology*, or the natural history of the human species; the complete science of man, body and soul, including sex, temperament, race, civilization, etc."—*Providence Press.*

"A work which is most comprehensive in its aim, and most admirable in its execution. The patience and judgment bestowed on the book are everywhere apparent; the mere list of authorities quoted giving evidence of wide and impartial reading. The work, indeed, is not only a valuable one on account of the opinions it expresses, but it is also most serviceable as a book of reference. It offers an able and exhaustive table of a vast array of facts, which no single student could well obtain for himself, and it has not been made the vehicle for any special pleading on the part of the author."—*London Athenæum.*

"The book is no cursory and superficial review; it goes to the very heart of the subject, and embodies the results of all the later investigations. It is replete with curious and quaint information presented in a compact, luminous, and entertaining form."—*Albany Evening Journal.*

"The treatment of the subject is eminently practical, dealing more with fact than theory, or perhaps it will be more just to say, dealing only with theory amply sustained by fact."—*Detroit Free Press.*

"This interesting and valuable volume illustrates, to some extent, the way in which the modern scientific spirit manages to extract a considerable treasure from the chaff and refuse neglected or thrown aside by former inquirers."—*London Saturday Review.*

D. APPLETON & CO., Publishers.

DATE DUE

NOV 3 '87			